Teaching the Digital Generation

Frank dedicates this book to his wife Lynda. To the real scholar in the Kelly family for supporting and tolerating my focus on this book.

Ted dedicates this book to his wife Heather. Her amazing support, thoughtful input, and intelligent criticism of ideas have made me a better writer, a more effective teacher, and a better person.

Ian dedicates this book to Arthur and Marion Jukes. Thanks for all your support and encouragement over the years; and to my son Kyler, who has helped me see the world through a different lens and brought me kicking and screaming into the 21st century.

Teaching the Digital Generation

No More Cookie-Cutter High Schools

FRANK S. KELLY **TED McCAIN** **IAN JUKES**

Foreword by Michael Hinojosa

The new city scene (Cityscape) is from the following source:
Cliptures Volume 1—Business Images
Copyright 1988
Dream Maker Software
4020 Paige Street
Los Angeles, California
U.S.A.
90031

The images for the people, car, factory are from the following source:
Task Force Clip Art for Macintosh
Copyright 1989—1994
New Vision Technologies
38 Auriga Drive, Unit 13
Nepean, Ontario
Canada
K2E 8A5

For information:

Corwin Press
A SAGE Company
2455 Teller Road
Thousand Oaks, California 91320
www.corwinpress.com

SAGE Pvt. Ltd.
B 1/I 1 Mohan Cooperative Industrial Area
Mathura Road, New Delhi 110 044
India

SAGE Ltd.
1 Oliver's Yard
55 City Road
London EC1Y 1SP
United Kingdom

SAGE Asia-Pacific Pte. Ltd.
33 Pekin Street #02-01
Far East Square
Singapore 048763

Printed in the United States of America

Library of Congress Cataloging-in-Publication Data

Kelly, Frank S., 1941-
Teaching the digital generation : no more cookie-cutter high schools/Frank S. Kelly, Ted McCain, Ian Jukes.
p. cm.
Includes bibliographical references and index.
ISBN 978-1-4129-3926-3 (cloth)
ISBN 978-1-4129-3927-0 (pbk.)
1. High school teaching—United States. 2. Educational technology—United States. 3. Educational innovations—United States. I. McCain, Ted D. E. II. Jukes, Ian. III. Title.

LB1607.5.K45 2009
373.11020973—dc22 2008021949

This book is printed on acid-free paper.

09 10 11 12 10 9 8 7 6 5 4 3

Acquisitions Editor: Debra Stollenwerk
Editorial Assistant: Allison Scott
Production Editor: Veronica Stapleton
Copy Editor: Barbara Ray
Typesetter: C&M Digitals (P) Ltd.
Proofreader: Dennis W. Webb
Indexer: Sheila Bodell
Cover Designer: Michael Dubowe

Contents

Foreword

Having introduced Ian and Ted to Frank several years ago as part of a bond planning process, I read the draft of this book with some sense of responsibility. Given that their collaboration contributed greatly to the success of that bond program, which ultimately produced two high schools of real interest instructionally and architecturally, I opened the draft with a sense of anticipation. I was greatly encouraged by what I read.

I have deep concerns for the future of public education. These concerns have grown as I have served as superintendent in several very different school districts over the last decade. I led one suburban district near Austin with about 9,800 students as it grew from one to two high schools; then another near Houston with about 28,000 students as it grew from two to four high schools. Today, I'm superintendent of the Dallas ISD with 30 high schools and 158,000 students of enormous diversity and with worrisome graduation rates. Working for these school districts has provided me with a wide range of perspectives of how high schools operate.

The evolution of my concerns for education makes this book particularly relevant to me. It has become clear that our high schools are not working as well as they once did. On average, our nation's high schools graduate fewer than 70% of their students, and unfortunately, students in urban districts like mine fare much worse. Even the students who do graduate often need remedial work to succeed, whether in college or in the workplace. In Texas, the largest cities are growing in population while their central school districts have shrinking enrollments. Parents and students are choosing other education options. The likelihood is that this will only get worse in the future as change in the world accelerates. The future of public schools, particularly the future of our high schools, is by no means assured. Educators desperately need leadership to address the pressing challenges they face today.

That is the reason this book is so timely and encouraging. Not only have the authors outlined powerful forces that are combining to profoundly challenge education, they also take the bold step of pointing educators toward possible solutions. The ultimate contribution of this book may not be in the details of its thoughtful proposals, but in the declaration Frank, Ted, and Ian set out in its title—*No More Cookie-Cutter High Schools*—that there are many different ways to create high schools that work. No single design or strategy will meet the needs of all students in the future.

Whether operating an existing school or planning a new one, we need to start with a singular focus on the needs of students to be served and only then devise the instructional methods, the programs, and the facilities they will require for success. The effectiveness of a school needs to be measured not in terms of the range of programs and facilities offered, but in terms of the success realized by each individual student. This requires diverse types of schooling for our increasingly diverse clientele.

Inherent in the concept of having different types of schools is the idea that students and parents must be able to choose the school best suited to their interests and needs. Where you go to school should not be based simply on where you live. This further implies that, over time, the types of schools will evolve—they will change and grow. High schools in this context cannot be the static institutions that they have been generation after generation.

In January of 2008, the Dallas ISD announced plans to make our high schools feel smaller, more personal, and more connected to work and careers. The plan calls for them to do the following:

- Create "career academies" that integrate core and career studies to make schools more relevant and engaging for students.
- Allow students to apply to any high school in the district offering programs of interest to them.
- Require students to take more college-level courses.
- Break large campuses into smaller units to make big, crowded schools feel more personal.

All of that is very much in the spirit of this book. I hope that after you've read it, you will be less certain about what constitutes a high school and more inclined to seek new ways to make high schools work in the 21st century.

Michael Hinojosa, EdD
Superintendent of Schools
Dallas Independent School District

Acknowledgments

SHW Group—for its resources and support of our work on this book.

About the Authors

In 2002, the SHW Group and the firm's Director of Planning, Frank Kelly, were at work with the Spring ISD (near Houston) on a long-range plan to serve the district's growing enrollment. The planning began with a visioning process to help the district think conceptually about where they wanted to go over the next decade. Recalling the forward-looking content of the book *Windows on the Future,* Spring's Superintendent, Michael Hinojosa (now Dallas ISD Superintendent), suggested engaging the authors Ted McCain and Ian Jukes to stimulate discussions about the future and applications for technology in education.

That first collaboration was a great success—Spring passed a $257,000,000 bond program that ultimately included two innovative new high schools—and led to similar efforts in several other districts. Working together on plans for the future, we invariably found ourselves talking all at once about instruction, technology, time, architecture, and money—and noted that, when it came to education, we could not keep those topics separate: each affected the others.

We found that our diverse backgrounds and common interests in education made for exceptionally lively discussions, and a book seemed a productive rationale for prolonging those. We began to consider broad ideas related to K–12 education, but soon focused on high schools—by any measure the least successful of our public schools, widely criticized and debated, and constrained by traditions.

An architect, Frank S. Kelly is Director of Planning/ Programming and a Principal of the SHW Group, an architectural, planning, and engineering firm focused on architecture for education. SHW's practice extends across much of the country with offices in Texas, Michigan, and Virginia.

Frank taught design in the School of Architecture at the University of Tennessee and has worked with architectural classes at both Texas A&M and Rice University. With particular interest in the relationship between instruction and facilities, much of his architectural experience has focused on the planning, programming, and design of K–12 schools. He frequently lectures at school conferences on instruction and has written a number of articles for education journals. His projects have been recognized by design awards from the architectural profession and educational organizations. In 1984, he was elected to the American Institute of Architects' College of Fellows for his work in design.

Frank S. Kelly, FAIA, SHW Group, LLP, can be reached at fskelly@shw-group.com.

First and foremost, Ted McCain is an educator. He has taught high school students at Maple Ridge Secondary School in Vancouver, B.C., for 28 years. Although he has had several opportunities to take other jobs both inside education and in the private sector, he has felt his primary calling is to help prepare teenagers for success as they move into adult life. Ted continues to teach at Maple Ridge Secondary; he is now the coordinator of the Maple Ridge Secondary School Digital Art Academy, where he teaches digital art courses in PhotoShop, 3D modeling and animation, special effects for film, Web site design, and music composition and sound engineering.

In 1997, Ted received the Prime Minister's Award for Teaching Excellence. Ted was awarded this prestigious Canadian national award for creating his innovative "4 D" approach to solving problems, his unique use of role playing in the classroom, and his idea of progressive withdrawal as a way to foster independence in his students.

In addition to his work as a high school teacher, Ted has taught technology and graphic design courses at a junior college. Ted has also consulted with school districts and businesses for more than 25 years on effective teaching for the digital generation and the implementation of instructional technology. Ted has now joined the Thornburg Center for Professional Development in Chicago, Illinois, as an associate director. In this role, he shares with educators his passion for the critical need for schools to adapt to the new digital reality in order to prepare the next generation for life in the 21st century.

Ted McCain, Coordinator of The Maple Ridge Secondary School Digital Art Academy & Associate Director of the Thornburg Center for Professional Development, can be reached at tmccain@shaw.ca.

Ian Jukes has been a teacher, administrator, writer, consultant, university instructor, and keynote speaker. He is the Director of the InfoSavvy Group, an international consulting group that provides leadership and program development in the areas of assessment and evaluation, strategic alignment, curriculum design and publication, professional development, planning, change management, hardware and software acquisition, information services, customized research, media services, and online training as well as conference keynotes and workshop presentations. He also works with organizations and communities that have lost their market or economic base and wish to explore possibilities for preferred economic futures.

But Ian is an educator first and foremost. His focus has consistently been on the compelling need to restructure our educational institutions so that they become relevant to the current and future needs of children. As a registered educational evangelist, his self-avowed mission in life is to ensure that children are properly prepared for the future rather than society's past. As a result, his primary focus is on many of the pragmatic issues that provide the essential context for educational restructuring. Over the course of the past 10 years, Ian has worked with clients in more than 40 countries and made more than 8,000 presentations, typically speaking to between 300,000 and 350,000 people a year. His Committed Sardine Blog is read by more than 80,000 people in 75 countries, and can be found at www.ianjukes.com.

Ian Jukes, The InfoSavvy Group, can be reached at iajukes@mac.com.

Introduction

WHY WE WROTE THIS BOOK

We wrote this book because it is vitally important that education respond to the dramatic changes taking place around the globe. You can't look at the modern world without recognizing that something really big is happening in the way life is lived—the way we work, the way we play, the way we communicate, the way we view our fellow citizens, and the way we learn. The 21st century is a fundamentally different environment that is demanding completely new ideas for how things get done. These sweeping changes are occurring so rapidly and are of such magnitude that education must quickly adapt or face the very real prospect of becoming irrelevant. For example, at a recent leadership institute for a diverse group of superintendents from across Texas, an urgent concern was raised by those in attendance that unless drastic changes are made, public education has less than a decade before serious problems will emerge. All of the superintendents agreed.

It is absolutely critical that everyone involved in education realize that change is not optional for schools today. But embracing the kind of fundamental and pervasive change that is needed to keep schools relevant in the world of the 21st century is a real problem for educators because schools have operated the same way quite successfully for such a long time. The problem is TTWWADI.

THE PROBLEM OF TTWWADI

It is amazing how many things we do from habit. Once we discover a way to be successful at something, it's human nature to latch onto the process that yielded the positive result. After we put forth the effort to make a decision to behave in a certain way, or perform a task at a specific time, or follow a particular procedure to do a job, life becomes much easier when we continue to follow the steps that lead to our success. In his book, *Future*

Shock, Alvin Toffler (1970) calls these habits programmed decisions that were made so long ago and repeated so many times that they have become rote. He uses the example of a commuter who long ago discovered by a painful process of trial and error that the best time to leave for work was 7:35 a.m. Now, years later, that commuter has left at that time so often that he no longer even thinks about it. In fact, he can't even remember what the reasons were for leaving at that time. All he knows is that if he leaves at 7:35, he'll get to work on time. No thinking is required. And that's the point—he did the thinking long ago, discovered a way to be successful, and now just repeats the steps that led to his initial success. It's quite literally a no-brainer.

What is even more amazing is how we can accept and internalize the decisions made by others. We join an organization or work for a company and find ourselves doing things without really knowing why. Everyone continues to do things a certain way because it's been done that way for as long as anyone can remember. Besides, it's much easier to keep following the same path than it is to try to change things. What is remarkable about this is that the reasons for doing something in a particular way can be lost altogether because the original decisions were made so long ago. Consider the following example of how continuing down the same path for a long time can become so entrenched, not only is the original rationale lost, it no longer applies.

Today in North America, the spacing between the rails on railroad tracks is always 4 feet, 8 1/2 inches—a rather odd and seemingly arbitrary number. One legend as to why this particular spacing is used is because that's the rail spacing they used to build the railroads in England, and English expatriates built the railroads in the new world. So why did the English use that measurement for the spacing? It was because the English railcars were built by the same people who built the horse-drawn wagons in the pre-railroad era. That's the axle width wagon makers had always used, so they just kept on using it when they built the first railroad cars. Why did the wagon makers use that particular axle width? They did this because, if they used any other axle spacing, the wagon wheels would break on the sides of the established wheel ruts on English roads. So, where did those old rutted roads come from? The first long-distance roads in Britain and Europe were built by Imperial Rome for the use of the Roman military, and they have been in use ever since. Why did the Romans use that particular axle spacing? That was the width of the two horses that were used to pull the chariots. Thus, the North American standard railroad track spacing of 4 feet, 8 1/2 inches derives from the original specification for an Imperial Roman war chariot.

And there's more. There's a new twist to the story about railroad track spacing and horses' behinds. When we see a space shuttle sitting on its launch pad, there are two big booster rockets attached to the sides of the main fuel tank. These are solid rocket boosters, or SRBs, which are made at the ATK Thiokol Propulsion factory in Utah. The engineers who designed the SRBs might have preferred to make them a bit fatter, but the SRBs have to be shipped by train from the factory in Utah to the launch site in Florida. The railway line from the factory runs through various tunnels in the mountains. The tunnels are slightly wider than the railroad track, and the railroad track is about as wide as two horses' behinds. So, a specification for a major design feature of what is arguably the world's most advanced transportation system was determined over 2,000 years ago by the width of two horses' behinds.

What is important to note is that the original decision that led to the specification for the space shuttle propulsion system was made in a world where railroads and space travel were never considered. Although it may have made great sense to use that specification in ancient Roman times, there is no compelling reason to use it today. In fact, there are compelling reasons for using a completely different measurement today that would be of much greater utility for modern purposes.

Whether this is the true story or not has been lost in the annals of history, but we think the story of the development of the spacing of railroad tracks is an apt metaphor for the public school system. The way our schools are designed, the way they operate, when they operate, and the way teaching is accomplished are all based on decisions that were made a long time ago. Many of those decisions originated in a time before computers, before television, before airplanes, before satellites, and before brain research. Today's public education system originated in an era when more than 90% of young people still lived on farms or in rural areas. Consequently, education was institutionalized as a seasonal enterprise. Schools adopted the six-hour day and the nine-month calendar to accommodate farm life. Summers were reserved for harvesting crops and other agricultural activities. Even as we progressed through the Industrial Age of the 20th century, many of the attributes of schools for agricultural life persisted. More astounding is that many of these attributes persist today. And similarly, many of the attributes of Industrial Age schools persist in today's schools in the world of the Information Age. Just like the spacing of the rails for our trains, the school system is based on decisions that were made for another time.

An important question to ask is why hasn't education changed as the world has changed around it? How can you explain the steadfast refusal of most people in education to embrace anything more than superficial changes to the way schools operate? We perceive that the school system is under the influence of a powerful force that compels it to continue on its current course. This is a force so potent that few have been able to break free of its grasp. What is this force that is making education so impervious to change? It's TTWWADI, and it has awesome power over people. What exactly is TTWWADI? It stands for **T**hat's **T**he **W**ay **W**e've **A**lways **D**one **I**t, and it is a mindset that develops as people form habits of behavior, both personally and professionally. Over time, TTWWADI becomes a powerful force that thwarts change as new people embrace doing things the way they have always been done without examining where the original decisions came from. People just accept the preexisting mindset because it's the path of least resistance. Once a course of action is determined, staying on that course becomes habitual.

Take a good look at our education system and you will quickly discover that much of what happens in schools today is done from habit. The school system runs on an enormous number of programmed decisions that were made by people who aren't around anymore. Those people who shaped the school system into what it is today did their thinking in another time and discovered ways to be successful in educating children for a world that no longer exists. But because of the incredible power of TTWWADI, the people currently running schools continue to repeat the steps that lead to the system's past success. And they unconsciously adopt the long-established thinking that lies behind why our schools function the way they do. Just think of words like classroom, teacher, instruction, lesson, textbook, and test. These terms don't even have to be defined for new educators because it is assumed that everyone knows what they mean. For the vast majority of people, working in the school system today is a no-brainer. They work very hard and with great passion in very difficult conditions, but they don't have to think hard about how the system operates because it's been that way for such a long time.

Now this is not a problem when things don't change very much or change very quickly. That was the case for the early and middle parts of the 20th century, and at that time schools did a good job of preparing students for the rest of their lives. However, as we entered the latter part of the 20th century, the world began to experience increasing change due to rapidly growing technological development. But as the world began to shift to a totally new life experience, schools continued on as before. As a result, schools started to encounter more and more difficulties in achieving success in teaching kids. Today, schools are having serious problems. The entire school system is straining under the pressure being exerted on it by a world on the move. There is mounting evidence that the schools designed for the 19th and 20th centuries are not working well in the modern digital world. But remarkably, there is no widespread panic among educators, no anxiety over the 21st-century challenges facing education, no huge concern about the relevancy of what and how teachers teach. In fact, there is not even any real discussion of these pressing issues at all. Instead, demonstrating the extraordinary power of TTWWADI, most people working in the school system carry on with business as usual.

This simply cannot continue. We cannot carry on preparing students for the farms and factories of yesterday while the world jumps to light speed with biotechnology, nanotechnology, neurotechnology, global high speed wired and wireless networks, and incredibly powerful personal portable devices. We strongly believe that schools must prepare kids for the world of tomorrow—the world where they will spend the rest of their lives. So we have been inspired to add our voices to the call for substantial change to our schools—change that needs to begin immediately, if not sooner!

A SUMMARY OF WHAT WE ARE TRYING TO SAY

The new digital world is having a profound impact on modern students. They actually think differently than older people who did not grow up in the digital environment. Educators must adapt their approaches to instruction and the organization of their schools to address this new reality if they hope to engage students in learning today and into the future.

We want our readers to understand and believe that there are many ways to organize high schools—not just one. We need our readers to understand and believe that the industrial model is not the standard school suitable for most students. We want our readers to understand that all the other models described here are not merely "special" for small numbers of "special" students. We need our readers to understand that there should be no "base," "standard," "normal," "conventional," or "traditional" high school. In creating new high schools, our assumptions must start from scratch every time for every community.

This book is not a comprehensive catalog of high school models from which to make selections. Rather, it is intended to provide illustrative examples exploring viable possibilities. There are clearly many variations on the models described, not to mention many other models we've yet to imagine. The challenge is not just to find new ways to make high schools, but also to muster the courage to seek them out.

It is clear that the industrial model high school is ill suited to the needs of most 21st-century students. If we are going to prepare our students for the world that awaits them beyond school, rather than the world we are familiar with, we must transform or close the industrial schools we have and stop building more—and we need to do it now!

There is little risk in pursuing new ideas for high schools. Industrial model schools have served students increasingly badly for decades. For example, in the United States we graduate only about two-thirds of all high school students. In urban districts with substantial low-income or minority populations, we graduate less than half. And many of those who do graduate leave academically deficient, unprepared for the world that awaits them after school and requiring remedial instruction to be able to survive in college and life. It is a far greater risk to stick with what we already know does not work rather than to explore new alternatives.

The future of public high schools is not assured. Given the statistics we cite later in the book, growing worldwide competition, mounting political pressures, and the emergence of truly viable alternatives, we should not assume that high schools as we've known them for generations can or will survive for another decade.

There are many great ideas and examples for making more effective high schools, including many that have been around for decades. The issue is not figuring out what *might* be done, but having the courage to do it.

This is not about funding. The industrial model school is costly to build and costly to operate—and considerably more costly when you consider the percentage of kids it fails. The related social costs of its low graduation rate are immense. Entire cities are being shaped, and property values being affected by people fleeing dubious urban center schools to enroll their kids in suburban schools they perceive to be better. As fundamentally contradictory as it may seem, we have urban school districts with declining enrollments in cities with growing populations. All the models examined here can do more for less—the issue is courage, not money.

In *The March of Folly* (1984), American historian Barbara W. Tuchman set three conditions for a folly:

- Doing something contrary to your own self-interest,
- Doing it despite readily available knowledge that it is contrary to your own self-interest, and
- Doing it when you have a choice to do something else.

She cited several examples:

- The Trojans taking the wooden horse into their city.
- The Renaissance popes provoking the Protestant secession.
- The British losing America.

Will some historian in the middle of the 21st century look back on our educational system and its high schools and observe that we knew there were problems, knew how to remedy them, and had the means to do so—but did not? We hope not. Instead, it is our desire that this book will, in some small way, inspire educators to respond positively to the challenges facing education in the 21st century. It is our sincere desire that this book will provide a useful resource for educators wanting to explore new ways of organizing schools to meet the needs of modern students.

Please note: Although we have focused on ideas for high schools in this book, much of what we have written also applies equally as well to elementary and middle schools.

Accompanying Web Site

A Web site in support of this book is available at www.nomorecookiecutterschools.com. This site contains a blog, articles, downloadable handouts, photos, videos, podcasts, recommended readings, additional materials, and contact information. Please visit the Website for further resources, links to valuable education sites, and interesting articles related to teaching, learning, and school design.

PART 1

"Conventional wisdom is that it takes great strength to hold on to something. In my view, it takes the greatest strength to let go of something you have done the same way for a long time."

Ted McCain

1

Schools Must Change

The world we live in has fundamentally changed. Our students have moved into the Information Age. Meanwhile, our high schools continue to operate on the ideas and assumptions from the Industrial Age. As a result, there is a fundamental disconnect between students and the schools they attend.

- The industrial efficiency envisioned for teaching in the early 20th century is not reflected in learning efficiency for students in the 21st century.
- The learning styles of today's digital kids are significantly different than those for whom our high schools were originally designed. They work, think, and learn differently—and our schools were not designed for them.
- Instruction is primarily based on teachers talking in classrooms, textbooks, memorization, and content-based tests; schools are becoming increasingly out of sync with the world around them.
- Schools focus on linear, sequential, left-brain thinking in a world that requires both left- and right-brain capabilities.
- The segregation of skills and tasks that typified the industrial approach is reflected today in our approach to creating schools for the future—and it does not serve us well.

What's the definition of insanity?

Doing the same thing you've always done, but expecting or wanting or needing completely different results. If we continue to do what we've always done, we will continue to get what we've always got.

WHY SCHOOLS ARE THE WAY THEY ARE

How many of you recognize this scenario from your own high school experience? A teacher returns to her high school after a weekend. She walks to the school office and checks her mailbox. Then she heads for her classroom. After turning on the lights and adjusting the window blinds, she puts her binder on the lectern and opens it to the lesson plan for first period. Kids start arriving and wander to their desks. The bell rings, the teacher takes attendance, and she places the absentee list on the hook on the outside of the door. Then she walks over to the lectern and begins talking about the topic to be covered. Students listen until she gives them an assignment to be done using the textbook for the course. The teacher tells students to pay particular attention to this assignment because there will be a test on the material next period. Sound familiar?

Of course it does, because that scene is repeated over and over again each day in our high schools all across North America. Teachers and students meet in classrooms. Teachers talk and students listen. Students are given work to do using textbooks that focus on committing content to memory. Students are motivated to do the work of memorization because their performance on tests will be recorded.

Teachers are completely comfortable with teaching this way because it was the only approach to instruction that was modeled for them in high school, or university for that matter. Education has happened this way for so long, no one questions it. It's just assumed that this is the way it's supposed to be.

Those who work in the school system are victims of TTWWADI—**T**hat's **T**he **W**ay **W**e've **A**lways **D**one **I**t. Schools, especially high schools, have operated the same way for such a long time, most people who work there don't really know the reasons why they do the things they do.

So how did schools get to look like this and when did it happen? Let's have a quick look at the historical roots of our schools.

Believe it or not, the mindset for the current structure of our 21st-century schools is partly based on decisions that were made in the days of the horse and buggy, the kerosene lamp, ploughs pulled by oxen, and the first production lines. For example, the yearly calendar for our current school system was set in the United States and Canada in the late 1800s, and it is based on the agricultural cycle in which students were released for three months each summer so that they could help harvest the crops.

The basic organization of schools and the school day dates back to the early 1900s, when the world was excited about the success of Henry Ford's assembly line. This method of production was based on the ideas of Scientific Management developed by Frederick Winslow Taylor. With such dramatic improvements in productivity at Ford, there was great excitement in applying Taylor's ideas widely across society. Schools were not exempt. According to Linda Darling-Hammond in *The*

Right to Learn (1997), in 1908, William Wirt came up with the idea of the "platoon school."

> Hoping to save on wasted plant space and solve overcrowding in schools, Wirt devised a system in which students circulate through the school from one classroom to another, with different teachers teaching them different subjects for short periods of time. (Darling-Hammond, 1997, p. 41)

Under this system, schools became modeled after the assembly line, and teachers began to specialize and teach only one subject, over and over again, all day.

According to Darling-Hammond, in 1890, the only nonteacher in most school districts was the superintendent. By the 1920s, however, schools based on Taylor's ideas had developed a new class of managers called principals, who were to do all the thinking. The role of the teacher was restricted to conducting routine instructional tasks following procedures developed by the principals. The Taylor system was criticized for the number of unproductive people his plan introduced into a system. That has certainly proven to be the case in education, where today non-teaching personnel constitute more than half of the workforce in the U.S. education system.

Also in the early years of the 20th century, decisions about teaching, curriculum, assessment, and learning passed from the hands of teachers to administrators, commercial textbook publishers, and test makers, who were not concerned with the needs of individual students. Instructional standards were introduced into education at this time as well. These standards were to be used with extensive tests so the teacher could know at all times whether instruction was progressing as it should.

Taylor's ideas caused a great reorganization in society. People fell into distinct groups based on the roles they played in the economy. In the same way, it quickly became the role of the school to sort students in order to prepare them for the roles they would assume on leaving high school. Educators created different tracks for students performing at different levels. Harvard University president Charles Eliot identified three distinct roles in industrial life in 1909, each of which required a different form of education. A small number of the most intellectually gifted students would become managers and leaders. A larger number of students would become skilled workers and merchants, and the vast majority of students would become manual laborers. In the 1920s, IQ testing was introduced into education and quickly became the main tool for sorting students into the various tracks in school.

As early as 1926, behaviorist theories were put into practice in schools. B.F. Skinner further modified this thinking in 1954. The basic idea behind the behaviorist approach to learning was that by giving students only small, discrete portions of information in a predetermined sequence, performance would improve. The key to this approach was short responses that would be learned by rote with immediate positive reinforcement for correct answers. This approach focused on the memorization skills that were critical for the Industrial Age production line life of the time. Schools rapidly adopted it, and, although subsequent research in cognitive psychology has identified considerable limitations to behaviorist thinking, this approach to learning persists to the present:

> A recent international evaluation of mathematics and science curriculum found that US curricula and textbooks cover far more topics with less depth and more repetition, and with less attention to higher-order thinking skills, than those in most other countries. (Darling-Hammond, 1997, p. 52)

Designs for high schools changed to support this new assembly-line approach to instruction that resulted from Taylor's ideas of Scientific Management. Schools very much resembled a production line, with workers specializing in subtasks of the instruction process. Teachers abandoned the holistic approach in which they had taught many subjects to a wide range of ages. They began teaching a single subject to students who were all the same age. Schools were organized into departments to further the specialization of teachers. Teachers were given classrooms in which they would teach for short periods of time, typically an hour. A bell would ring, and the students would move from one specialist to another. The basic layout of the high school we have today, with its hallways, classrooms, and departments, was created before the Great Depression.

There are many who believe that the high schools of today are radically different than the schools of the early 20th century. They point to computers, networking, air conditioning, skylights, video surveillance, telephones in classrooms, digital phone and PA systems, digital whiteboards in classrooms, and a multitude of other improvements as proof that schools have changed. Although there have been changes, most of them are superficial. The underlying assumptions and organization of the school into classrooms, hallways, and departments that was instituted so long ago remain unchanged. Further, the basic instructional approach of teachers talking to students as they sit passively in their seats continues to be the main teaching strategy of the vast majority of educators.

It is amazing to review this history and realize that so many aspects of our current education system are deeply rooted in Industrial Age life of the early 1900s. As we have seen, most of the ideas that form the basis of our current schools were well established by the 1920s. That means schools have looked the same for more than 80 years! And because the basic instructional strategies have not changed significantly over that time, the assumptions behind school facility design have not changed that much either.

WHAT'S WRONG WITH THAT?

Quite simply, what's wrong is that the world has changed and schools have not. The world outside school has shifted to the Information Age, but most schools are still operating on the ideas of the Industrial Age. Capitalizing on the astounding power of new electronic tools, the world outside of education has moved beyond the idea of mass production that was the hallmark of Taylor's assembly-line approach to life. We are now in the beginnings of a whole new era of technologically driven mass customization and the age of the individual.

This new age represents a shift in life experience of enormous magnitude. It is affecting virtually every aspect of our lives, and it has already significantly altered many of the traditional foundations for our schools. For example, the technology of the modern world has radically changed the nature of information. Remember that information, especially textual information, makes the school world go around and has been the major focus of instruction for more than a hundred years. Schools, more specifically teachers, have traditionally been the source of the important information students require to do their schoolwork and to prepare for their future life in the workforce. But now the Internet, through Google and a multitude of other online searching tools, has made vast amounts of information readily available to students in their bedrooms, on the bus, at their friends' houses—anywhere they can connect to the Internet via a cable or wireless device. They can retrieve specific details in seconds. But not only has the access to information changed, there has also been a major shift in the kind of information that is available. The digital world has quickly left behind the black-and-white text-only information most of us grew up with and facilitated access to full-color graphics and video accompanied by stereo sound.

In addition, access to information has rapidly progressed from the linear, paper-based information of the 20th century to the fully hyperlinked, random access, digital world of online information sources. Further, through online cameras, simulations, and games, more and more, technology is allowing people to have firsthand experiences of events, to communicate with other people, and to observe and manipulate natural processes. Learning about the world has become dynamic, relevant, and fun.

Plus, the sheer amount of information in the world has gone berserk. It is growing exponentially. We are being infowhelmed. *The Expanding Digital Universe* (IDC, 2007) says that according to research from the University of California, Berkeley, the world produced five billion gigabytes of digital information in 2003. That's like a stack of books that reaches a third of the way from the Earth to the sun. But that's nothing! According to *The Expanding Digital Universe,* the world generated 161 billion gigabytes of digital information in 2006. That's 161 exabytes of data—that's like 12 stacks of books that reach from the Earth to the sun. Or think of it as three million times more info than in all the books ever written. And all that happened in just one year! But it doesn't stop there. Estimates are that by 2010 the world will generate 988 exabytes of digital information (IDC, 2007).

But the real story concerning information in the modern world is not just about the *amount* of data being produced. It's about the ability to search for the information you require. Google, Yahoo, and other search engines allow users of the Internet to zero in on specific material from an enormous database of information posted on Web sites around the globe. The ability to find the information you need from these online sources without having to leave your home, office, or classroom has significantly changed the notion of research in just a few short years. But even more momentous changes in information access are on the horizon.

Of great significance is the creation of an online digital library of great literary works. In his article for the *New York Times,* Kevin Kelly (2006) says Google started this project off when it announced in December 2004 that it would digitize all of the books in five major research libraries (Stanford University, Harvard University, Oxford University, the University of Michigan, and the New York Public Library). Google is now partnering with several major publishing companies to digitize vast numbers of out-of-print books and excerpts from books currently in print. Others have joined in the effort to create this online digital library. Also in 2004, Raj Reddy, a professor at Carnegie Mellon University, began scanning books from his university's library. His Million Book Project has a goal of digitizing a million books by 2008. Superstar, a company based in Beijing, has scanned every book from 200 libraries in China, representing half of all the books published in the Chinese language since 1949. Just think of what will be available when students begin doing research online. But the real power will be in the ability to link digital information. Kevin Kelly puts it this way:

> Turning inked letters into electronic dots that can be read on a screen is simply the first essential step in creating this new library. The real magic will come in the second act, as each word in each book is cross-linked, clustered, cited, extracted, indexed, analyzed, annotated, remixed, reassembled and woven deeper into the culture than ever before. In the new world of books, every bit informs another; every page reads all the other pages. (Kelly, 2006)

There will be awesome new possibilities for research when digital books are seamlessly linked together. Just imagine being able to jump to each book in a bibliography to see the context of quotes, or being able to assemble all of the passages from all digital books on a specific term or concept, or accessing all of the works with an opinion on a particular issue. And we are only talking about print here—what happens when recordings and film are linked to the books in the same way? Students in school desperately need to be taught strategies for effectively handling this kind of information growth and the new tools that are emerging to access it.

But as important as this online information library is, there is an even more important aspect of the Information Age for educators to consider: the impact the online digital world is having on the thinking patterns of young people. Kids today are growing up in a radically different environment than kids did as little as 10 or 15 years ago. They have been exposed to online digital tools for their entire lives. The use of such devices as computers, digital cameras, hand-held digital assistants, cell phones, scanners, printers, wireless devices for the home and those you store in your pocket or wear on your body, and a myriad of other networked digital tools and social networking software is as natural to them as breathing. They are completely comfortable with powerful software tools that allow them to send e-mail, chat with text or video, surf the online world, search online resources for specific information, download music, movies, drivers, demos, etc., play games both independently and networked with other game players around the world, write essays and reports, edit digital photos, and a whole host of other tasks. Kids today are immersed in an online digital experience.

It is critical for parents and educators to grasp that this digital immersion is changing the way kids think. These digital tools provide kids with an unprecedented level of interaction and immediate feedback. As a result, kids today crave interactivity in their lives. They love to play electronic games because they provide so much more than just sitting watching TV. These digital tools also are a gateway to the world through connections to the online world. Whether it's through a computer or a cell phone, kids today have a strong desire to be networked with others across the room, down the hall, across the city, or around the world. And digital tools provide kids with a sensory-rich world full of color, sound, graphics, and video. Consequently, unlike their parents, kids today want multimedia before they want text-only information. And they want multiple points of entry into informational sources and nonlinear pathways through informational space.

But there is even more for parents and educators to consider. This new digital experience that has sprung into being in the last few years has actually altered the neural pathways in kids' brains. Brain research has progressed significantly in the last 10 years because of the ability of powerful new FMRI scanners to scan a person's brain noninvasively while they are in the process of thinking. This research has revealed that young people who have grown up digital have developed a cultural brain. Because they have grown up with digital bombardment as an everyday part of their lives, they process the same information differently than their parents or teachers.

Today's generations operate at twitch speed because of constant exposure to video games, hypertext, and all of the other experiences that reflect an increasingly digital world. As a result, digital learners have had far more experience at processing information quickly than the older generations have, and they're better at managing high-speed information. To borrow a phrase from the movie *Top Gun*, digital kids have "a need for speed."

This is especially the case in terms of visual information: kids are more visually oriented. They receive and process visual information more effectively than their elders. It is critical that parents, teachers, and administrators understand that these kids think differently than they do.

But in the face of these fantastic changes in the world and the impact they are having on the minds of young people, schools have steadfastly resisted any major alterations to the way instruction takes place. Students are still expected to sit in classrooms and listen to teachers talk. Information access is still provided largely through black-and-white handouts and textbooks. Content-based tests, still the main evaluative tool teachers use, emphasize memorization while largely ignoring other important learning. Remarkably, despite the fact that the world has changed so dramatically, schools persist in operating on ideas from another age. As a consequence of this intransigence, schools are becoming increasingly out of sync with the world around them. And this is having a very real, negative impact on how students view the relevancy of school to the rest of their lives.

There are a number of alarming indications of just how bad this situation has already become. The problem is a fundamental disconnect between students and the schools they attend, particularly as it relates to how and what students are taught as they progress through the school system. Today, more than one-third of students and almost half of minorities drop out before they complete high school. Many more of those who do graduate are learning disabled or delayed. What's more, they're increasingly turned off. According to a recent study (National Center for Education Statistics, 2002, p. 72), only 39% of 12th grade high school students believe that schoolwork will have any bearing on their success in later life, only 28% believe that schoolwork is meaningful, and a mere 21% believe that their courses are interesting. These statistics are even more shocking when one realizes that these are only the opinions of those students who have remained in high school for four years. Students who have found the high school experience the least relevant have already exited the system in huge numbers.

And for those students who do stay in the system, current instructional techniques are not proving to be effective. In a 2005 survey for the National Association of Manufacturers, 55% of business respondents said schools are deficient in preparing students with basic employability skills (attendance, timeliness, work ethic), 51% cited math and science deficiencies, and 38% cited reading and comprehension deficiencies (National Association of Manufacturers, 2005).

The response to these concerns from many teachers, parents, administrators, and politicians has been to go back and teach basic skills. The idea seems to be that if we just get students of today to master the skills that served the older generation well, then the kids will be well prepared for the modern world.

Unfortunately, this nostalgic view of education usually does not work as well as expected because more often than not, the basic skills to be taught are determined by what worked when the teachers or parents went to school in the 20th century. Going back to the basic skills needed for success in the late Industrial Age doesn't make sense in the Information Age of the 21st century. There are new basic skills that are needed to survive in the online, digital world. It would be like teaching students how to ride a horse and then expecting them to know how to drive a car. Given the definition we provided at the beginning of this chapter, this would qualify as insanity.

Why? Because the digital tools of this new age have radically changed the way things are done. It's not that there is anything wrong with the basic skills that were needed for success in the 20th century. In fact, they are still very important. It's that those skills alone are not enough to prepare students for the reality of the new workplace. Bill Gates captured this when he said the following:

> America's high schools are obsolete. . . . By obsolete, I mean that our high schools, even when they're working exactly as designed, cannot teach our kids what they need to know today. Training the workforce of tomorrow with the high schools of today is like trying to teach kids about today's computers on a 50-year-old mainframe. It's the wrong tool for the times. Our high schools were designed fifty years ago to meet the needs of another age. Until we design them to meet the needs of the 21st century, we will keep limiting, even ruining, the lives of millions of Americans every year. (Gates, 2005)

If you take the time to read what people like Tom Peters, Ray Kurzweil, Thomas Friedman, Daniel Pink, Marc Prensky, Alvin Toffler, Jeremy Rifkin, Frank Levy, Donald Tapscott, James Canton, John Naisbitt, Richard Murname, and a whole host of others are saying, you will quickly realize that students today must be equipped with skills that enable them to handle the radically different and constantly changing, technologically driven, bewildering and exciting working world of the 21st century.

Many educators, parents, and politicians have a great deal of difficulty understanding that the world is that different than the world they experienced when they grew up. Does education have to change that much? After all, if school was OK for me and my generation, why won't the same schooling be OK for kids today? It's easy to understand why so many older people have missed the significance of what has happened. This major shift to the online Information Age happened suddenly. In the early 1990s, a number of exponential trends came together with remarkable rapidity to provide us with the amazing online world and relatively inexpensive digital tools to access it. In the few short years since then, the ways people communicate, do business, get information, and entertain themselves have all been radically transformed by this online digital revolution.

This has some startling implications for the older generation. If you graduated from high school before the early 1990s, then you will have a difficult time relating to the life experience of kids today. And it is critical that you understand that your high school experience, while it may have been a good experience for you, cannot be used as a good example for what schools should look like today. The sudden shift to the online digital world has rendered that experience irrelevant to modern students.

So how should we respond to this new world? How can education address the disconnect students are experiencing with school today? How can we change to ensure that schooling will remain relevant as we go further into the 21st century? There are five major shifts that must take place immediately if we are going to come up with effective solutions to the problems schools face.

We Must Shift Instruction to Focus on the Higher Level Thinking Skills Needed for the 21st Century

As we mentioned previously, memorization was a key focus of Industrial Age schools. This was important because memorizing policies and procedures was vital for the vast majority of Industrial Age workers. Only those employees at the management level were required to think independently. But in the technologically rich work environment of today, many of the manual labor tasks done by the Industrial workforce have been automated. Tom Peters (2001) states:

> The age of the blue collar automaton hanging out in that Ford or U.S. Steel factory, then spending a couple of hours at the pub, then going home and sleeping it off . . . and then robotically returning to work . . . is dead. Long dead. (Peters, 2001, p. 10)

But it's much more than the traditional blue-collar jobs that are at risk in the new economy. Many white-collar jobs in accounting, engineering, medicine, and other fields are being outsourced to well-educated, low-salary workers in other parts of the world like India and China. Thomas Friedman, a journalist for the *New York Times*, tells in his book *The World Is Flat* of his surprise at discovering that his profession was not exempt from this aspect of the new world of work.

> Thank goodness I'm a journalist and not an accountant or a radiologist. There will be no outsourcing for me . . . at least that's what I thought. Then I heard about the Reuters operation in India . . . outsourcing elements of the news supply chain. (Friedman, 2005, p. 10)

This is a substantially different world than the one most of us experienced growing up. What we face is a world of work that is a radically different than the one of the 20th century and one that is not familiar to teachers, administrators, parents, and politicians. In this new world, workers will work individually and in teams on an entrepreneurial basis, empowered by new technological tools. The online world will be the gateway to this new workplace, and it will be unlike anything we have ever seen before. Just listen to what Thomas Malone and Robert Laubacher wrote in *Harvard Business Review* about how workers will operate in the future:

> The fundamental unit of the new economy is not the corporation, but the individual. Tasks aren't assigned and controlled through a stable chain of management, but rather are carried out autonomously by independent contractors—e-lancers—who join together into fluid and temporary networks to produce and sell goods and service. When the job is done . . . the network dissolves, and its members become independent agents again, circulating through the economy, seeking the next assignment. (quoted in Peters, 2001, p. 11)

Richard Worzel, writing in *Teach* magazine, said the following about the workplace of tomorrow:

> The world of work is automating rapidly, and routine work of all kinds is disappearing. Tomorrow's workers will survive on the basis of their unique talents, plus their ability to innovate, create, market, and sell their ideas in the global marketplace. They will probably be self-employed, even if they work under contract for a large corporation. (Worzel, 2006, p. 7)

This is a whole new ball game. People will survive on their wits. They will rely on themselves, working as independent entrepreneurs. They will increasingly deal with online information. They will use powerful portable digital tools to get and process information as they need it wherever they are. They will use it to communicate and network with clients and coworkers. Whether this occupies all of their time or is only a part of what they do, an ever-increasing number of people will require a much higher level of thinking skills to do the information processing and problem solving to function successfully at work.

In *A Whole New Mind,* Daniel Pink (2005) examines recent brain research to discover the secrets of how people think. Pink's goal is to determine the kind of thinking that will be needed for the 21st century. He starts by outlining what has been learned about the two hemispheres of the brain. He summarizes this research by saying the left brain handles details, logic, sequence, literalness, and analysis—breaking things down into their components to see how they work.

On the other hand, the right brain handles emotional expression, context, and synthesis—the weaving together of components to see the big picture to gain meaning and significance. Schools have traditionally focused on reinforcing left-brain thinking, and with good reason: It was the basis of the incredible success of the Industrial Age.

Taylor's idea of breaking complex tasks down into manageable subtasks and having workers specialize in doing specific subtasks is at the heart of Scientific Management. Breaking tasks down into their components is largely a left-brain activity.

So, too, is the linear, logical, beginning to end, sequential reasoning required to do work in this environment. Workers don't need to see the big picture. They just need to master their part in the process. Don't think, just do as you are told and memorize the procedures you are responsible for was the mantra of Industrial Age workers. From assembly-line workers to office workers to high school teachers, this was the approach that was needed for success. In that world, only a very few managers needed the big-picture thinking skills. And so schools focused on left-brain thinking in their instruction to the overwhelming majority of students to prepare them for the realities of life after school.

But along came the Information Age, in which many of the tasks of the Industrial Age have been automated or outsourced.

Increasingly, we are left with jobs in which people have to see the significance in information to determine the big-picture meaning of what is being said. Then workers have to take that newfound knowledge and apply it to solve problems and accomplish a task. This kind of thinking requires people to use the capabilities of the right side of their brains working in concert with their left brain's functions to be successful. This environment requires all workers to have the higher level, big-picture thinking skills that only managers needed in the Industrial Age.

And there's the rub. Schools must shift gears to catch up to this new world. Schools cannot continue the current traditional focus on low-level detail recall as the main thinking skill for students in a world that is crying out for workers with high-level thinking skills. Thinkers must use both sides of their brain to be truly effective at applying the full capacity of human reasoning to 21st-century tasks. That means we must change the focus of what we teach to encompass much more than we do now. A recent report on 21st-century skills stated this clearly:

> Even if every student in this country satisfied traditional metrics, they still would remain woefully under-prepared for success beyond high school. (Partnership for 21st Century Skills, 2006, p. 2)

In addition to teaching the wrong skills, the traditional emphasis on low-level memorization has a stultifying effect on the students who must endure teaching whose goal is content recall. In this approach to instruction, success is measured in higher scores on tests that rate a student's memory. To prepare students for such exercises, teachers often resort to drills to improve content recall. The problem is that these mind-numbing exercises take the enjoyment out of learning. This is captured in a quote from W. James Popham:

> [M]any teachers, in desperation, require seemingly endless practice with items similar to those on an approaching accountability test. This dreary drilling often stamps out any genuine joy students might (and should) experience while they learn. (Popham, 2005, p. 41)

This is not what we want to do to our children. Instead, we want to cultivate in them a love for learning that will be so strong that it will sustain them for a lifetime. We want them to see that the relevance of what we teach them in school is so compelling that they can't wait to get at it. To do this, we must make a significant shift in the kinds of skills we emphasize in our instruction. We must shift our focus to the higher level thinking skills that are needed for success in 21st-century life.

We Must Embrace the New Digital Reality

Over the last 10 years, the school system has spent a substantial amount of money on technology. Some think that the job of equipping our schools must be just about done. They are wrong on two accounts.

First, technological change is increasing. This means that equipping schools with new technology will always be with us. Because the role of the public school system is to be the great equalizer in society, ensuring that those who are economically disadvantaged are given the same opportunities as those from wealthier households, it is critical that we embrace the idea that doing our best to give schools the newest technology possible will be an ongoing goal in the 21st century.

Second, we must continue to focus on technology to keep our schools relevant to the society in which they function and to address the already existing problem of the disconnect between students and school. Even before the online revolution, schools were having difficulty reaching their students and convincing them of the usefulness of schools. Now that the world outside school has made a quantum leap into an entirely new way of doing everything from work to entertainment, there is an expectation that education will keep up. Schools that continue to teach to an Industrial Age way of life will be dismissed outright by their clientele of 21st-century digital kids.

Educators have not grasped how pervasive technology has become for kids today. One of the most significant realities of digital tools is that increasing power is continually becoming available at decreasing cost. As a result, in addition to using desktop and laptop computers, kids today are also surfing the Internet, sending e-mail, sending text messages, and talking to one another on inexpensive cell phones and other handheld devices. This digitally charged environment has become so much a part of the daily experience of the majority of kids today that it is affecting the way they think. You can't speak their language unless you understand their world, and today that means embracing the new digital reality they live every day.

Why is it so important for educators to embrace this new digital world? Why is it so important to speak the new digital language of modern kids? Because connecting with the world students experience is at the very heart of what we know about learning.

Brain research has demonstrated that for new learning to stick in a student's long-term memory, the student must make a connection between the new information and something she already knows. Therefore, for teachers to teach effectively for long-term memory recall, they must use examples, illustrations, and stories that come from the kids' world—ideas the kids can relate to.

So what does it mean to embrace the new digital reality? Nothing less than jumping into the digital world with both feet. This means that everyone who is involved in teaching kids and designing the schools they attend needs to catch up to these new digital kids. For teachers and administrators who communicate directly with kids, this means firsthand experience with communicating with e-mail, chatting with instant messaging, surfing and searching the Internet, reading and publishing blogs, texting with cell phones, going online with cell phones, taking and sending pictures with cell phones, playing electronic and online games, listening, watching, and creating podcasts, and a whole range of other activities kids take for granted.

This is also the case for school district staff who make decisions about the allocation of learning resources, teaching training, and the assessment of learning. In fact, if we want to ensure that schools become relevant to the kids of today and tomorrow, then everyone in education from the classroom teacher to the superintendent must address the critical need for educators to catch up with the kids they teach. It can't be optional.

If the adults involved in education are willing to do this, it will have three enormous benefits. First, as we mentioned above, instruction in the classroom will become more relevant to students because it will be linked to their world. It's very simple—if we can't relate to the digital world of our students, then we can't make schools relevant.

Second, by exploring the digital world, teachers will be able to discover powerful new electronic tools that will enhance the learning experience for their kids. These include games, simulations, new ways for students to publish their work, entirely new ways to access and process information, and new ways for students to communicate and collaborate. Some of these tools exist today, and more will certainly appear in the near future. Third, teachers will be able to bring the wisdom of their life experiences to guide students in using the new digital tools that are cascading onto the market. Right now, the kids are way ahead of adults in the use of digital tools, so they are defining the parameters of the how, when, where, what, and why these tools are used.

We Must Address the Shift in Thinking Patterns of Digital Kids

It is the normal experience of the majority of kids growing up today to be immersed in this digital world. From a very early age, kids are surfing the Internet, downloading files, playing games, doing online chatting, blogging, and engaging in a multitude of other digital activities. The impact of this experience on the minds of young people has been nothing short of phenomenal.

The reason for this impact has to do with a relatively new discovery about how the brain works. It is called neuroplasticity, and it is the brain's amazing ability to reorganize how it processes information based on new input. If the brain encounters a new kind of input for sustained periods of time on a daily basis for an extended period of time, it will reorganize neural pathways to handle the new input more effectively. This is what happens when a child learns to read. With sustained exposure to textual input on a daily basis, the child's brain reorganizes how the brain processes this new input so the brain can make sense of it.

In the same way, kids growing up in a digital world are being exposed to new kinds of input from digital experiences for sustained periods of time on a daily basis. Consequently, their brains are reorganizing to handle the digital environment more effectively. This is creating a huge problem in our schools. Kids are quite literally thinking differently than those who teach them.

Here are just some of the differences that already exist between the way digital kids process information and learn because of their digital experiences and the way nondigital adults teach. Digital learners prefer receiving information quickly from multiple multimedia sources, but many nondigital teachers prefer slow and controlled release of information at conventional speed and from limited sources. Digital learners prefer parallel processing and multitasking, but many nondigital teachers prefer singular processing and single or limited tasking. Digital learners prefer active, engaged learning, but many nondigital teachers have more experience with passive learning such as lectures. Digital learners prefer processing pictures, sounds, and video before text, but many nondigital teachers prefer to provide text before pictures, sounds, and video. Digital learners prefer random access to hyperlinked multimedia information, but many nondigital teachers prefer to provide new info linearly, logically, and sequentially. Digital learners prefer to network simultaneously with many others, but many nondigital teachers prefer students to work independently before they network and interact.

Furthermore, kids today are developing a high level of skill with new technologies that nondigital adults do not value or even recognize. These adults dismiss the abilities kids acquire from playing games, using cell phones, surfing the Internet, etc., and complain about the skills they don't have. They fail to realize that the skills kids do have are vitally important for younger people to survive in the digital world they live in and are increasingly a part of business and life.

You can quickly see the magnitude of the problem we face in trying to teach digital kids effectively. And because children have much more time to use, learn, and master new digital tools than adults do, educators face the prospect of a clientele whose brains are continually being reorganized as new digital experiences emerge from the relentless technological development in the modern world. It will be imperative for educators to monitor the way kids use new technology if they hope to keep their instruction effective.

However, although we will always be playing catch up with students, it is already clear that there are some significant changes we can make to our approach to instruction that will greatly improve our effectiveness at reaching digital students. First, our instruction must shift from a predominantly lecture format to one that focuses more on discovery learning. Digital kids are used to learning by doing, by manipulating, and by interacting with digital experiences. Thus, even though just talking at them never was the best way to teach, it will prove increasingly ineffective at communicating concepts and content to our students. Instead, students need more hands-on learning activities that allow them to use the rapid-fire, trial-and-error approach that enables them to master digital tools.

Second, teachers must make a significant shift away from text-based learning materials. They must embrace photographs, especially with color, video, and sound as the primary vehicles for conveying information to students. These are not only the preferred means of communication for students today, they are much more powerful ways to get messages across than traditional textual material. Research by 3M shows that the brain is able to process visual information 60,000 times more quickly than textual information. Robert L. Lindstrom, in *The Business Week Guide to Multimedia Presentations* (1994), explains that the brain is much more suited to processing visual information than any other. He states that nerve cells devoted to visual processing account for about 30% of the brain's cortex, compared to 8% for touch and 3% for hearing (Lindstrom, 1994, p. 2). Those creating the new digital experiences kids are exposed to are keenly aware of the visual processing preference of the brain and craft the new tools to provide maximum visual content. Consequently, kids are becoming increasingly visually oriented and adept at processing this kind of communication. Therefore, it is critical for educators to shift the way they communicate in schools both to capitalize on the power of visual information and to keep instruction relevant to their clientele of digital students.

Third, we must provide students with more access to hyperlinked information that can be navigated randomly. This is the underlying structure of the World Wide Web, and kids learn to travel in this kind of informational space from an early age. Although it is foreign to most adults, it has great power to support learning. It allows a person to follow cognitive links as they develop. It is a kind of learning that young people are completely comfortable with. To many adults, kids employ seemingly nonsensical strategies to discover the information they need. But they can find information in seconds that would take hours, perhaps longer, using the strategies of their parents and teachers.

Fourth, we must allow students to network and collaborate with each other and with experts from around the world on an ad hoc basis. Kids are interacting with people in the online world from an early age. Although most adults cannot understand their need to constantly be connected using e-mail, cell phones, instant messaging, and texting, communicating with people in a virtual world is natural to kids today. Plus, many adults have no idea of the kind of collaboration that takes place when kids play online games. But this kind of networking is second nature to digital kids, and they use this collaboration to joint problem solve and accomplish tasks. In fact, collaborating in this way will be an essential skill for success in the ultraconnected world of the 21st century.

Taken together, these shifts in instruction lead us to question one of the fundamental assumptions of Industrial Age schools—that the classroom is the best way to organize a school and provide instruction. Certainly many of the most effective learning activities in the future will be provided by technology. There are strong indications that the online world will soon be providing much more than the two-dimensional experiences we currently get from computer screens. It will be critical that educators continually monitor new developments in technology and evaluate their potential to enhance student learning. It will be equally important that educators consider how schools could be reorganized to maximize the learning experience of students.

These shifts in instruction also point to the need for massive teacher retraining. Unfortunately, universities generally have not anticipated the kinds of changes we have discussed in this chapter. As a result, teacher training programs continue to prepare young teachers to teach in Industrial Age schools. But it is clear that teachers need new skills to be able to function in 21st-century schools. These skills include hands-on interactive learning, visual literacy and graphic design, the use of both stand-alone and networked digital tools for deep learning activities, information processing, and assessment strategies for measuring higher level thinking.

We Must Broaden Evaluation to Encompass Activities That Provide a Complete Picture of Student Learning

The problem with the way we evaluate student achievement is captured in an analogy that Dave Master (1999) uses in his presentations. Dave's wife, a nurse, has told him that you can get a good picture of a person's health by measuring his height and weight. But, Dave asks, would you go to a doctor who only took your height and weight and then said here's a complete picture of your health? Of course you wouldn't!

Everyone knows that a doctor can get a complete picture of a person's health only after poking and prodding and doing a multitude of tests. Yet when it comes to getting a picture of a student's achievement, the school system operates much like the doctor who just measures height and weight. We simply don't do enough measuring to get a complete picture of student learning. Nowhere is this more the case than in the United States, where current federal legislation for education has greatly narrowed the definition of success in school.

Just as the thinking is flawed by only looking at height and weight as the measure of a person's health, the thinking behind the No Child Left Behind Act in the United States is severely flawed in its focus on written standardized tests as the major, if not the only, instrument for measuring student achievement. Although it is laudable that we hold schools accountable, this act has two significant problems.

First, the focus on text-based tests with mainly multiple-choice answers is far too narrow to give a complete picture of a student's learning and skill development. A complete picture of student learning would be a portfolio of student work that would measure such things as skill in debating, skill in performing scientific experiments, the ability to see the meaning in information retrieved from various sources, the ability to use a variety of digital tools to accomplish real-world tasks effectively, the ability to evaluate the messages in photographs and videos, skill in solving real-world problems, skill in publishing information on the World Wide Web in an effective graphical format, and a whole host of other skills that do not show up on the standardized tests that are used today. It's presumptuous for us to say that current test scores are a complete indicator of student learning. In fact, they are only a small part of learning a student should do in school.

Second, the skills that are measured by the standardized tests required by the No Child Left Behind Act are not the skills that students will need for success in 21st-century life. These standardized tests overwhelmingly measure information recall and low-level understanding of concepts. As we have already discussed, low-level memorization skills are not as important in the Information Age as they were in the late industrialized life of the 20th century. Students now need higher level thinking skills if they are going to be successful in life after school. However, these are generally not measured in schools, especially since the No Child Left Behind Act narrowed the definition of success in school to test scores on text-based, multiple-choice standardized tests.

Therefore, we must broaden the focus of our instruction to include the new skills young people will need for 21st-century life. However, the reality of school life is that students and teachers will focus on whatever is being measured. "Is this going to be on the test?" is a common question from students who want to know where to put their effort. Similarly, teachers will ignore teaching concepts, content, and skills that, although important, are not going to be measured on standardized tests because they know that their effectiveness as teachers will be gauged on how well their students score on the tests. Thus, if we want to change the kind of teaching in our schools, we must change the way we measure student achievement.

In addition to changing the focus of student evaluation, we must also look at massive teacher retraining. Teachers will need new skills to empower them to teach effectively in the digital world of the Information Age. They need not only the skills to harness the power of the new modes of communication that are cascading into daily life, but also the ability to equip students with the new thinking skills they will need for success in the postgraduation world This will require a huge shift in focus in teacher training programs. It is critical that we begin immediately to equip teachers with skills in information processing, visual literacy, problem solving and higher level thinking, ad hoc collaboration, effective graphic design skills, and a deep understanding of how technological tools can enhance the learning process.

We Must Increase the Connection Between Instruction in Schools and the World Outside

One of the biggest problems we face in education is convincing students that what we are teaching them is relevant to their lives and important for them to learn. This is especially the case with much of the theoretical, decontextualized content contained in many of the curriculum guides for high school courses. Therefore, we must make a concerted effort to help students see the connection between learning and the world at large. There are two significant changes educators must embrace to address this issue. First, teachers must make the effort to relate their instruction to the real world outside the walls of the school. The key point here is that the kids must understand not just the content, but also the context of how that content is applied in the outside world.

Second, schools must make it a priority to provide students with real-world experiences while they are still in school. This can involve inviting speakers to come into the school, but it is much more effective if you can get students out of the school environment and let them experience the nonschool world. Traditional field trips are still a valid way to get kids to see the larger world. Students benefit greatly from working with mentors who have real-world jobs. Job shadowing provides students with a more in-depth experience of what people do in various occupations. To ensure that students see the relevancy of what they are learning, schools need to be much less insular than they are today.

Technology can already be of great assistance in making connections with the world outside school. Students can communicate with mentors via e-mail, instant messaging, and video chatting. They can also use digital simulations to get real-world experiences. Incredibly realistic simulations are already being used in many places in the working world. Pilots train in simulators that are so realistic that trainees quite literally begin to sweat and panic when things go wrong. This kind of virtual experience will proliferate rapidly in the near future.

To make the shift necessary to address the five issues we have just discussed, we must be willing to look at alternatives to the traditional organization of Industrial Age schools. We need to reconsider our longstanding assumptions about teaching and learning, about where, how, and when they may occur, and the resources that are put in place to support learning. We need to reexamine the use of time—the school day, the school timetable, and the school year. It is also clear that we must embrace new methods of instructional delivery to prepare our students for life. The bottom line is that schools must change.

WHY IS THIS IMPORTANT IN A BOOK ABOUT CREATING 21ST-CENTURY LEARNING ENVIRONMENTS?

You might be thinking that this is all well and good, but what does any of this have to do with me? And it's just that kind of thinking that highlights a huge problem with the way schools are designed. There are so many people specializing in subtasks in the process that the overall big picture gets lost. We have observed that students and learning often get overlooked when new schools are being created. Here are some responses we have heard from people involved in designing schools.

> "I work in the facilities department for the school district. I don't need to know about all this instructional stuff. I just work on the technical specifications for new schools. It's the job of the architect to come up with a workable design. My job is to nail down the technical specifications for schools to ensure we don't waste money. There's a lot more to designing a school than just focusing on teaching. And you know, the Department of Education won't fund experiments. Besides, we tried doing something new in one of our schools a while ago and as soon as new staff came to the facility they wanted to change it back to a traditional school. Teachers won't change so why should we talk about doing anything different with the design of a school?"

> "I'm an architect. It's my job is to take the specifications given to me by a school district and plug the numbers into my spreadsheets to determine the parameters of my design. It's not my job to know about any of this stuff about digital kids. That's the job of the

school district. Besides, most of the school district facilities staff we deal with don't even talk to the instructional people about these things, so why should we?"

"I'm a district business manager. I watch the finances. It's my job to fund the construction and operations of the school within the revenue available to our district. Sure I care about how the school works and looks, but my big concern is keeping design and construction on budget. We have very little flexibility when it comes to expenditures."

"I'm a district facilities manager. My job is to deliver the school on time, on budget. I don't know about instruction. In fact, curriculum and instruction people drive me crazy. It would be a whole lot easier if they just let me create the box and they can decide what to do inside after I'm done."

"I'm a director of curriculum and instruction. I'm not interested in how the construction of facilities takes place. I find it incredibly difficult dealing with the facilities people in our district because they don't value what I do. I don't even try to talk to them anymore about new methods of instruction. They just give me the classrooms and I train the people to teach in them after the school is built."

"I'm a high school principal. I don't have time to worry about instruction. Teachers will have to figure that out for themselves. I'm worried about making sure the new facility has adequate staff parking, a student drop-off and pick-up area, proper building security, a working bell system, and a great PA system. I have to make sure we have the school facility ready on time for school start-up, especially the football field and the gym."

"I'm a high school teacher. They don't consult me when they design a new school. All I get to do is decide where the white boards go after my classroom is built. And I don't know what all the fuss is about the way teachers teach. I teach the way I was taught—I tell students what they need to know to pass the tests from the Department of Education. Besides, if they want me to teach differently, then the school district has to train me. What I really need is more storage in my classroom and a photocopy room and a staff washroom near by."

Remember that these are actual responses we've heard from people when talking about designing schools. Round and round it goes. It's much easier to point a finger and play the blame game than it is to change. The problem is that kids are stuck in the middle and have to attend the schools that are the result of the collective effort of all these people who are involved in the design process. And that is the reason it is vital that everyone who is involved in designing schools consider the information we have presented in this chapter. Not only does this information have huge implications for how we must shift instruction to be effective in the 21st century, it also has enormous implications for how schools are organized and constructed. If we want to design truly effective schools, then we all must come to grips with these pressing issues.

Let's recap what those issues are. First, we are currently spending millions of dollars on building new high schools that will last for 40 years or more that are designed on ideas that date back to the early 1900s. Other than some network cables, high-tech communications, and air conditioning, the high schools of today amazingly resemble the schools of our grandparents. Second, schools based on these old ideas are not working well with modern students. The combination of an average dropout rate of one-third, a lack of interest in those who stay, and dissatisfaction in the working world with the skills of graduates is an untenable situation that cannot continue. Third, it's going to get worse very quickly. We are facing a new clientele that continually adapts with the ever-changing world of digital wizardry. Schools are already out of step, and the gap is widening.

In the face of these concerns, we certainly cannot continue to design and build schools the way we always have and expect everything to be OK! Remember the definition of insanity we gave you at the beginning of the chapter? Insanity is doing the same thing you've always done, but expecting or wanting or needing completely different results. According to that definition, believing that existing high school designs based on old ideas will serve 21st-century students well certainly qualifies as insane. The question is, are we going to let old, traditional teaching and learning approaches be the underlying foundation for how we design and operate the new schools we build, or are we going to embrace new ideas about teaching and learning that will be suited to the new digital world of the 21st century and create new facilities that reflect this new thinking? More often than not, we simply move an old mindset for what a school is into a new facility. But when you consider the material we have presented in this chapter, it is obvious that the old mindset will not do the job we want it to do. It is clear that we need to do something different if we want to meet the needs of modern kids.

BACK TO BASICS

But where do we start to address these issues? There is a story told about legendary football coach Vince Lombardi. Each year at the beginning of training camp, he would take all of his players, rookies and veterans alike, out onto the football field and hold up a football. The objective of this game, he would say, is to get this ball across the other team's goal line while keeping the other team from getting it across ours. Lombardi knew that it was important to start with the basics and build from there. So let's go back and re-examine our assumptions about the basics of designing schools and build our ideas for new schools from there. What are we all about in the public school system? We are about equipping kids with the skills and knowledge they will need for success as they live their lives in the 21st century. Thus, the core activity in schools is instruction. Everything else, although still important, must either support instruction or operate in such a way that it does not interfere with instruction.

It is imperative that we look at innovative new ways to design schools to ensure that the younger generation is given the best opportunity for success in life. But it is critical to remember that the physical design must be driven by what takes place inside. The physical design must support the main activity that occurs in a school—instruction. To come up with the new designs schools need to be successful in the 21st century, it is essential that everyone involved in school planning and design adopt the motto, "instruction must drive construction." So before we can even begin to look at what a new structure might look like, we must clearly grasp the changes that will be taking place in the kinds of activities that will be occurring inside.

If you consider the implications of what we have just presented about the new world of the Information Age and the nature of digital kids, it is clear that educators must come up with new instructional approaches if they hope to reach their students and keep schools relevant. Consequently, innovative new school designs will be needed to support these new approaches to learning. These new designs can be effective only if everyone involved in planning new schools takes the time to consider how best to instruct modern students for life in the 21st century. Teachers must do this, of course. But it also means that school district facilities staff and architects and even parents, students, and the community must be engaged in the discussions about new instructional models and strategies for organizing schools.

Don't dismiss this book because it seeks to integrate all sorts of topics we usually think are unrelated. Otherwise, you just might end up creating the same kind of school we've had for almost a hundred years instead of the new environments students so desperately need.

Reflect on Your Community and Its High School(s)

- How do the basic instructional methods in our community's high schools differ from those in the high school you attended?
- How is instruction in our high schools geared to the minds of today's Information Age students?
- How are we using Information Age resources for learning in our high schools?
- How do plans for the future of our high schools reflect the new digital world and new mindsets of students?

2

Changing the Process of Designing Schools

The process by which we create schools shapes the teaching and learning environments we design.

- Many of the most important decisions that define new schools are often based on assumptions stemming from the way we've done things in the past, not the way we might do them in the future.
- Getting everyone who has a real interest in how the completed school will function working together to define requirements and to create the design is critical to the process. These stakeholders include district and campus administrators, teachers, facilities and technology personnel, parents, and students.
- Start by defining a broad vision for the future of the school related to learning, then delve into the details required to realize your aspirations.
- Be certain that the architectural design reflects the vision related to learning, and that after construction, the operation of the school carries out the vision for the students.

School buildings must change because instruction must change. We need creative new designs that will support 21st-century learning. But how do we do this? Savvy businesspeople know that if you want to change a product, you must change the process that was used to produce that product. The same is true if you want to build effective new schools—you must change the process of planning and designing new facilities. Thus, it is imperative that we examine the way we currently design new schools and suggest ways to modify our approach to yield the innovative new learning environments that will meet the needs of the students of tomorrow.

HOW SCHOOLS ARE DESIGNED TODAY—STEADY AS SHE GOES

Early in the first chapter, we stated that much of what gets done in schools is based on TTWWADI (That's The Way We've Always Done It). TTWWADI is a mindset that develops when things have been done the same way for so long that everyone assumes they must be right and should be continued into the future. This mindset leads to an unconscious acceptance of the status quo. Thus, people continue to follow a procedure even if the reasons for that procedure are no longer valid.

TTWWADI is alive and well in the way we currently plan and design schools. Everyone involved has made so many assumptions about what schools look like and what people do inside them that efforts focus on a myriad of important, but not central, issues. This process is essentially the same one that has been followed for years, and it's based on 20th-century thinking. Those involved in the process accept it without question. Consequently, it cannot produce the schools we need for the 21st century.

Let's take a quick look at the way schools are designed today. The first step of the process is defining the requirements to be met by the design of the facility—what architects call programming (not to be confused with software). The program states the problem, and the design is the solution. Working from the approved design, the architect prepares construction drawings and specifications (the blueprints) that the contractor uses to build the project. Yogi Berra's admonition that, "if you don't know where you are going, you'll probably end up somewhere else," is perfectly applicable here. If the program is ill defined, the completed building won't meet the needs of teachers and students. Writing a good architectural program is a critical step in creating a new school. The problem is that architects often have a very difficult time writing these programs. There are several reasons why.

First, for all sorts of good reasons related to different types of expertise and the immense amounts of important work to be done, school districts typically have separate departments to address instruction and curriculum, technology, and facility and maintenance responsibilities. Although instruction should drive construction, in most districts these departments report separately to the superintendent and often operate quite independently, at times with conflicting priorities. Charged with getting projects done within budgets and schedules, facilities personnel sometimes think instructional staff, with their evolving needs, complicate their jobs.

Maintenance staff want facilities built of the most permanent, durable, and serviceable materials, whereas instructional staff may want change and flexibility in the building. In turn, instructional personnel may feel that facilities staff are unresponsive to their charge to help kids learn. Technology personnel focus on providing hardware and software for instructional staff who aren't quite sure what to do with it. This adds complexities and costs for the facilities staff. As districts and their departments grow larger, these divisions widen to the point that new or renovated schools are created almost entirely through facilities departments with little or no input from instructional or technology staff. Architectural programs may be generated by consultants, furnished by state agencies outside the district, or simply reproduced from previous projects, stamped out like cookies from a cookie cutter. Educators and architects may have little or no contact and no discussions about instructional issues that should shape the building design.

Second, architects struggle to get educators to talk about instruction. When meeting with teachers, Frank has often thought that disguising the fact that he's an architect would make it easier to elicit information useful for design purposes. Once teachers know he's an architect, they want to talk about architecture. This invariably leads to discussions centering on the shortcomings of their existing spaces (too small, too dark, too hot or cold, insufficient storage, etc.) and very little about how they really want or need to teach in the future. However, in defense of teachers, many architects and school district facilities staff are similarly focused on important, but secondary, details. Many teachers have learned from bad experiences on previous building projects that their input is not really wanted in any significant way. Consequently, they become cynical because they know that they have little say in what their workplace will look like. For many teachers, facilities staff, and architects, instruction will definitely not shape construction.

Third, educators, facilities staff, and architects often bring to each project preconceived ideas about what a school should be based on their TTWWADIs. As a result, many of the most important instructional concepts that should shape high schools are rarely discussed at all. In many cases, it is assumed that core instruction will

- be teacher directed and teacher centered,
- occur in classrooms,
- address one discipline at a time,
- serve groups of approximately 25–30 students,
- happen in equal periods of time over a nine-month school year, and
- be focused on content.

The question is rarely "how do we want to teach?" but rather "how many classrooms do we need?" With these assumptions plus the graduation requirements and target enrollment, a knowledgeable architect can compute the number of core classrooms needed with no input from educators.

Consequently, far less time is typically spent defining program requirements for core instruction than for elective career and performing arts subjects and extracurricular athletic programs. These priorities are subsequently reflected in the design of the school, as core subjects are housed in rows of generic classrooms, while elective, arts, and extracurricular classes are housed in individually designed, specialized spaces.

This current process for designing schools will not give us the new schools we need for the students of tomorrow. There are too many assumptions about the nature of instruction and learning, the use of time, the role of technology, and the physical organization of the school.

The universal acceptance of these assumptions by school district facilities staff, teachers, administrators, architects, parents, and politicians means the current process of school design is certain to result in schools that look, feel, and operate like schools have for nearly a hundred years.

That is simply not good enough. We need to change this process of school planning and design for the sake of the kids who will use them as a springboard into their future lives. And we need to make this change immediately.

SHIFTING THE DESIGN PROCESS FOR SUCCESS IN THE 21ST CENTURY—START ASKING QUESTIONS

What is currently lacking from the school design process is a way to set aside old assumptions about teaching and learning in order to allow people to develop new visions for the future. We cannot aspire to create schools that we cannot envision. So how do you create a new vision for what a school should be? You start by asking questions. It is critical that you ask these questions long before you start thinking about what a new facility will look like. Many people reading this book will want to skip over this chapter and get to the material in the chapters describing the models for schools. That is a mistake. The only way to determine which of the ideas in those chapters will apply to a particular school is to follow the process we outline here.

Engage the Right People at the Right Time

If instruction is to drive construction, then you must start the design process by engaging the people who will be touched by the teaching and learning that will occur in the school. These should include the following:

- students,
- parents,
- teachers,

- school district instructional staff,
- campus administrators,
- school board members,
- community members, and
- businesspeople.

Ask the Right Questions

This is the key to creating a new vision for a school—asking questions. Not just any questions, but a prioritized list that puts first things first. You take the Vince Lombardi approach we mentioned earlier: start with the basics and build everything on that foundation. What are the basics of a school? The prime tasks of a school are teaching and learning. Therefore, you start the visioning process by asking questions about instruction and learning. Here are the five categories of questions that must be asked to create an effective new vision for a school. It is vital that they be asked in this order to ensure that priorities are maintained.

What should teaching and learning look like in a 21st-century school?

How can technology foster this kind of learning?

What noninstructional components should be incorporated into the school?

How can time be used differently to support what we want the school to be?

How can the physical facilities be organized to bring this vision to reality?

The three authors of this book have been doing visioning exercises together for school districts and planning organizations for several years. We have discovered that the discussions regarding vision benefit greatly from having some guidelines to provide an initial context and direction. Here are some guiding principles for creating a new vision for a school that can be used as a starting point for discussions:

1. **Start by looking at kids and learning.**

   This is a critical point. Traditionally, the process of creating new schools has focused on teachers and instruction instead of kids and learning. But if we want to create schools that tailor instruction for maximum effect for digital learners, we must begin by looking at modern kids and how they learn. There is a growing body of research on digital learning styles and preferences as well as research on how the brains of today's young people function. This mounting body of work indicates that if we want to be effective in teaching modern students, then we need to look at different approaches to instruction.

2. **Learning must prepare students for a world of constant change.**

   Today's students will graduate into a world unlike anything we have ever seen before. Twenty-first-century life will be fundamentally different than the experiences most of us had growing up and exponentially different than life today. Astounding technological development is driving continual and ever-increasing rates of change. In this environment, we cannot look at the world of today, but must envision the world of tomorrow and the skills and knowledge students will need for success in that future world. We must provide students with strategies for handling a world that is always on the move.

3. **Learning must focus on 21st-century thinking skills.**

   Students require new basic skills to survive in 21st-century life. These skills include problem solving, decision making, time management, assessing the relative importance of information, and applying learning to accomplish real-world tasks. An ever-increasing number of people will need higher level problem-solving abilities as an entry skill for the workplace. Memorization skills, although still needed, will decrease in importance in the age of anytime, anywhere access to online information sources.

4. **Learning must include 21st-century fluency skills.**

   The explosion of the quantity of information available to the average person has already made information literacy skills a necessity in the modern world. But we must prepare students to go beyond being just literate with 20th-century information skills to being fluent with these skills. Fluency means that these skills have been learned so well that their use is immediate and unconscious. Like riding a bike: kids don't think about it, they just do it.

   As for which skills should be taught, students need to learn much more than just information retrieval skills. They need to be taught how to process the information they retrieve to determine its significance in order to apply this knowledge to real-world tasks. Further, as development of the online world progresses, students will need skills to process the new forms of information that will emerge. We live in a graphical world. Students must be taught to communicate as effectively in the visual environment, as the older generation was taught to communicate in the text-based world. This means schools must include such skills as visual fluency, graphic design, and video production as basic skills that are taught to all students.

5. **Learning must reflect the new digital reality.**

   Instructional approaches must incorporate the latest technological tools to maximize the learning experience for students. In the very near future, online technology coupled with artificially intelligent software will transform the learning environment with powerful tools for discovery learning. Teachers must use the latest digital tools for engaging students in the task of learning. Learning tasks should be designed to use whatever digital tools are available for information retrieval, information processing, information publishing, simulations, and learning games. All teachers and students must have their own digital device to use anytime, anywhere. Technology must be as integral to high school teaching and learning as it is to the world outside schools.

6. **Learning must be interdisciplinary.**

   The time of breaking things down into components and studying them independent of one another has long passed. True understanding comes only from a holistic approach that allows the student to see the interrelationships between the components of a process or system. Schools must move beyond the mindset of departments and provide interdisciplinary learning. What we are saying is that schools need to make meaningful links between what students learn in science and what they learn in math and what they learn in social studies and what they learn in languages.

7. **Learning must be shaped for the individual.**

   The Industrial Age approach to instruction was "one size fits all" even if it didn't fit very well. This approach is not very effective at meeting the needs of individual students. Research clearly indicates that kids learn at different rates and in different ways. If we want schools to be as effective as possible, then we must shape learning to the individual. In addition, students are growing up in a "made for me" world. They increasingly require, want, and expect their educational experience to be tailored to their individual needs, interests, and personal digital learning styles.

8. **Learning must engage 21st-century digital kids.**

   Digital kids learn differently and have different learning preferences and styles than young people from previous generations. Traditional approaches to instruction are tolerable for digital kids, at best. At worst, they are tedious, boring, and counterproductive. New schools must look at the digital learning preferences of modern students and develop instructional approaches that incorporate digital, online, multimedia experiences into learning activities and resources.

9. **Learning must be connected to the outside world.**

   Students are most engaged and motivated, and learn best, when they understand the relevance and application of their studies. Reaching out from the school to the world outside will have two benefits. First, connections with the larger world outside the walls of the school will provide students with the real-world context for their learning. Second, teachers will be able to see clearly why and how instruction must change to keep up with changes in modern society.

10. **Learning opportunities should be available 24 hours a day, seven days a week.**

    Anyone who has had teenagers knows that they keep hours that are frequently not in sync with the rest of the world. Kids are often ready to do their schoolwork after midnight. Schools should accommodate this by allowing anytime, anywhere access to learning resources and research materials. Online technology can facilitate this kind of access to the resources of the school. This will require a rethinking of the kinds of resources the school should provide. With digital technology providing access to learning resources from across the globe, the need for high school libraries with printed materials will diminish significantly. Web portals provide one-stop access to a wide range of educational resources for students much the same way Wal-Mart provides one-stop access to a wide range of products for consumers. In response to this, librarians must become digital research experts rather than just archivists. Therefore, much of the space traditionally allocated to libraries should be put to other uses.

11. **Time, not learning, should be flexible.**

    Prisoners of Time stated, "For the past 150 years, American Public Schools have held time constant and let learning vary" (National Education Commission on Time and Learning, 1994, p. 5). Because individual learning rates are different, when we require all students to complete their learning on a particular topic or course within the same period of time, some students excel, some struggle, and some fail. If time is the constant as it is in most schools today, then learning becomes the variable. Think of this way: most people can travel 100 yards. Some will sprint it, some will jog it, some will walk it, and some may have to use a wheelchair. But the important point here is that given enough time, all can accomplish that task. The same principle applies to education. If we make mastery learning the target, and adapt our learning environments to support that goal, more students can be successful more of the time. The goal of schools must be learning for all students regardless of how long it takes.

12. **Students should assume responsibility for their own learning.**

    The need for constant supervision is largely generated by boring instruction on subjects that students see as irrelevant. When students see the value of their studies and the opportunity to succeed, they assume real responsibility for their time and conduct—and the teaching and learning environment can be extraordinarily different. High school instruction and time should be organized to help students exercise that responsibility.

13. **Every student should have a close working relationship with at least one adult in the school.**

    The student and adult should work together closely and frequently throughout the student's school years. The adult should guide and support the student's studies, and also communicate with the student's parents. If treated as individuals and provided with close support, virtually every student can succeed.

14. **Students should have their own personal place to work.**

    Learning is the most important work done in high schools. Students must have more than lockers and temporary seats in classrooms in which to do that work. Every student must have access to a comfortable place on the campus to do individual independent work during the course of a typical school day.

15. **Assessment must encompass both knowledge skills and higher order thinking skills.**

    Content instruction alone may suffice for short-term memory and success on standardized tests, but if the content does not have personal relevance, it becomes boring for students and difficult to use in the real world. Written tests seldom require real-world applications of that content. Beyond numeric grades, assessment must measure both facts learned and the application of those facts to solve real-world problems. Assessment strategies must therefore be widened to include a broad range of measures for student achievement. This will provide a more complete assessment of all of the learning a student does in school. It will also ensure that teachers do not discard important learning activities simply because their outcomes are not stipulated. Assessment of higher order thinking skills must be an integral part of the teaching and learning process.

16. **All students must be prepared so they can go on to some form of postsecondary studies.**

    A high school diploma will not suffice for most jobs in the 21st century. It is critical that students, parents, and educators grasp the importance of ensuring that high school graduates are prepared for entry into postsecondary programs. To make this a reality, academic rigor in high school must not be "dumbed down" just to get students through. This will ensure that high school graduation will enable students to go on to further education if they choose to do so.

17. **The configuration of spaces within the school building must be highly flexible.**

    Just as ATMs and the Internet have changed the time, place, and method of how people access financial services, new instructional technology will change the when, where, and how students access educational services. Given the accelerating pace of change in virtually every aspect of our society, it is probable that any high school built today will need to be modified substantially multiple times over its life to support evolving learning needs. We must create durable, long-lasting school building shells that contain highly flexible inner spaces defined by easily modified partitions and furnishing systems that can be changed inexpensively in the future.

QUESTIONS FROM THE FUTURE

We often begin the design process by asking participants in visioning discussions to answer questions about their district as if they were meeting 10 years in the future to reflect on the process that has taken place. Ten years is an appropriate timespan because that is the same timeframe demographers often use to project changes in enrollment. It is far enough into the future to require imagination, yet it is too far to simply extrapolate from current events and trends. Yet, it is not so far into the future that participants think that it is beyond the impact of their work.

In a decade, current school district kindergarten students will have entered high school. It will take almost half of that 10-year period to design and build a high school, and its first graduating class will finish very near the end of the decade. Here are some of the questions we use to get people thinking beyond TTWWADI:

Ten Years in the Future: Question 1

How is learning different for our students today than it was 10 years ago? How have instructional methods changed? How has the learning environment changed?

Ten Years in the Future: Question 2

How are our students the same or different from the way they were 10 years ago? What are the skills, attributes, characteristics, and behaviors with which all of our students are graduating today (10 years in the future)? How do students exhibit these skills, etc.?

Ten Years in the Future: Question 3

How are our teachers the same as and/or different from the way they were 10 years ago? What are the skills, attributes, characteristics, and behaviors that all of our teachers are using to facilitate student learning? How do teachers exhibit these skills, etc.?

Ten Years in the Future: Question 4

How are teaching, learning, and assessment more learner-focused instead of subject-focused than they were 10 years ago? Are teaching, learning, and assessment focused on classes of students or on individual students? How did we make these changes? What challenges did we encounter, and how did we overcome them?

Ten Years in the Future: Question 5

How are we using technology to support teaching, learning, and assessment? How is that different than it was 10 years ago? What challenges did we encounter, and how did we overcome them?

Ten Years in the Future: Question 6

How did we get our community to understand and support a new vision for teaching, learning, and assessment? What strategies did we use to overcome the challenges we encountered?

INSTRUCTION

Within the context defined by the questions from the future, there is a further set of detailed questions about how the school is to function. In asking these secondary questions, we want to elicit more than yes/no, either/or responses from participants. The goal is to have people consider when various instructional factors are appropriate. Here are some examples.

General Issues

- What strategies can teachers use to focus more on individuals rather than on entire classes of students?
- What techniques can teachers use to effectively teach to groups of varied size or individuals?
- What methods can teachers use to provide varied time as needed for the teaching method, subject, and student instead of allotting the

same amount of time every day for every subject for every teaching method for every student?

- What differentiated instructional techniques can teachers use to provide multiple and varied modes of learning depending on the subject and students?
- What teaching, learning, and assessment strategies can teachers use to help reduce the students' dependence on the teacher as the primary knowledge source?
- What techniques can teachers use to move from the traditional primarily stand-and-deliver model of instruction to being guides for students as they assume responsibility for their own learning? Does this change with an increase in the use of technology?
- What strategies can teachers use to work with those in other fields to help integrate their students' learning?
- How can high schools be planned to move from departments or disciplines to interdisciplinary groups?
- How can school spaces be planned or reorganized to accommodate multiple modes of instruction?
- How can the school day be reorganized for teachers and students to provide some unscheduled time to work together and independently in order to allow students to obtain help as needed and to pursue areas of interest?
- How can the school day be reorganized for teachers and students to provide flexible periods of time for students to complete their learning activities? How can schools provide varied levels of teacher support as needed to help students succeed within the given time?
- How can teachers create effective learning environments that students find relevant and engaging?
- What methods can be used to allow student achievement to be demonstrated and authentically measured by means other than traditional written tests and letter grades?
- What strategies can schools use to allow a focus on both teaching content skills and higher order thinking? Explain the reasoning behind your answer.

Instructional Methods and Spaces

- What different types of spaces other than traditional classrooms can be designed to allow seminar or small groups, individual study, hands-on laboratories, project-based instruction, and/or virtual instruction?

Technology

- What types of personal digital tools can schools provide to students in order to enhance teaching, learning, and assessment?

- What strategies can we use to ensure that these tools are placed in students' hands?
- Will there be a need for general-purpose computer labs? Will there be a need for specialized labs for graphics, animation, CAD, desktop publishing, and so on?
- Will there be a need for specialized distance learning spaces?
- If every high school student has her own digital device, what implications does this hold for teaching, learning, and assessment?
- If every high school student has his own digital device, what implications does this hold for high school facilities and the use of time?

Individualized Instruction

- How will instructional methods, learning environments, and student schedules reflect and respond to individual learning styles?
- What strategies can be used to ensure that every student has a personalized learning plan?

Time

- As we modify the way teachers teach and students learn, how should we organize the school day and year? How will the use of time facilitate more individualized, personalized instruction? How will the use of time be affected by the increased use of technology?
- How will the length of the school day and year change?

Counseling, Advisories

- How do we ensure that every high school student be well known by at least one adult on the campus?
- How will counselors or advisors interface with students? When? Where?

Organization of Instructional Spaces

- How should the core instructional areas be organized spatially:
  - by discipline or department?
  - in multidisciplinary groups?
  - in houses (schools-within-a-school, small learning communities)?
  - in multidisciplinary academies focused on special subject areas?

- If the school is organized around some form of small learning community, should each community serve a single grade or multiple grades?
- If the school is organized around some form of small learning community, how should core subjects such as English, social studies, math, and science be taught? What other subjects should be included as well, and how should they be taught?

- How should other school functions relate to this organization of core spaces:
  - o administration?
  - o assistant principals?
  - o counselors and advisors?
  - o library?
  - o food service?
  - o career technology programs?

Where Should High School Instruction and Learning Occur?

- How do high schools make the connection to what happens outside the school and outside school hours? What resources might they use to make this work?
- What strategies should the school district use to allow mentors or apprenticeships outside the school to help with instruction? What are the implications for the use of time and space in the school?

Flexibility of Teaching and Learning Environment

- How important is long-term spatial flexibility? Does the district need or desire the ability to substantially reconfigure the internal layout of the high school in the future? What are the implications for the configuration of the school? What are the implications for construction materials and building systems?
- Should the configuration of the building provide natural light and windows in some or all instructional spaces? Or should natural light be provided in spaces where it is beneficial for instruction—art, for example?

Teaching Spaces, Working Spaces

- Should every teacher have a workspace in his or her own instructional space, or should teachers float to some extent?
- How do the nature and location of teacher workspaces relate to instructional methods, schedules, and technology?
- Does every workspace in the school belong to a teacher or administrator? Where do students do their work and construct learning projects?
- Should each discipline or department have a workroom?

Library/Media Center

- What functions should be housed in the library/media center?
- How will the roles of the library and librarians in the school change as the use of technology increases?

- How does the district ensure that libraries be accessible after hours for students and the community?
- Will students be able to access school libraries from their digital devices from anywhere in the school? Will they be able to access the library from outside school?

School and Community

- Beyond their instructional responsibilities, how can the school building and its site provide services for the community?
- What kinds of new services beyond classrooms, playing fields, pool, tennis courts, gym, library, auditorium, and computer labs can the district and school provide?
- How can the school facility be used by a community college or other educational groups during or after normal high school hours?
- What types of health care, social services, childcare, or other community services can be located on the campus?

Visual and Performing Arts

- What visual and performing arts programs and spaces should be included:
  - painting?
  - drawing?
  - sculpture?
  - digital graphics and photography?
  - band?
  - orchestra?
  - choir?
  - drama and theater?
  - dance?
  - debate?

Career Technology

- Which career technology programs will this school offer? Will the programs be the same at other district high schools?
- How should the career technology spaces be located relative to the core instruction spaces? Will they be integrated with the core spaces where appropriate? Or will they be separated as their own department?

Athletic Programs and Facilities

- Which athletic programs and sports will the school provide? What facilities will be needed to support them?

- Which athletic facilities that are central to the district could be shared by multiple schools:
  - o football stadium?
  - o baseball?
  - o natatorium?
  - o others?
- What high school or central facilities will be accessible to the community after school hours?
- Will athletic programs be scheduled within or outside of the school day?

Seating Capacities

- If the high school is to contain assembly spaces, what are the required seating capacities:
  - o auditorium?
  - o gym?
  - o lecture hall?
  - o cafeteria?
  - o stadium?

Student Storage

- Should the school provide individual lockers for students?
- If not lockers, should other storage provisions be included?

THE KEY TO EFFECTIVE VISIONING

The key to effective visioning is to question everything about a school. It is amazing how much of what we currently do is accepted without thinking. Although it may seem like you are wasting time instead of getting on with the real work of designing the school, the visioning process is the only way to break out of the traditional mold of school planning and to design the new schools we need for the future. The vision must be clearly and thoroughly documented as a reference for every subsequent step in the design and construction to follow.

The visioning process is the first and single most important step in setting the direction of the school and avoiding Yogi Berra's dilemma ("if you don't know where you are going, you'll probably end up somewhere else"). But make no mistake, creating a new vision for a high school is a difficult undertaking. The challenge stems from the power of TTWWADI. The current mindset for what a school looks like and how instruction should take place has been around for so long and is so entrenched that it takes great effort to break out of the box of this thinking. Further, even if you are able to get people to embrace new ideas about school design, they often shrink back from the implications of those ideas after a few days because the school that would be created as a result of the new thinking would be significantly different than anything they have ever seen before. Instead, they retreat to ideas and designs that are much more in line with what schools have always been, even when they know that these schools serve many students poorly. As we have done visioning exercises with school districts embarking on building a new high school, we have found that it is imperative to have everyone involved in the visioning process keep asking themselves if the ideas being put forward are more about their own comfort level or about preparing kids for the future.

Keep Priorities Straight as the Architectural Program Is Written

Once the vision has been defined, it becomes the task of the school district facilities staff and the architect to capture that vision in the details of the architectural program. It is very easy for those writing the program to get sidetracked by the myriad of issues that must be addressed. In the process, it may be convenient for the program writers to ignore some of the vision for the school. However, there is great risk if the vision for the school is altered or abandoned in the process of writing the program. The goodwill of those involved in the visioning process will be lost if they discover that their input was disregarded. The cynicism created will be much worse than if those people had never been asked to participate in the visioning process in the first place. Writing the architectural program must not be taken lightly. It is, in fact, a hugely important step because it must capture the vision while balancing all of the agendas of the various participants. The school board and members of the community must see that their desires for innovative approaches to instruction focused on 21st-century skills are addressed. Teachers need to know that their input will actually have a significant impact on the design. Administrators need to know that the entire process will reflect district policies and aspirations. Technology staff need to know that budgets and schedules have been considered. Facilities staff need to see that maintenance and operational issues have been included. The architectural program that is produced by this process must address in equal measure instructional, budgetary, and scheduling objectives and balance each against the others.

Integrate the Instructional, Technology, and Facilities Staff Directly Into the Conceptual Design Process

No matter how complete the program, the design process will invariably raise instructional possibilities and problems no one imagined. Just as the program was created in the district, so should the design concepts be created and explored in the school district, even on-site if possible, with the instructional, technology, and facilities staff fully engaged in weighing the options. The great benefit from including these people in the design process is that there are no surprises with the design because people from the school and district have been involved as it was developed. Just as the program informed the design, the design may in turn inform the program. In the end, it is the school that is created that counts.

Sustain the Vision

One of the hazards of designing high schools is that the architectural program and design are often created long before those who will operate the school are identified or even hired. Typically, only after construction for a new high school is well underway will the staff be assigned to their new posts. These people must then adapt themselves and the way they work to their new teaching environment. After the facility opens, the original school board members, administrators, and teachers change constantly. Each new person inherits a building that represents the vision of others who have now departed. It can be a bewildering experience. Without anything to guide them, new people naturally use their own thinking about how to use the facility and question the planning prowess of those who made the original decisions. Without guidance, more often than not traditional approaches to instruction and facility use are implemented in the new building. Unfortunately, the original vision for the school is lost in the process.

School districts and architects need to provide all those who will use the building with information on the original vision that shaped it and how its spaces are intended to be used to support instruction. Architects and contractors have long provided operating manuals for the mechanical equipment in schools. Similarly, architects should provide those who will actually bring the building to life with an owner's manual to help them understand how it is supposed to work to serve its real purpose—teaching kids. When the full faculty has been assembled, the owner's manual can be used for staff development. If the visioning, programming, and design have been successful, the school will embody new ways to teach and learn. Faculty with experience in other schools may have to learn new roles, new ways to teach, new uses of technology, and new ways to use time. Completing construction is not sufficient to realize the original vision for the school. The teaching staff must be equipped to sustain the vision over the years as they work with students.

A New Role for Architects—Change Agent

Historically, architects have helped clients define and document their aspirations and functional requirements for their building projects. The process is called programming, and it has been much the same for every type of structure including schools. The role of the architect has been primarily reactive in nature. Architects listen to their client's wants and their budgetary and other constraints and then respond with an architectural program that balances those desires and limitations.

However, we see a new role for architects to assume in the school design process—that of proactive change agent. Some architects are able to contribute more than reactive documentation to the school programming process because they have been involved in many more building projects than most school district and instructional staff. Although teachers and administrators may have few opportunities to create new facilities in an entire career, experienced educational architects are continuously involved in planning new schools that meet a wide range of instructional needs. For example, Frank's firm has designed more than 260 new schools in 97 school districts in the last five years. Such experience enables these architectural firms to bring a wider perspective to the visioning, programming, and design process. Ultimately, the client must make the final decisions about their program, but the decision-making process can benefit greatly from all that the firm has learned from other projects. In addition to understanding architecture, architects must be fluent with instructional concepts and their design implications to contribute meaningfully to the development of the vision and program for a new school. In so doing, the architect can have a positive role in creating more effective schools for the 21st century.

As we mentioned earlier, the three authors of this book began implementing this new visioning and design process in school districts in the Houston area several years ago. What we have discovered in these visioning exercises has been exciting. In fact, starting with the visioning exercise as the first step in the planning and design of a new school has had an amazingly positive effect on the focus of discussions concerning ideas for the new building. People are actually starting the process by talking about instruction and what they want it to do for kids instead of where the whiteboards should go or how big the student drop-off area should be.

However, taking the vision that is developed during these exercises and translating it into new school facilities have been more challenging. We have found that the pull of TTWWADI can take the energy out of many good ideas, and most of the schools that have been built have not been significant departures from what we currently have. But although the schools are not radically different, they are different. The important point here is that the visioning process has empowered school districts to take the first steps in making real changes in what high schools look like and how they operate. By continuing with the visioning exercises at the beginning of the design process for each new facility they build, districts will continue to make progress toward the goal of creating the truly new and innovative schools that are required to meet the educational needs of the students of today as well as those of tomorrow. To help those struggling with what high schools could be like in the future, we have included concepts in the following chapters in an attempt to spark thinking that goes beyond the tired ideas behind the schools of today.

Reflect on the Process by Which Your School District Creates Its School Facilities

- How do you define a broad vision for teaching and learning to guide the creation of new schools? How do you avoid creating the design of new schools on assumptions based on how you've done schools in the past? What issues and questions do you consider?
- How are your administrative, instructional, facilities, and technology personnel engaged in the process of defining the functional requirements for your facilities?
- How are your administrative, instructional, technology, and facilities personnel directly engaged in the facility design process?
- After a new school has been constructed and school is underway, how do you sustain the original vision for teaching and learning around which it was designed?

3

No More Cookie-Cutter Schools

Given the exponential pace of change and the state of our schools today, we must rethink what a high school should be each time we plan a new school. We simply cannot continue to allow the industrialized, cookie-cutter approach of the early 20th century to fail to serve the diverse and evolving needs of 21st-century students.

- Each high school must be customized to address the needs of the community in which it operates. What works in one community may not work in another.
- No single teaching and learning approach can serve the needs of every student. Schools need to tailor teaching and learning to individual students.
- Schools must offer more choice—where students attend, and what, how, and when they learn.
- Significant change is difficult to effect and still more difficult to sustain.
- Although there are challenges and potential risks to changing, the greater and more certain danger is continuing to operate high schools that fail a third or more of our students and leave many others ill prepared for postsecondary schooling and work.

In the chapters that follow, we explore ideas for high school design that go beyond the typical school we have today. But we must remind you that the focus cannot be on the material we will present there. In fact, those ideas don't begin to make sense until you have first developed a vision for what you want a school to be. A vision for the kind of instruction you see meeting the needs of students and the community both now and in the future. A vision that results from following the process we outlined in Chapter 2.

In the past, there was a single approach to high school design that naturally developed from the mass-production mentality of the assembly line oriented Industrial Age. Although it was a great step forward in providing high school education to large numbers of students, it could not and never did meet the needs of every student or the desires of every parent.

Now that we have had a century of experience with this "one size fits all" approach to designing high schools, it has become obvious that the assumptions it is based on have serious shortcomings in handling the demands for individualization in the new Information Age.

Students and parents are becoming increasingly dissatisfied with the inflexibility of schools. Recent developments such as vouchers, charter schools, virtual schools, magnet schools, home schooling, online learning, and a growing list of nontraditional educational choices are indications that we are not meeting the needs of all of our students in the public system.

To a large degree, this trend toward alternatives to the traditional public high school is a result of a combination of unresponsive schools and the increasing choice to which people are becoming accustomed in the world outside the school system. The Industrial Age notion of comprehensive school design was that all schools were similarly designed, equipped, and operated—stamped out as though they were made with a cookie cutter. But this is not an adequate way to deal with the diversity of students that attend a school. And because there is not just one generic kind of student with uniform interests and life goals, it is foolish to think there is one school design that will meet the needs of all those who attend.

In the Information Age of the 21st century, schools will be customized to meet the specific needs of each community in which they operate. This tailoring of schools to meet specific needs will be part of a much larger trend of mass customization that is already beginning to sweep over the modern world.

In *Free Agent Nation,* Daniel Pink (2001) talks about the astounding level of customization available to us in the technologically infused life we are beginning to experience. There are a multitude of examples of how choice has already become a part of the approach businesses have towards their customers. Here are just a few:

- Technological advances in food cooking mean that you can now go into a fast food restaurant and customize your order.
- Automobile companies will let you go online and customize a vehicle as it is moving down the production line.
- Levi Straus will let you custom order clothes that are made to fit.

- Frank has been getting custom-made shirts from Lands' End for the last few years.
- Web sites will allow you to create your own designs for wallpaper, business cards, T-shirts, or kitchen cabinets.
- Apple's iPod allows you to customize your playlists. By going online, you can customize the music content you listen to by downloading the song files for the kind of music you prefer.
- CRAYON.net allows you to **CR**e**A**te **Y**our **O**wn **N**ewspaper with the information customized to match your own specific needs and interests.
- The Expedia Web site (and several others) allow people to create their own customized travel itineraries.
- TiVo allows you to customize your television experience.
- Kitchenaide allows customers to order from a wide range of colors for household appliances.

As a result of the rapid move toward customized products, there has been a huge shift toward just-in-time production in manufacturing. This means there has been a drastic reduction in inventories of premade items because premade goods have been manufactured without customer input. In *The Long Tail,* Chris Anderson (2006) discusses these and many more examples from the new era of customer choice.

In the same way, education must be caught up in this trend of tailored goods and services if it is to keep pace with the world of the 21st century. Instead of fitting students into the existing school system, we must shape schools to fit the needs of students. If we hope to create schools that fit into and reflect modern society and adequately prepare students for their life in that society, it is critical that we consider what this trend will mean for education. What will it mean to have tailored schools?

SCHOOLS MUST OFFER MORE CHOICE

The trend toward tailored goods and services in the modern world will mean that schools will have to offer much more choice to parents and students than they currently do because, as we have just outlined, increasing choice will be one of the hallmarks of 21st-century life. Technology is providing an unprecedented level of choice for an ever-increasing range of products and services. The trend toward more choice in life will naturally lead people to demand more choice in the schooling their children or they themselves receive.

Students and parents will increasingly demand that their schools provide educational programs that are customized to the individual aspirations of a single student. Each school and school district will have to make a huge shift in attitude toward students, parents, and the community. Schools will have to become far more client driven than they are today.

Just as businesses continually monitor their customers to keep in sync with their changing demands, schools and school districts will have to treat kids and their parents as customers and continually monitor their preferences for the kind of education that will best meet their needs. Phil Schlechty made this point a number of years ago in *Inventing Better Schools* (1997).

This shift in thinking has already begun in schooling that takes place outside the public school system. Why is there such growth in the range of alternatives to traditional public schools? Why are these alternatives attracting so many students? Why are there long waiting lists for openings in these institutions? It's because these schools are much more client driven than typical public schools.

A recent interview Frank had with the principal of an exceptional magnet school in Houston was quite revealing in terms of the shift in mindset needed to make that school run. The school has an exceptional record of student achievement and has five applicants for every space available. Frank asked the principal what he thought was the secret to the success of the school. The principal responded that kids are forced to attend most high schools, but that he has to attract kids to his school because they are not compelled to come—they must *want* to come. He observed that his school has to be one of the very best high schools in the country if he hopes to get any kids at all.

To do this, the school has to continually reflect on the services it provides students and adjust its approach to ensure that it meets the needs of its students. This represents a colossal shift in thinking from the mindset of the vast majority of school administrators and school district staff. It is critical that school districts come to terms with the idea that the virtual monopoly that public schools have had until now in providing K–12 education is not at all assured in the future.

Once schools are more client driven, they will discover that students and parents will want choice in three major areas. First, they will want options in the focus of instruction. Individual students may want to have their studies focus on a specific area of interest. This may be a science focus for medicine or engineering, or a visual arts focus for drawing and painting or sculpture, or a sports focus on athletic development, or a business focus on accounting or marketing. Students will also demand that they be able to take courses that are not currently offered at the school.

Second, students will want a choice of instructional delivery. Some students will choose a self-paced, self-directed approach to instruction. Others will want a project-based, group-oriented approach. Some students will prefer an approach that incorporates mentors from real-world jobs. Other students will want to do their learning using online resources and tools.

Third, students will want a choice in the time in which their instruction takes place. Life in the 21st century is becoming more complex, and people will increasingly want to fit their schooling around their individual schedules, both daily and over the school year.

So the million-dollar question is, "how can we meet the diverse needs of our clientele in one school or in one district?" To do this, we must abandon the cookie-cutter approach to school design. Many effective alternatives to the comprehensive public high school have emerged, proving that there are options aside from the traditional approach to school design. Therefore, effective schools and districts must offer multiple instructional approaches to students.

For example, regardless of the size of a school district, with creative use of technology, a single high school could offer a variety of learning opportunities including virtual schools, community mentorships, an extended school day and school year, academies, a school within a school, or just about any combination of the models outlined in subsequent chapters. All of these models are intended to address the interests and needs of individuals or specific groups of students. In the following chapters, we outline a number of different ideas for organizing high schools that begin to address the needs of modern students. The question is not which one of those models is the best, but which one is best for a particular community. In fact, the question should be refined even more to be, "which features of two or more of those models can be combined with any new ideas we haven't covered, and altered to create just the right hybrid to meet the needs of a particular community?"

The point is that we must get beyond the idea that all high schools must look and operate the same way, that there is something that could be considered a standard high school and every other variation is something special for kids with unusual needs. This will also mean that school districts will have to embrace the idea of multiple school designs within a single district. This will certainly increase the choice of instructional options for students.

But this strategy will also force school districts to embrace a much more flexible approach toward the way schools operate. No longer can a school be built and be expected to operate in the same basic way for 30 years or more. Even with the best efforts in gauging the instructional needs and desires of their students and creating the various school models to meet those needs, some school designs may prove to be more effective than others.

In addition, changing demographics, new technological developments, and a myriad of other factors may render some school designs less or more effective over time. Just as businesses modify their products and services to meet the changing needs and desires of their customers, school districts will have to monitor the instructional needs and aspirations of their students and change the way schools operate as required. If a model for instruction proves to be less effective, then that school must be reconfigured and realigned to a model that will work.

Abandoning the cookie-cutter approach to school design goes even further than this. Within a school district with multiple high schools, different schools could specialize in different instructional approaches. For example, within a single district there might be a virtual school; a community mentorship school; a school with an extended school day and school year; a school with an academy focus on medicine, business, fine arts, or athletics; or just about any combination of the models we describe later in the book. Again, all of these models are intended to address the interests and needs of individuals or specific groups of students.

School districts will also have the responsibility to vary school models according to the learning preferences of their students. A client-driven school district will monitor which school models are most popular and effective with students and parents and adjust school organization to meet demand. This is how successful businesses operate. If there are 1,000 students applying to go to one school with 500 seats and only 250 students applying to go to another school with 500 seats, a strong message is being sent to the school district. Client-driven school districts create schools that are based on how students learn, not where they live.

SCHOOLS MUST DEAL WITH UNPRECEDENTED CHANGE

The previous section dealing with increased choice in schools probably gave many school planners and designers fits as they began to wrestle with the implications of how school districts could possibly embrace those ideas in the everyday details of planning, designing, building, and operating the high schools in their community.

Unfortunately, there's even more to consider. In fact, what we are going to discuss now will have even more far-reaching implications than dealing with the increased choice we just covered. What we must now consider is that the very nature of change is changing in the 21st century.

In the 20th century, especially the mid-20th century, change was predictable. It followed a relatively linear growth pattern as shown in Figure 3.1. Growth in the power of technology, for example, could be predicted from past or current changes. This made change manageable. It was fairly easy to extrapolate into the future and see where things were headed. This kind of change persisted for many years. Planning for schools was straightforward in this environment, and because the rate of change remained quite stable for a long time, planners got used to being able to easily predict where things were going.

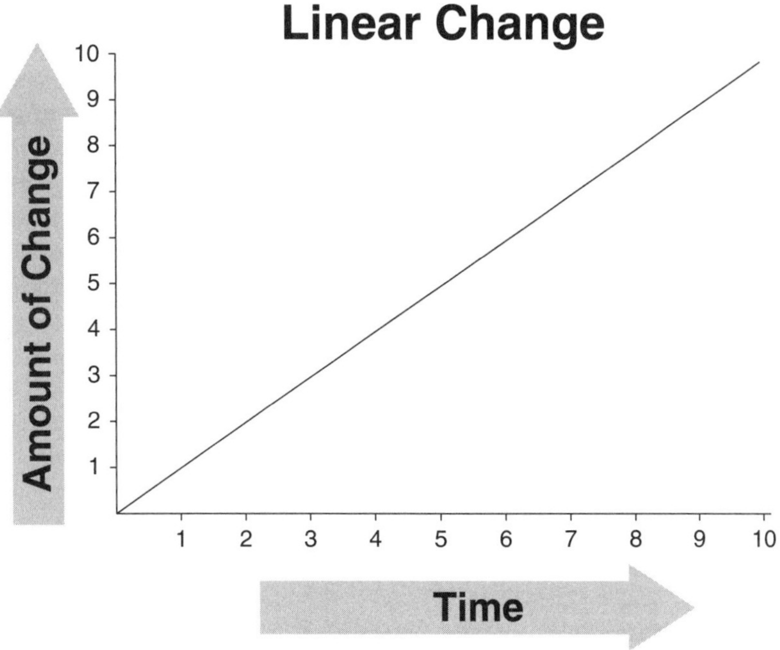

Figure 3.1

However, something dramatic happened in the latter part of the 20th century that made planning for schools much more difficult. Technological development increasingly changed the way the world operated. Sudden developments burst onto the scene with great power. One of the best examples of this is the rapid emergence of the World Wide Web as an integral part of everyday life. It was developed in the early 1990s, and it exploded into everyone's consciousness in the summer of 1995 shortly after a powerful free program called Mosaic was released (re-released as Netscape Navigator in 1995). In the short time since then, the World Wide Web has grown into an essential tool for business, education, and personal use that couldn't even have been imagined in 1995. The world seemed like it had changed overnight. New methods of information access, marketing, and instruction rocketed into action, rendering many old approaches and procedures obsolete.

How could a development with such global impact have exploded onto the scene so rapidly? Even more troubling is how something of this magnitude could happen so quickly without anyone knowing it was about to happen. What was going on? What was going on was a radical shift in the way change takes place. In a very short time, we have gone from the linear and relatively predictable change of the late Industrial Age to the exponential and highly unpredictable change of the Information Age.

So how is exponential change different from linear change? Linear change occurs when development increases by a fixed increment. For example, if the power of a computer is increasing in a linear fashion, then each day you add a fixed increment to the number representing its power. This was shown in Figure 3.1. But if you are experiencing an exponential growth in the power of the computer, then each day the power might double or triple from the previous day. This kind of change based on the daily doubling of power is illustrated in Figure 3.2. Notice that the growth in power in the exponential change graph develops slowly for a while, then makes a dramatic swing upward as the doubling really kicks in. Once this occurs, the power increases each day are astounding. This explains why the development of the World Wide Web exploded into our lives. It was increasing in size and power exponentially.

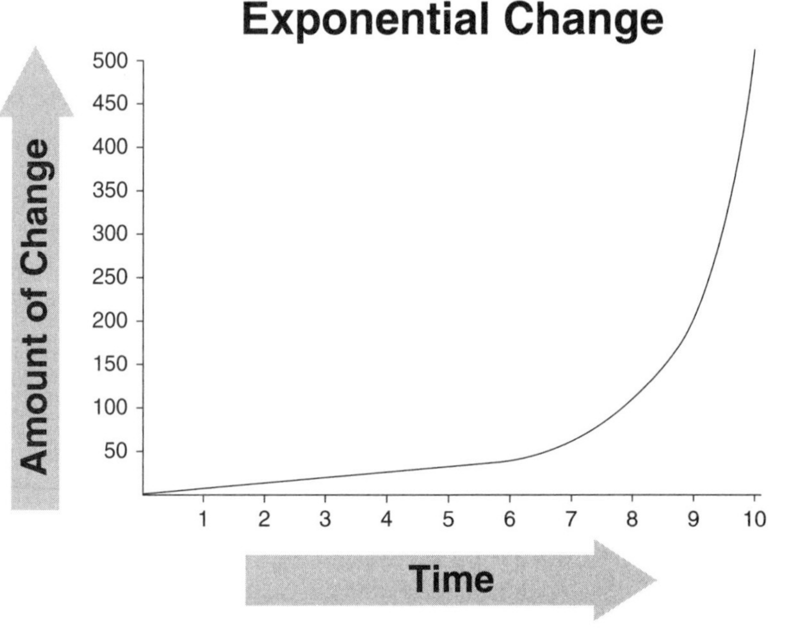

Figure 3.2

In *The Singularity Is Near*, Ray Kurzweil (2005, p. 21) states that there are more than 75 exponential trends occurring in technological development in the world today. Taken individually, these trends are thought provoking. Taken collectively, these trends are absolutely staggering in their implications for life in the future. The exponential nature of the change means that in the 21st century, it will become increasingly commonplace for overwhelming developments of enormous power to appear suddenly.

Further, Kurzweil indicates that not only will change be increasingly exponential in nature, but there will be more of it in many more areas of life than we have seen previously. It will truly be a world unlike anything we have ever experienced before.

What will this mean for school planning and design? It will mean that the old ways of doing things will quickly become obsolete. Those who persist in using the old tried-and-true approaches of the 20th century will encounter more and more difficulties and feel more and more stress as the world experiences more and more exponential change.

Ideas developed for the Industrial Age simply won't work in the Information Age. We must employ new approaches if we want to have any hope of succeeding in designing effective schools in this new era of change. What is needed is nothing short of a radical new mindset for school design.

No longer can we think of schools as static facilities that are built and then essentially left standing with minor renovations for 30, 40, 50 years or more. New school designs will have to be incredibly flexible to accommodate the shifting demands of the 21st-century world as it experiences exponential change.

Some businesses are already using facilities that are designed to function in an environment of change. Just think of the conference facilities at hotels. They have movable walls and other features that make it easy for hotel staff to reconfigure the conference space to meet the needs of their various clients.

For years, shopping centers and office buildings have been designed with customizable interior spaces. Walls are made out of easily removed metal studs, ceilings are made out of easily removed suspended tiles, and the mechanical, electrical, and network systems are constructed in the ceiling so they can be easily accessed and modified. When new clients want different interior spaces, the building owners can reconfigure the structure to meet their needs.

Schools planners will have to adopt a similar mindset when creating new facilities. One thing we can count on in the 21st century is change, so schools must be designed with change in mind. This will radically alter the way we approach the design of school facilities. In the past, we have typically spent more on school buildings to ensure that they last a very long time. Extra money is often spent on the cost of masonry partitions, terrazzo floors, and the like. In the future, however, we will spend less on some materials as we recognize that the interior spaces will be changed multiple times over the life of the building.

This will require a major departure from the current thinking that school districts have toward their school buildings. They must come to see the interior of a school as temporary. Although this is new for school districts, it is exactly what office building developers have done for some time. They plan and budget for the shell of the building. Everything inside that shell is considered temporary and related to the specific needs of the tenants, who will change numerous times over the lifespan of the structure.

The notion of continual change will force school districts to alter their thinking even further. As we have seen, change, especially the exponential change we are seeing in the modern world, will be sudden and not easily predicted. This is the worst nightmare for the traditional mindset of school planning. But dealing with rapid and unpredictable change is not new.

Look at how businesses are dealing with the rapid and unpredictable changes in technological development. Although they do not always know what the changes will be, businesses know that new computers will continue to hit the market and their new power and features will compel their use. To handle the continual turnover of high-tech equipment, many businesses no longer purchase the equipment. Instead, they lease or even treat them as consumables with a very short lifespan, typically two to three years. These businesses do not think of technology as capital goods, but treat it more like office supplies. At the end of the lease, they return the computers. If they have treated them as consumables, then the businesses give the computers to employees to take home. In either case, this allows the business to replace the computers with the latest, most powerful models available. This keeps the businesses up to date with the rapidly changing world of computer technology.

Because the world of the 21st century will be a rapidly changing environment for education, school districts will have to consider this option as well. Knowing that schools will have to change to meet the changing needs of their students, school districts may decide to rent or lease space for schools. This would allow schools to move to more suitable locations when the term of their lease is up or at least put the burden of renovations on the building owner if they want to keep the school as a tenant.

Schools and school districts will take on a radically different look when they embrace these ideas. The bulk of core instructional spaces could be housed in typical office or retail leased facilities. Districts may choose to sign shorter term leases for certain programs so they can move to more suitable facilities as their needs change. School districts may own only highly specialized spaces such as science labs, art studios, theaters, music halls, and specialized spaces for career education programs. Some districts may choose to own physical education and athletic spaces and fields, whereas others may leave these to community groups.

THE REAL ISSUE FACING SCHOOLS

It should be clear that all those involved in creating new learning environments will face some amazing challenges in the 21st century. It should also be clear that schools cannot stay the same if we hope to keep them relevant, effective, viable, and filled with kids. If we want the innovative schooling that will be needed to keep high schools relevant for learners in this new age, then we cannot continue to create them using ideas and approaches that were developed in another age for a world that no longer exists. That means schools must change. And there, as the Bard would tell us, is the rub.

The most important issue facing schools today is not how to incorporate the fantastic new technology we have discussed. It's not adjusting to the new ways digital students think. It's not implementing the new planning approach we outlined. It's not even deciding which of the models for high schools discussed in subsequent chapters to use.

No, the most important issue facing schools today is the reluctance of those in control of education to let go of what they are used to, whatever their role in the system. Teachers must let go of instructional approaches that were designed to work in the Industrial Age schools of the 20th century. Administrators and school district staff must let go of traditional ideas of managing students. School district facilities staff and architects must let go of their preconceived ideas of how schools operate and what schools look like.

It really boils down to an issue of comfort. It took a lot of time and effort for people to acquire the skills necessary to make the school system work the way it does now. Many have invested their entire careers learning how to teach in the Industrial Age schools we have today. Others have invested their professional lives in obtaining the knowledge and skill required to plan and design these 20th-century facilities. And because schools have remained the same for such a long time, people have become very comfortable with the way things are done. The status quo is firmly entrenched in the way schools are financed, and in the laws governing curriculum, student assessment, school accountability, the length of the school year, as well as in labor laws, family habits, community self-images related to sports, and so forth.

Now we come along and say that the world of the 21st century will be radically different from the world that most of us grew up in, that it will require a major shift in the way we think about education. This upsets the apple cart. Making the shift to a 21st-century approach to school design will be a challenge for anyone who is used to doing things the old-fashioned way, and the more time a person has invested in the old way of doing things, the greater the challenge will be. Simply put, making the shift will be uncomfortable. It will force people to start examining what they think about students, learning, instructional strategies, school organization, and school design all over again. It will require time and effort. It will be messy. It will also be easier to cling to and defend the way it's always been done.

One of the metaphors we use in our visioning exercises with school districts is comparing people's minds to rubber bands. Our goal at the beginning of our visioning sessions is to stretch the rubber band by examining what is happening in the digital world and the impact it is having on our kids, the things we discussed in Chapter 1. We ask people to consider the implications these developments should have on the way we teach, the way we assess, the way we plan for new schools, and the way we design new facilities. Without exception, we have found that the teachers, administrators, district staff, board members, businesspeople, students, parents, and community members have seen that we cannot continue to do things the way we do them now. Our initial visioning sessions are very stimulating as the people involved get excited about new ideas for how schooling could take place. By the time we have finished exploring what 21st-century schools could look like, the rubber band has been significantly stretched!

Then something remarkable happens. The people involved in the visioning session, especially those who work in the school system, begin to grasp the significance and the implications of the changes that they've envisioned. To make the vision become a reality will require people to make substantial changes in the way they currently do things. They begin to realize that this will require real effort. They begin to understand that this will be extraordinarily uncomfortable. Consequently, they start to second-guess the wisdom of creating such a wild new vision for their schools. And the rubber band snaps back.

Then those involved in developing the new vision start getting feedback from those who were not directly involved in the visioning exercise. The vision that was developed in the first session is written up for others to see and distributed for feedback. Some will respond positively, but the majority of responses will be negative.

Here is a sample of actual responses we have heard to new visions for 21st-century schools:

> "Are you crazy? You can't expect teachers to teach that way."
>
> "Do you have any idea how much this will cost?"
>
> "Yeah, those are great ideas, but they'll never work here."
>
> "What makes you so sure the world is going to be that different in the future anyway?"
>
> "I've been through all this before. This technology thing is just another fad like open classrooms. It will pass and things will return to normal in a little while."
>
> "If schools were like that, I couldn't use all the lesson plans I've developed."
>
> "The Department of Education will never let you do something like this."
>
> "What will happen to test scores?"
>
> "People aren't trained for this kind of school. What were you thinking?"
>
> "What's wrong with the schools we have now? They were good enough for me so they should be good enough for kids today."

We have found that the majority of people respond from their comfort zone. As they begin to grasp the magnitude of the change required to make this new kind of schooling a reality, they begin to see how much time, effort, and struggle it will take. They respond accordingly.

The end result is that the new vision is reeled in so it isn't so challenging. The new learning that was seen as so important when the original vision was created is now questioned and its new features dismissed. People come up with all of the reasons why it can't be done instead of looking for all the ways it could be done. Teachers attack the new kind of instruction because it doesn't look like anything they have ever seen before. Parents don't like the new schools because they don't look like the schools they attended. School district staffs don't like the new ideas because they can't see how to manage students in such a new environment. Everyone sees only problems with the new vision for learning. By the time the facilities people and the architects get through with the planning for the next school, the vision has been seriously watered down or lost altogether.

Why? Because the status quo is so firmly entrenched, it is much easier to keep doing things in schools the way they always have been done than it is to change. You must remember that schools have been the same since before everyone alive today was born. People have literally grown up with schools as they are.

Embracing the kind of change we see that is needed for the 21st century will require rethinking much of what we have taken for granted for so long. When confronted with this kind of change, most people retreat to what is familiar. They deny that the change is needed, they ridicule those who espouse such nonsense, they avoid dealing with the implications of such change, they dismiss the need for considering new ideas, and they point to any problems as reasons for dismissing the change outright. Why? Because it is easier than getting down and doing the hard, messy work of changing the longstanding and ineffective way we have taught our kids and the way we have designed the schools they use.

Here is a powerful reason we know that change is avoided in the school system. Most of the ideas in this book about reorganizing schools are not new. Yes, we have added some of our thoughts to each of the models, and we have extended the idea of school design to include the Cyber School, but most of the models for school organization we cover are just the repackaged ideas of others. And their ideas are not new.

For example, recognizing the need to teach students differently, J. Lloyd Trump wrote *Images of the Future* in 1959. Since then, there have been many who have come to similar conclusions about the state of schools and the need for change. Yet despite the mounting body of work pointing to the need for substantial change in our schools, those responsible for education have steadfastly resisted most of the calls for new forms of instruction.

What is most troubling about this situation is that those responsible for schools have decided to ignore the calls for change and continue with traditional approaches despite the growing evidence that schools are performing very poorly. Here are just a few of the grim statistics regarding the performance of schools in the United States.

- "Almost one third of all public high school students and nearly one half of all blacks, Hispanics, and Native Americans fail to graduate from public high schools with their class" (Bridgeland, DiIulio, & Morison, 2006, p. 1).
- "The United States has one of the lowest high school graduation rates among industrialized nations" (National Governors Association [NGA], 2005, p. 3).
- "On state assessments of English and mathematics, roughly one in three high school students fails to meet standards" (NGA, 2005, p. 3).
- "Nearly a third of high school graduates who go on to college require immediate placement in remedial education courses" (NGA, 2005, p. 3).
- "The percentage of 9th graders that make it through the education process: 68% of them graduate from high school, 40% of them immediately enroll in college, 27% of them are still enrolled in their sophomore year, and 18% graduate from college" (NGA, 2005, p. 3).
- "84% of employers say K–12 schools are not doing sufficient job preparing students for work—in Math, Science, Reading and Comprehension—even in attendance, timeliness, and work ethic" (National Association of Manufacturers, 2005, p. 16).
- "Nearly half of Texas students entering college now must take remedial classes" (*Houston Chronicle*, July 7, 2006, p. B1).

These statistics paint an incredibly damning picture of the performance of schools. But if those in education have resisted any major changes even though the poor performance and need for change have been well documented, it makes us conclude that people in education are choosing, consciously or unconsciously, to hold onto inefficient, underperforming approaches to instruction rather than embrace the change that is desperately needed because that is the most comfortable thing to do.

That illustrates the difficulty of breaking out of the mold of current thinking about education. It also illustrates the power of TTWWADI. We have done things the same way for so long in schools, and people have become so comfortable with the way things are, that change is extremely difficult. Like the width between the rails of train tracks, the way we teach students is accepted without question because it's been that way for so long. Conventional wisdom is that it takes strength to hold on to something. However, the truth is that it takes the greatest amount of strength to let go of something familiar.

WHAT CAN BE DONE?

Is the situation hopeless? Far from it. But it will take real effort if we want to get the school system out of the deeply entrenched ways of doing things that are the status quo.

Where do we begin? The starting point is to embrace the new planning process we outlined in Chapter 2. As you begin to ask questions about where the world is heading, the implications of technological development, and the digital world kids are experiencing, a new vision for what learning could and should be will naturally emerge. If you are having trouble getting started, get help. There are people who have been helping school districts develop new visions for 21st-century schools for several years. Seek them out.

Do not rush through the visioning process. It has been our experience that school districts that have not taken the time to create a new vision for learning encounter a great deal of resistance. This invariably occurs because they have not involved everyone associated with the design and operation of new schools in the visioning process.

A key step of the process of effecting change in an organization is the development of a collective vision that comes from real dialogue with all those who will be affected by any departures from established ways of doing things. If those people are not involved in the visioning process, they will not fully understand the reasons for the changes being contemplated. Consequently, they will resist any move away from what they are currently doing.

Although it takes time and money to bring everyone into the visioning process, it is the key to bringing about significant change. Once all the stakeholders have had the opportunity to be involved and have real input, you can then produce a vision document that captures the new direction for your schools. Use this document as a standard to measure any work on new facilities. And be sure you take the time to fully create a comprehensive new vision for schools before spending a dollar on planning or construction.

Developing a new vision for schools is hard work to be sure, but don't be fooled into thinking the work is done once the vision has been created. In fact, the hard part is what comes next. It will take great courage, steadfast commitment, and a lot of just plain hard work to sustain the vision. The rubber band can still snap back.

Make no mistake about this—the process of transferring the new ideas for instruction and learning into actual practice with students is the critical and most difficult part of shifting schools to new approaches to education.

You will have as critics all those who are married to traditional methods for instruction and conventional school design. Their opposition to the new vision will rise as they begin to see that they will have to make personal changes as schools shift away from the familiar 20th-century designs and methods of operation.

To counter the criticism that will inevitably come, those advocating the new vision must understand that changing longstanding approaches to learning will require a concerted, long-term effort. We cannot view transferring vision into practice as a one-shot, short-term thing. Without continual encouragement and assistance, people will slip back to what is familiar and comfortable.

To create new schools for the 21st century, all those involved must receive support and training over a period of years, long after a new building has been constructed. It will be hard. It will be a struggle. Many will complain. You will wonder at times why you ever started with this harebrained idea of creating new schools. It will be incredibly important to remember the number one reason you started looking at new approaches to instruction and learning—our children and their success in the unfamiliar, technologically infused world of the 21st century.

We began the first chapter with the following definition of insanity: *Doing the same thing you've always done, but expecting or wanting or needing completely different results.* We see this insanity being lived out daily in the schools our children attend. We have written this book in an attempt to bring sanity back to the way we design 21st-century schools. We firmly believe that if you embrace the new planning process we have outlined and apply some combination of the school models that follow, you will create the innovative new facility designs the school system desperately needs to engage modern students and to prepare them for their life in the future. We can't wait to see the kinds of schools you create.

Reflect on Your Schools and How They Serve the Diverse and Changing Needs of Your Students

- Assess your own personal comfort level with the way schools are today. Whatever role you play in designing or operating a school, are you resisting new ideas because they will force you out of your zone of comfort and familiarity?
- How do your high schools reflect the diverse needs of the students they serve? How are your instructional methods and offerings different from school to school?
- How do parents and students decide which high school to attend in your district? Do they have choices of schools and instructional methods?
- How are your high school instruction and facilities planned to accommodate the exponential change occurring in the world in which your students live?
- When a new school opens, how do you assure that the vision that shaped the school will be realized in its long-term operation?
- What percentage of your students graduate from high school? How do those who graduate fare in college and at work? Over time, are these acceptable for your community?

PART 2

"There is nothing more difficult to take in hand, more perilous to conduct, or more uncertain in its success, than to take the lead in the introduction of a new order of things, because the innovator has for enemies all those who have done well under the old conditions, and lukewarm defenders in those who may do well under the new."

Niccolò Machiavelli, *The Prince* (1513/2005, p. 27)

4

Models for High Schools

High schools are complex institutions in which teaching, learning, time, technology, facilities, and costs are integrally related, each dependent on and affected by the other. Part 2 of *Teaching the Digital Generation* describes 11 models for widely different ways to make high schools. This chapter includes the following:

- A guide to reading the graphics that describe each model.
- Concepts for time (school day and year) that may be applicable across multiple models.
- A description of the graphic scales provided to assess the models according to the principles for high schools set out in Chapter 2.

Reading the Diagrams

Each model is described by an annotated diagram that explains conceptual relationships between instruction, time, technology, and facilities. These are not floor plans and are not to scale.

Instructional/Spatial Organization
Notes and diagrams describe how the school is organized instructionally and architecturally.

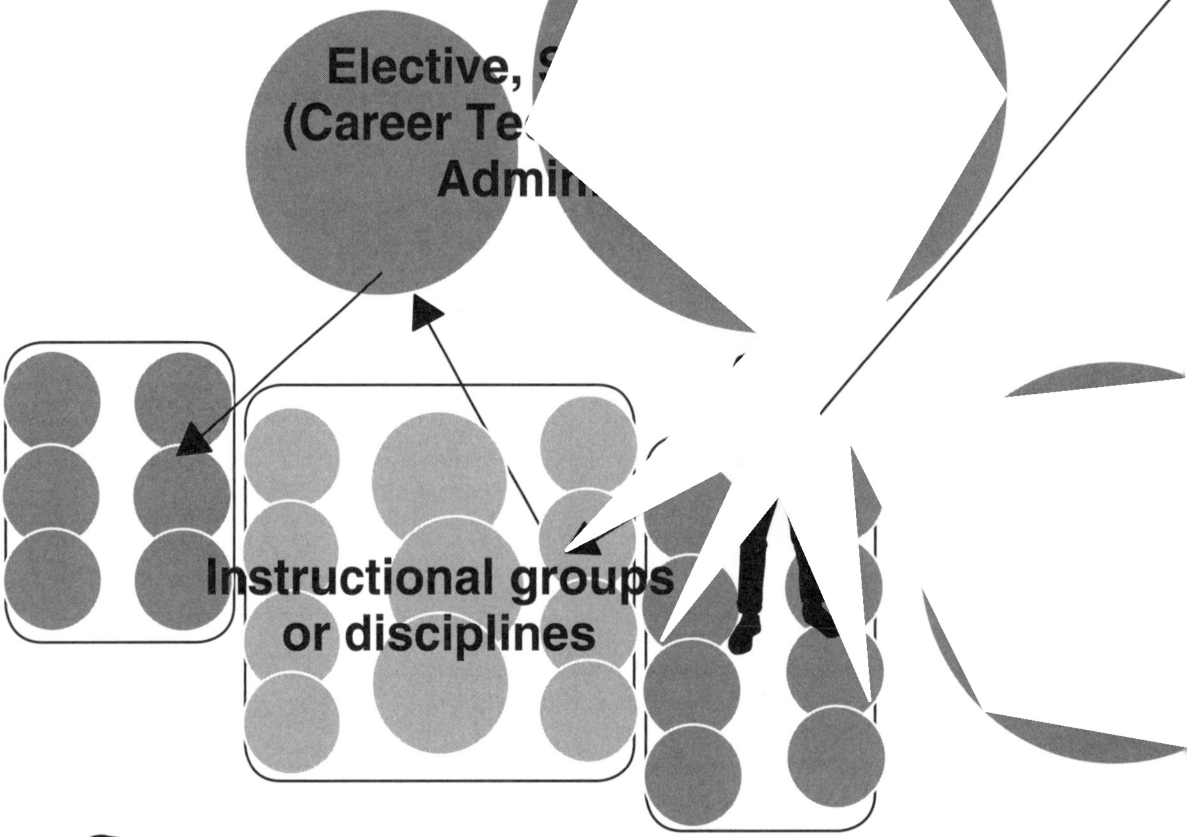
Elective,
Instructional groups or disciplines

Students and Technology
The student may or may not have personal digital devices depending on the model. Where they do, it is assumed that every student has continuous personal use of the devices anytime, anywhere.

Students
The instructional path that a student may take over the course of a typical day. They indicate the scale of the environment in which the student works. Different instructional concepts create very different environments for students and teachers.

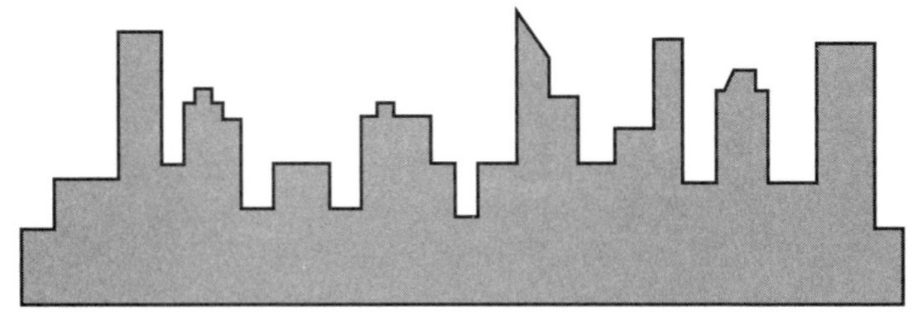

Real-World Instructional Resources
Several models integrate real-world resources both on and off the campuses.

School Size, Scalability
Notes explore the relationship between the instructional program and the size of the school. Some instructional progams may work whether the school is large or small. Others may work on only one scale. The size of the school has implications for what it may offer in some programs.

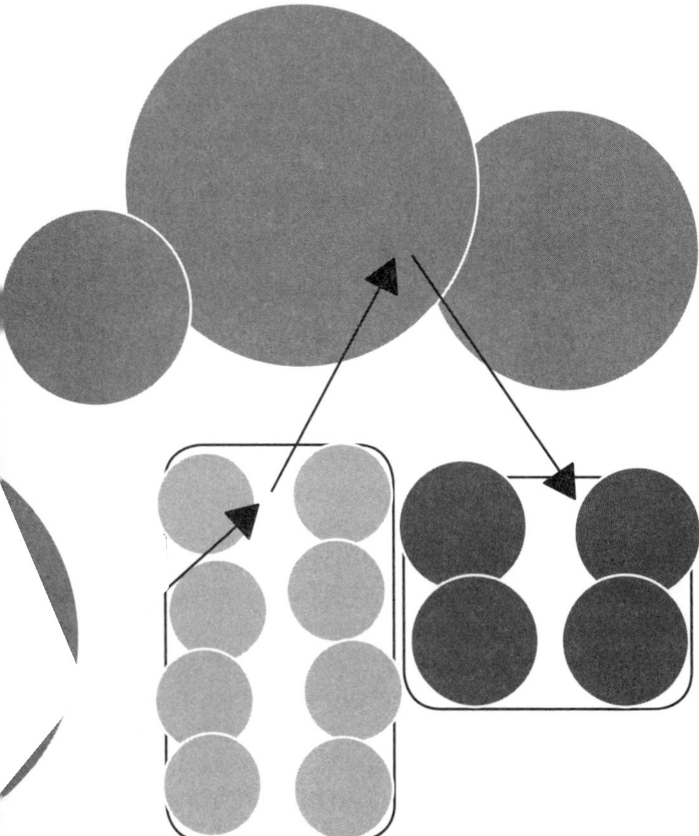

School Days
This diagram shows the days in the school week and how each day is organized. Black segments of time are scheduled for specific purposes. White segments are flexible periods of time that may be used by teachers and students as needed for teaching and learning. The number of segments may vary, but the real issue is the percentage of time fixed by the schedule vs. by the teachers and students.

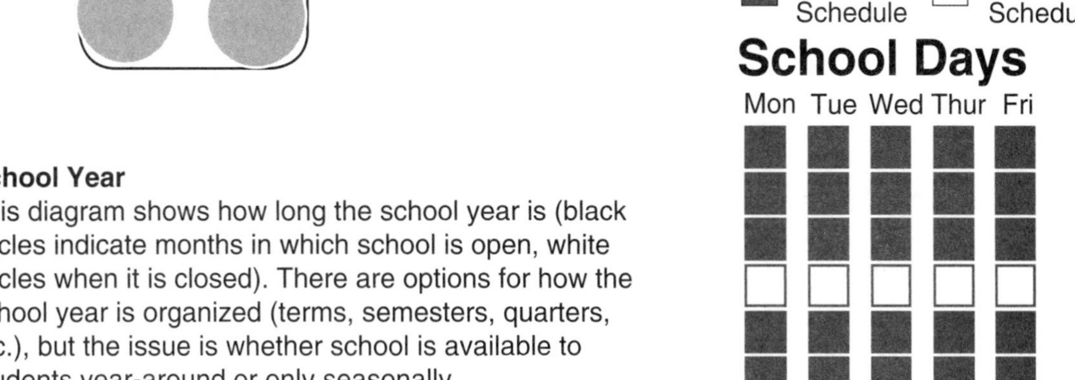

School Year
This diagram shows how long the school year is (black circles indicate months in which school is open, white circles when it is closed). There are options for how the school year is organized (terms, semesters, quarters, etc.), but the issue is whether school is available to students year-around or only seasonally.

School Year

J F M A M J J A S O N D

Spring Semester

Fall Semester

A premise of this book is that we have, for a very long time, misread the nature of the high school "problem." In *Windows on the Future* (2001), Ted and Ian argued that schools have been treated as if they were trains—linear and incremental. Educators have added and subtracted cars, and juggled the content of others, while the basic nature of the train remained unchanged. But keeping the school train on the track (a 20th- or even 19th-century metaphor) allowed graduation rates to plummet and the ranking of our students among their peers in other industrialized nations to decline.

Great ideas that might have improved aspects of our high schools have been rejected outright or tried and failed because realizing them would have affected other parts of our schools—other cars on the train. Although the train metaphor may have characterized a viable proposition in the past, it will not suffice in the future. The elements of today's high school are integrally three dimensionally linked, more like those in a molecular structure: change one part and the others must change as well. So in Part 2 of the book, we have outlined models for high schools with integrated concepts for teaching and learning, time, technology, and facilities.

The chapters that follow delineate 11 models. In the first of these, we reflect on the Industrial Age high school as a point of reference for all the subsequent models. Chapters 6–15 explore models for high schools we believe are more appropriate for students in the 21st century. For each of these, we have provided diagrams that outline concepts for teaching and learning, the use of time, and the configuration of facilities. Following the description of the model, we review its implications for the teachers, students, and administrators in the school, for the architect who will design the facility, and for the funds required to build and operate it.

Each model explores varied concepts for teaching and learning, time, technology, spaces, and costs. Some of the models reflect concepts outlined in earlier books or practiced at existing schools, all of which we have identified.

But we do not intend this to be a definitive compilation of high school ideas. Even with our accumulated years of experience, research, and travels, hardly a month has passed without us finding some new idea worthy of consideration. None of the models exactly follows the precedents from which it evolved. We have modified all of them in significant ways to reflect the needs of students in the 21st century. Our intent is to leave the reader more aware of multiple ways to design high schools and how the critical relationships between their components reflect varied educational priorities.

SCHOOL YEAR AND DAY

Although components of some models are integrally linked and cannot be modified without affecting the entire model, aspects of other models, particularly time, may be interchangeable, which generates still more possibilities. We have shown a number of options for the school year and day. Although we propose forms of year-round schooling in all but one of the nine models, we might consider the traditional agrarian calendar in others; we note these along with implications for learning and costs.

In terms of both dollars and learning, it is difficult to justify closing schools 25% of each calendar year. Principal and interest payments on bonds and most operating costs (utilities, maintenance, insurance, etc.) continue to be incurred even when school buildings are idle. By operating schools only 75% of the year, either more or larger school facilities are required to serve the same enrollment. The nine-month school year has the same impact on costs for teachers. If schools operated year-round, teachers could teach more, meaning that either fewer teachers would be required or more students could be served. In either case, individual teachers could earn considerably more without increasing the cost per student to school districts.

The critical concept here is that schools would, in some manner, operate 12 months per year—schooling would be a continuous service. Both teachers and students could determine how much schooling they want each year and when they want that to occur. Some may elect to continue with the nine-month school year, but take the winter months off instead of the summer. Some may elect to be in school all year, but carry a lighter load so that they may pursue other needs concurrently. Some may elect to teach or study full time throughout the year in order to increase their compensation or graduate more quickly. All of these options would increase the efficiency with which we utilize school facilities and provide the opportunity to increase both annual teacher compensation and students' learning opportunities.

Coupling a nine-month school year with fixed school days and class periods gives time priority over learning. If every aspect of school time is fixed, then there is almost no flexibility to accommodate varied learning styles or modes of instruction, and the Carnegie Unit or seat time is left as the real measure of schooling.

In the 21st century, why should students and teachers be able to "go to school" only part of the year? Why not make school a continuous service instead of a timed, seasonal event? Why not allow teachers and students flexibility in their pursuit of learning? Could some teachers and students be in school 12 months per year and others only nine or even six? Could some teachers and students attend nine months per year but decide for themselves which three months to pursue other interests? Could some students attend 12 months per year and graduate earlier, whereas others attend nine or six months per year and take longer to finish? If time is not fixed, there are lots of possibilities to make schooling more responsive to the individual needs of students and teachers and more economical to operate.

The 10 models included in this book describe diverse ways to structure high school time.

School Year

- Nine-month agrarian year divided into varied increments.
- 12-month school year divided into varied increments.
- 12-month school year with continuous instructional services.
- 24/7/365 instructional services.

School Day

- Fixed periods in which students and teachers are fully scheduled each day.
- A combination of fixed periods and flexible time managed by the teachers and students.
- Fixed blocks of time for groups of related subjects with the use of those blocks determined by the teachers and students.
- Modular days with small increments that may be combined for varied purposes including independent work time for teachers and students.
- Days with no schedule during which students and teachers are responsible for managing their own time.
- 24/7.

In some models, the different ways to use time may be interchangeable, but in others a particular approach is critical to the concept. We have tried in each case to make that distinction clear.

The following 19 graphic scales describe the varied priorities that shaped each model. Although each scale spans a broad spectrum, neither end is necessarily good or bad, right or wrong, worst or best, highest or lowest. None of the models is ranked totally to the left or right sides of all the scales. Considered together, the scales are indicative of the complexity of making high schools.

FOCUS ON TEACHING OR LEARNING?

Teacher Centered **Student Centered**

?

Is instruction organized around teachers and instruction or students and learning?

GROUP OR INDIVIDUAL TEACHING AND LEARNING?

Group Teaching and Learning **Individual Teaching and Learning**

Do teaching and learning focus on groups of students or individuals with their special needs and interests?

TRADITIONAL TEACHING VS. DIGITAL LEARNING

Teacher, Text **Digital**

Is instruction primarily based on teachers and texts or on digital resources?

21ST-CENTURY THINKING SKILLS

Knowledge Skills **Content + Problem-Solving Skills**

Does instruction focus primarily on knowledge skills or does it include the application of those skills to real-world problems relevant to students?

ASSESSMENT

Content Skills **Content + Problem-Solving Skills**

Does assessment focus primarily on knowledge skills or the application of that knowledge to the solution of real-world problems?

LEARNING FOCUS

Traditional Content **21st-Century Literacies**

Does instruction focus primarily on traditional subjects, or does it include digital skills essential to learning and functioning in the 21st century?

INSTRUCTIONAL ORGANIZATION

Departments and Disciplines **Interdisciplinary**

Are the school's instruction and facility organized into departments or interdisciplinary groups?

APPLICATION OF LEARNING

Classroom Theory **Real-World Relevance**

Is learning focused on academic concepts and theories or the application of those in real-world conditions?

RESPONSIBILITY FOR LEARNING

Teacher **Student**

Does the student have a passive or an active role in the teaching and learning process? Does the student have real responsibility for her own learning and for the management of her time?

TIME—SCHOOL YEAR

Fixed, Traditional **Flexible**

Does the school operate nine months per year or all year? Is the year organized in fixed increments of time (terms, semesters, quarters, etc.), or does it afford flexibility to accommodate various student needs and interests?

TIME—SCHOOL DAY

Fixed, Traditional **Flexible**

Is the school day fixed in length? Is the school day divided into fixed increments (periods, blocks, etc.)? Are those increments marked by bells? Is the specific use of every hour stipulated or do teachers and students have significant time that they manage to address individual needs and interests?

STUDENT SUPPORT

Counselor **Teacher-Advisor**

Does the school have counselors who work with several hundred students or teacher-advisors who work with fewer than 20 students? Are all students well known by an adult who follows and supports their academic and personal life through their high school years?

STUDENT LEARNING SPACES

Teachers' Rooms **Personal Workspaces**

Do students work entirely in spaces "owned" by teachers (classrooms, labs, etc.) or do they have individual places in which to do the work of learning?

SPATIAL FLEXIBILITY

Durable, Permanent **Responsive, Flexible**

Does the spatial organization of the school and its facility contribute to long-term flexibility to accommodate changes in programs and methods of instruction?

SCALABILITY—SCHOOL SIZE

Large Enrollment **Small Enrollment**

Do the school's instructional methods and learning environment require a small or large enrollment? Will the concepts be functional at widely varied enrollments?

COURSE OFFERINGS

Core + Broad Elective Subjects **Core Subjects**

How do the school's academic focus, instructional methods, technology, and enrollment affect course offerings?

EXTRACURRICULAR ACTIVITIES

Extensive **Minimal**

Do the size of the school, the nature of its instructional programs, and the use of time permit or support extensive extracurricular programs including athletics?

COSTS—STAFF

High Cost per Student **Low Cost per Student**

			?			

Is the cost per student for instructional staff relatively high or low? Is the cost of total staff per student relatively high or low?

COSTS—FACILITIES

High Cost per Student **Low Cost per Student**

			?			

Is the building area per student relatively high or low?

In the following chapters, we describe 11 models for 21st-century high schools. As we noted earlier, each explores varied concepts for teaching and learning, time, technology, spaces, and costs. Our intent is to leave the reader more aware of multiple ways to make high schools and how the critical relationships between their components reflect varied educational priorities.

We've anticipated that our readers will find themselves, as each of us has during the writing process, tempted to choose favorites among the group of models. The title of our book and the third chapter are intended to dissuade all concerned from thinking that way—to lead us away from searching for "the" high school of the future to replace "the" traditional industrial high school of the past—to look for ways to make high schools as diverse and ever-changing as the students they serve. In the end, we hope after reading our book that you are less certain about what a high school is and more open to the consideration of different ways to assemble instruction, technology, time, architecture, and money to make high schools appropriate to the students they serve.

5

Industrial Age High Schools

Schools for a World That No Longer Exists

Industrial Age high schools try to meet the needs of every student. Their characteristics generally include the following:

- Instruction and spaces centered on teachers, disciplines, and the efficient delivery of instruction.
- A nine-month school year based on the agrarian calendar.
- School days divided into equal blocks of time for every subject and student.
- Instruction that primarily occurs in classrooms by discipline.
- Subjects that are substantially focused on knowledge and content skills.
- A schedule where students move from teacher to teacher, subject to subject each period, and where students typically work with different teachers every year in every discipline.
- Broad, diverse course offerings and extracurricular activities that afford students many choices.
- Large enrollments (2,000+) that are needed to justify diverse course and extracurricular offerings.
- A curriculum that generally predates the emergence of digital tools.

Industrial Age High School

Instructional/Spatial Organization
Both instruction and facilities are organized around disciplines/departments. Teachers work primarily with others in their discipline. The focus is on content/knowledge skills.

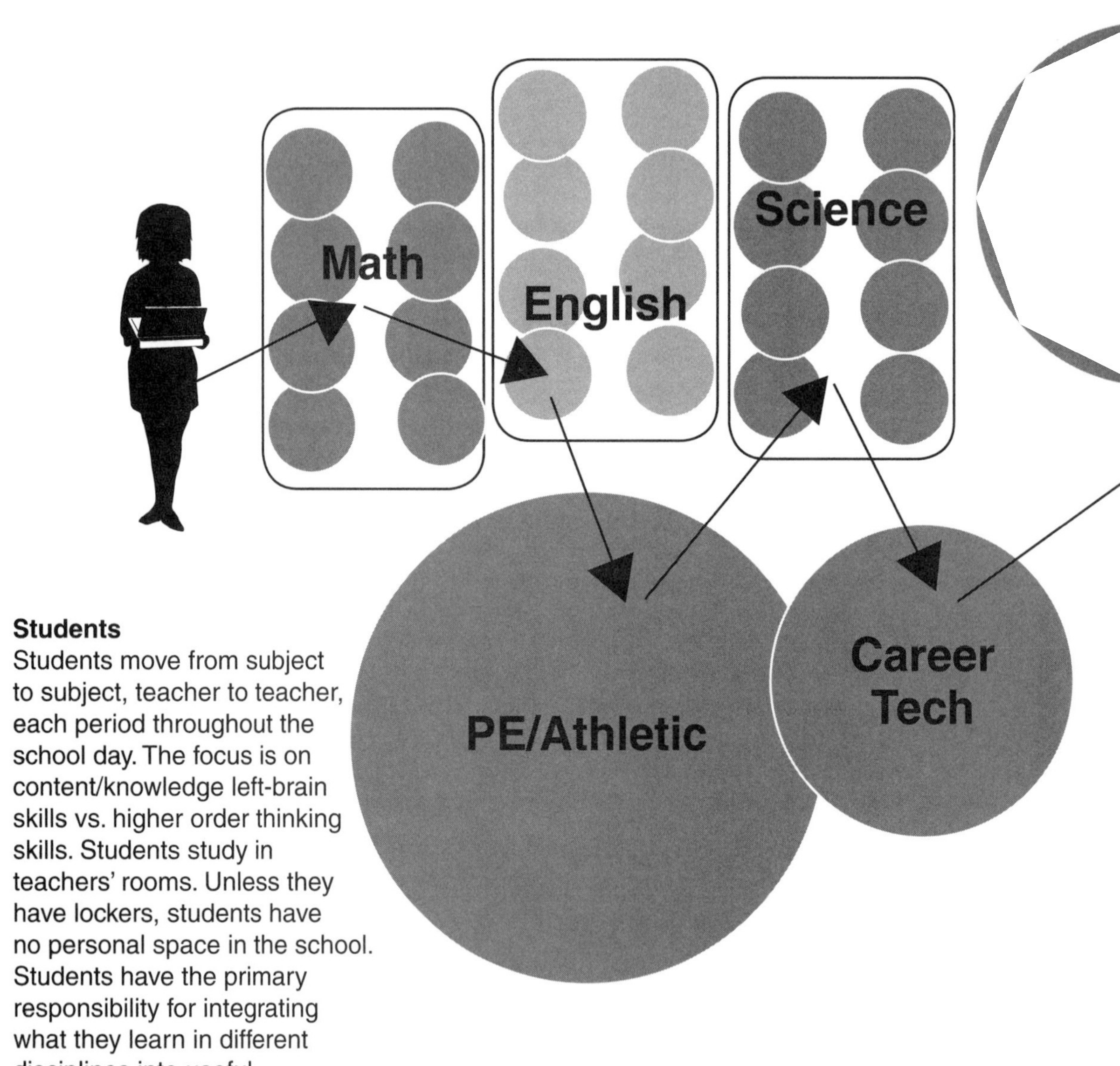

Students
Students move from subject to subject, teacher to teacher, each period throughout the school day. The focus is on content/knowledge left-brain skills vs. higher order thinking skills. Students study in teachers' rooms. Unless they have lockers, students have no personal space in the school. Students have the primary responsibility for integrating what they learn in different disciplines into useful real-world skills.

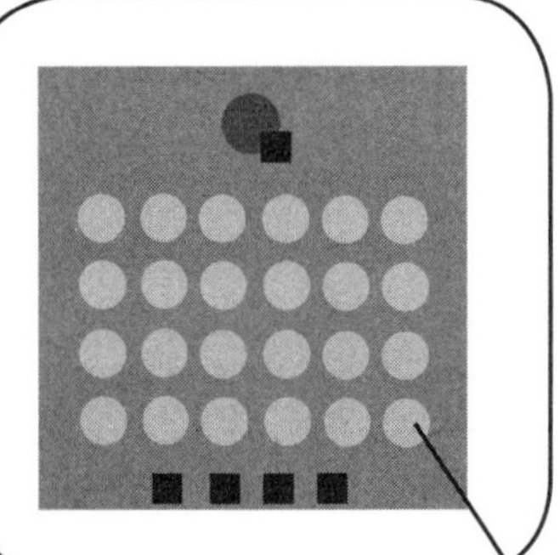

Classrooms
Virtually all instruction is in classrooms, each addressing 1 subject for 1 hour with 1 teacher and approximately 25 students. Most teachers prepare and teach in their classroom. There may be some technology for the teacher and students in the classroom. Instruction is primarily teacher centered.

School Size, Scalability
For teachers, the school is their classroom and department. For students, the entire high school is their context. They move from department to department, changing teachers every semester or year. The traditional school model has been used for both very small and very large schools. To be organized by departments and to support career, arts, and athletic programs, traditional high schools may be quite large—2,000 to 3,000 students or more.

Admin

Library

Visual, Performing Arts

Fixed Schedule

Flexible Schedule

School Days

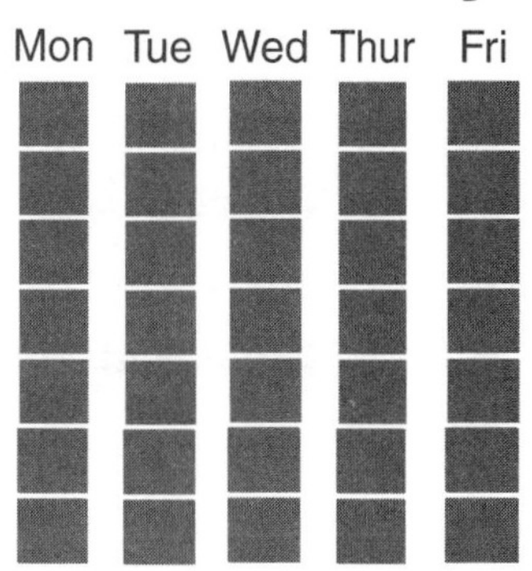

School Days
Every school day in every week is composed of the same time periods for every subject for every student. The number of periods/day typically varies from 4 to 8.

School Year
The 9–10 month school year is divided into 2 semesters totaling approximately 180–200 days. The school year, day, and instructional periods are fixed.

School Year

J F M A M J J A S O N D

Spring Semester

Fall Semester

We have already outlined the origins of the thinking that led to the design of Industrial Age high schools. These schools were a perfect fit with the industrialized world of the 20th century. They were so successful at educating students for that world that the design became a standard and quickly spread across North America and beyond. And these schools have been with us for a long time: they have been preparing students for life beyond high school for almost 100 years. But the success these schools achieved and the extended duration of being successful have led to an untenable situation in education today.

The world has made a huge shift into the digital Information Age based on a different kind of thinking than the Industrial Age of the 20th century. Success in this new age requires new and different skills than those needed for success in industrialized life. Plus, as we have documented, the digitally infused life of the 21st century is producing students who actually think differently than their elders. But just as this monumental shift has taken place, the entrenched Industrial Age mindset for what schools and learning look like has created a strong resistance to change in the school system. The adults in control of the system, from teachers to administrators to parents to politicians, demonstrate a nostalgic attraction to the Industrial Age schools of their youth. They continue to design and build schools based on thinking that no longer fully applies to or reflects life today. Worse, these schools continue to focus on skills that were valued for industrial life and ignore the skills that students really need for success in the future. From the best of intentions, with the increased testing in schools today, adults are reinforcing memory recall and the low-level thinking that was acceptable and appropriate for many positions in industrial society. The problem is that the schools of their youth were designed for a world that no longer exists. The rationale behind much of what is done in these schools no longer fully applies in the world of the 21st century. As the grim statistics that we outlined in Chapter 3 indicate, these schools are already not working well today. This will only get worse in the future. Assess the design of the traditional Industrial Age high school according to the guiding principles we outlined in Chapter 2 and you will quickly see that this type of school cannot effectively address the educational needs of the 21st century. Industrial Age high schools have had their run.

Industrial Age High Schools Are Characterized by the Following:

- Most instruction occurs in **classrooms,** each with one teacher and approximately 25–30 students focused on a single subject for a fixed period of time. Students move from class to class, subject to subject over the course of a school day.
- Instruction is **teacher centered,** with an emphasis on efficient teaching processes instead of individual learning outcomes. Students are

generally passive participants in the instructional process. Teachers and written texts are the major sources of content.

- The primary focus of instruction is **content and knowledge skills**—often substantially shaped by state- and federal-mandated tests.
- **Campuses are primarily self-contained**. All facilities, instruction, and activities are typically located at a single site. Campuses are usually closed. Most students are not allowed to leave campus until the end of the school day.
- **Comprehensive course offerings** and extracurricular activities include extensive core subjects, visual and performing arts, career technology, and physical education and athletics. The Industrial Age school seeks to serve all of the needs of all students.
- Most often, where a student may go to high school is determined by the **attendance zone** or catchment area in which the student lives. Students typically do not choose where they attend high school.
- Instructional spaces are organized around **disciplines** or departments, each of which is a separate area of the building. Teachers work primarily with others in their own discipline.
- The typical **school day** (approximately 6.5 hours total with an average of 5.6 hours of classroom time; National Education Commission on Time and Learning, 1994, p. 5) is divided into equal increments of time (average 51 minutes) for every subject, every day for every student. Virtually all school time is fully scheduled for every teacher and student. There is little or no flexible time to accommodate varied instructional methods or individual learning styles and capabilities. The unit of time is fixed regardless of whether students need more or less time to complete their studies. Generally, if students have not realized the learning objectives in the time allotted, they must repeat the entire course.
- The typical school day is divided into **six to eight periods**. Bells ring to mark the beginning and end of each class, and students circulate around the campus from class to class. At five to six minutes each, these transition periods consume 30–40 minutes or approximately 10% of each school day.
- Reflecting our agrarian past, the **school year** is typically 9 to 10 months allowing students to help with work on the farm.
- Typically, all teachers have their own **instructional space**—they do not "float" to spaces shared with others. Each space "belongs" to a teacher, and students move from teacher's space to teacher's space, subject to subject. Within their own spaces, teachers determine the configuration of furnishings, equipment, storage, displays, and teaching materials. Because, on average, teachers teach about 75% of the school day, and the school itself is open about 75% of the year, the typical instructional space is used 56.25% of the year (0.75 × 0.75 = 56.25%).

- Students use **seats in classrooms** during instructional periods, but are otherwise transients all day every day as they pass through teachers' spaces. Students do not have individual places in which to work. If students have lockers, they are the only part of the school identified with specific individuals.
- With the focus on individual disciplines and teacher-centered instruction, there is **little interdisciplinary teaching**, little development of problem-solving skills, and minimal exposure to real-world issues.
- With the focus on classroom instruction by disciplines, and with students changing teachers every year or semester, students have little opportunity to develop long-term, close **relationships with adults** on the campus. Counselors typically serve several hundred students.
- Industrial Age high school instructional concepts predate **digital technology** by 75 years or more. Although some technology is typically present in today's Industrial Age high schools, it is used to reinforce old assumptions about teaching, learning, and assessment. Technology has supplemented rather than transformed instruction. As they did in the past, the Industrial Age teaching methods could continue without the technology.
- Industrial Age high schools have **libraries** with collections of printed materials supplemented by computers that students may use for research via the Internet.
- To support comprehensive course offerings as well as extracurricular activities, the Industrial Age school often has a **large enrollment**. Schools with 2,000–3,000 students are typical, and there are much larger schools in some districts.

For the **teacher**, the Industrial Age high school requires a narrow focus on selected courses within a single discipline. Teachers typically have a small number of course preparations per term or semester. Teachers have minimal interaction with teachers and instruction in other disciplines. Becoming highly specialized, teachers in large schools may teach multiple sections of only one or two courses each year. As students move from course to course each year, teachers have little opportunity to get to know their students well. Methods for differentiated instruction may help teachers address individual learning styles, but the potential to teach individuals instead of groups is severely constrained within the context of classrooms, large class sizes, limited time, and fixed schedules. The teachers' "world" is primarily the department within which they work. Supervision and classroom management are important parts of the teacher's responsibilities.

For the **student** moving from department to department every day, the "school" is the entire campus—and for schools with more than 2,000 students and several hundred thousand square feet of building area, it is a very large place. With every school day fully scheduled, students have little opportunity to address personal interests and needs, or to assume responsibility for managing their own time and studies. With the focus on theoretical content within individual disciplines, it can be difficult for students to see the relevance and application of required courses for their own futures.

For **campus administrators**, the Industrial Age high school with several thousand students, teachers, and staff represents an enormous management task. However, that task is greatly simplified by the teacher-centered instruction, rigid schedule, and separation of the disciplines. Although changes in course offerings or schedules within the framework are easy to effect, the complexity of the overall structure virtually precludes significant changes.

For the **architect**, the Industrial Age high school is an exceptionally large and complex facility—more like a small town than a building. The key is to give clarity to the complex array of spaces so that students and visitors can find their way through structures with acres of interior space. Characterized as "egg crate" schools because of their long, double-loaded corridors and repetitive, generic classrooms, Industrial Age schools need strong focal points to avoid becoming mazes.

With regard to **cost**, the Industrial Age school was originally conceived to bring industrial efficiency to education. After a century of experience, it is still argued that big high schools are essential to serve large numbers of students economically. However, both of these arguments are true only if we agree to certain propositions. The traditional school is very efficient for delivering content, but considering graduation rates, comparisons with students in other countries, and the need for remedial studies in colleges, it is not very efficient with regard to learning and outcomes. If we measure efficiency in terms of cost per graduate instead of cost per student per year, the traditional high school is not very cost effective.

To house the comprehensive instructional and extracurricular programs typical of the Industrial Age school, **new facilities** are often very large. *School Planning and Management* magazine's *10th Annual School Construction Report* (Abramson, 2005) observed that the median area per student was 167 square feet and schools in the top 10% building area provided 240 square feet per student. A substantial percentage of those areas house elective and extracurricular instead of core instruction activities. In terms of the amount of space that is being built and the percentage of time (over the course of a year) that space is actually being used, facility construction and maintenance costs in Industrial Age high schools are higher than those for most of the other models that follow.

We have tried to be very clear regarding our concerns about the shortcomings of the Industrial Age high school today and about its prospects for the future, but we recognize that this instructional approach has served some students well. Schools with relatively homogeneous and affluent students from supportive, educated families and communities with high expectations achieve good outcomes consistently. But, the enrollment in most high schools today is much more diverse, and the industrial model fails more than 30% of all students and more than 50% in urban districts with lower income students. If high schools were a business and more than 50% of the product was defective, they wouldn't stay in business very long. Yet despite these acknowledged failures, traditional high schools persist.

Despite these terrible and widely acknowledged statistics, the industrial model is, practically speaking, the "definition" of what a high school is, and is used for almost every type of student in every type of community. We are still building them.

In planning a new high school or in the operation of an existing school, the question is rarely about who the kids are that need to be serviced or what they need to succeed. Often it is just about how many kids there are.

The issue is most often about instructional capacity, not the appropriateness of instruction for the kids to be served. Schools are predominantly funded via mandatory taxes and populated via mandatory attendance zones.

Students are expected to adapt themselves to the schooling offered. They are rarely seen as "customers" to be attracted, served, or pleased. Some high school educators see schooling as a "medicinal" process to be "taken," not an enjoyable, enriching, stimulating, engaging, motivating process that turns kids on. As a result, many educators spend more time thinking about supervision and control than about teaching and learning.

We should stop assuming that the industrial model is the "base school" that can serve all types of students, that it can be comprehensive, and that it can meet all the teaching and learning needs for all students.

We predict that in the not-too-distant future, Industrial Age schools will constitute a significantly smaller percentage of high schools than they do today. Consider the charter high schools currently being built and the precedents identified for the models that follow. They are generally far more focused on individuals and academic success and far less on mass-production instruction and extracurricular activities. This applies equally as well to virtual learning models.

So what are school districts to do with existing Industrial Age high schools that are increasingly ill-suited for teaching and learning in the 21st century? It will be a huge challenge and costly to modify existing schools for numerous reasons.

- Many Industrial Age schools are very large, with 2,000–3,000 students and more, and several hundred thousand square feet of building area. Although districts typically have numerous small-scale elementary schools, they usually have a relatively small number of large high schools, which makes realizing diversity in types of schools and instruction difficult. Serving diverse student needs with a few big schools may require each to function more like an assembly of small schools. Several of the models that follow explore this idea.

- Virtually all Industrial Age schools were designed to be solid, durable, and easy to maintain. Unfortunately, district facility personal and architects were very good at ensuring that this happened. We created buildings that in their configuration, materials, and systems were durable, but were and are not adaptable or flexible in responding to the enormous changes that have occurred and must continue to occur in the programs they house. For decades, other building types (such as office or retail structures) have been planned with the assumption that changes in the use and configuration of spaces will occur. But traditional schools have been built with the assumption that instructional methods will not change—that classrooms were and are forever. It was assumed that Taylorism and the industrial model would outlive our buildings. Sadly, that has been right for a long time. The durability we achieved with glazed tile and concrete block walls, terrazzo floors, inflexible mechanical, electrical and plumbing systems, and so on, has now become a huge constraint on our ability to adapt existing structures to future needs. Changes here will be difficult and costly.
- The classic egg-crate school with long, double-loaded corridors lined with essentially identical interchangeable classrooms, all with windows to the exterior (for light and ventilation before air conditioning systems), are inherently linear in character and difficult to reconfigure to create varied spaces to support varied modes of teaching and learning. They were perfectly suited to the linear thinking of the industrial model, but they constrain the use of multiple and flexible modes of instruction and technology.
- The need for paper-based libraries has already diminished and will become further reduced as more resources become digitized. Digital information is easier, faster, and cheaper to obtain, anywhere and anytime—and not just in the controlled space of a school library. There is a need to repurpose much of existing library space to better serve the learning needs of students. Librarians must become digital research specialists who can help kids find great information rather than archivists who see their task as protecting books from kids. Library spaces and stacks may become workspaces for students and teachers with amenities such as a Starbucks or Kinko's.
- Cafeterias in Industrial Age schools are planned on the assumption that all students are on fixed schedules—that they will eat at stipulated times between periods in great masses under close supervision. More individualized instruction and flexible schedules will dramatically alter the nature of food services. Eating spaces will need to be reconfigured more as student centers with the look and

feel of a shopping mall food court in order to accommodate eating, studying, and socializing over the full school day. Kitchens will need to be redesigned to serve more varied foods and beverages. Gang tables will need to give way to more flexible and inviting seating kids can enjoy.

- Spaces for performing arts and athletics programs typically make up a very significant portion of Industrial Age high school buildings, and the budgets to construct, staff, and operate them are equally large. Justifying and populating these programs and facilities are major determinants in the large enrollments of high schools. If high schools become more diverse in their instructional methods and course offerings and in their teaching and learning environments, and become more flexible in their use of time, they will either become smaller and more numerous or be subdivided into schools-within-schools or small learning communities.
- Where there is not the critical mass in a single small high school to provide a diverse range of programs, it may be possible for groups of small schools to collaborate to provide students with course offerings, field competitive teams, or offer extracurricular programs.
- Years ago, in Industrial Age schools, it was assumed that career programs were primarily to provide job skills and training for students who would not pursue postsecondary studies. Programs might include construction trades, agriculture, home economics, technology, or cosmetology. Career needs today are very different and much more diverse. Given that less than 30% of high school graduates go on to get a four-year university degree or two-year college certificate (McCain, 2004, pp. 13–14), career studies must now reflect individual interests and real-world prospects, and must be used to engage, motivate, and provide relevance for students in their core courses. The facility needs of these programs are very different, and they will change again and again over time. Many of these spaces need to be integrated with instead of separated from those for core courses. Many students may go off campus into the community for parts of these courses.
- Administrative offices are virtually always located at the "front door" to control access to campus, and almost all of the administrative nonteaching staff have offices in that area. Large Industrial Age schools require very large administrative staffs. More diverse teaching and learning methods and schedules organized in small learning communities require administrative staff to be dispersed throughout the school to have more meaningful contact with both students and teachers. Teachers may serve as advisors and assume much of the role traditionally held by counselors. Some people who have administrative responsibilities may also teach.

- Instruction and spaces in Industrial Age schools are typically organized around disciplines or departments. Science is usually in a separate area located near but still separate from other core subjects. Visual and performing arts, career programs, and athletics are usually located in separate areas of the building. Relocating science labs and other highly specialized spaces for arts and career programs can be very difficult, which limits the ability of the facility to adapt to new programs.
- Diverse learning methods, multidisciplinary instructional programs, small learning communities, and flexible time require very different and flexible organizational structures and spaces that allow programs to be rearranged in an easy and inexpensive manner.
- Elementary schools are typically small and closely related to a neighborhood, whereas high schools are more often isolated from their communities on very big sites surrounded by acres of parking lots and athletic fields. High schools, particularly in suburban areas, are generally isolated from both residential and commercial areas. Heightened concerns about security have further exacerbated the problem. In the future, isolated Industrial Age school buildings and sites will constrain access by students to community resources related to instructional programs. They will make it more difficult for students to access mentors, businesses, and institutions in the community who can enrich campus-based teaching and learning.

The industrial model was originally conceived to bring industrial efficiency to education, and educators persist in arguing that large, comprehensive high schools are more efficient and less costly to build and operate. *But* this is true only under the following conditions:

1. If we assume that a high school must have programs to serve every student and must have competitive extracurricular activities. If this is true, then big enrollments are a big plus. Costs for such programs are less per student when distributed across large enrollments. But small schools that focus on selected programs while excluding others, and on specific rather than all individuals, can easily match or exceed the facility and operating cost efficiency of huge schools.

2. If we assume that schooling should occur only 6.5 hours per day, 5 days per week, 180 days per year. If, however, we could imagine schooling occurring almost anytime, all week and all year long, then we would understand that our current limited time use of enormously expensive capital assets (facilities) is truly inefficient.

3. If we ignore the deplorable graduation rate of Industrial Age high schools. If, however, we measure the cost per graduate instead of the cost per Carnegie Unit delivered or Average Daily Attendance (ADA), we would have to include the cost of those kids who took classes but failed. We should not measure the cost of schooling by the dollars used to provide kids with seats and instruction, but the cost to help them learn and succeed. We should not ignore the human and monetary costs of school failures and dropouts in terms of lost wages or taxes, welfare, and incarceration and then imagine we are being efficient (Belfield & Leven, 2007).

Whenever new ideas for high schools are proposed, folks quickly and invariably ask what will happen if it does not work—and then they reference the open plan or open classroom schools of the 1970s. Open classroom schools failed not because of a flawed facility design, but because nothing changed about the assumptions about how teaching, learning, and assessment should take place in such a facility.

There is always some risk in trying new ideas, but we must weigh that against the risk of maintaining the status quo. That risk calculation seems easy today. We know with absolute certainty, through huge volumes of statistics and studies, that Industrial Age high schools are failing appalling numbers of students. What are the odds that new ideas could be worse? We know that there are many examples (see the precedents identified with models that follow) of new ways to make high schools that have realized terrific results in graduation rates and cost efficiencies. Surely, continuing to build and operate Industrial Age high schools is a far greater risk than seeking new alternatives.

But, there is another risk. We cannot assume that the future of public schools and high schools is assured or guaranteed—that parents, students, and the general public and taxpayers will continue to support and fund schools that do not perform well. We cannot assume that students and parents will agree to attend schools of dubious merit and that they will have no choices to do otherwise. We cannot assume that other providers such as charter schools and private schools will not continue to increase their share of the "market." We cannot assume that all funding will go to public schools. We cannot assume that where kids go will be set by attendance zones. Vouchers alone could make a profound change in where families seek schooling.

PRECEDENTS

In the models that follow, we cite references and precedents related to the concepts we describe. Given the probability that most of our readers attended Industrial Age high schools, and that many may now work in or with them, we leave it to you to recall your own precedents.

FOCUS ON TEACHING OR LEARNING?

Teacher Centered **Student Centered**

The traditional school is strongly teacher centered. Instruction is focused on the teacher and subjects within fixed time periods. The school is planned spatially around teachers and their work. The teacher is the expert, the source, broker of information, and the gatekeeper. The same teaching techniques are used for virtually all students.

GROUP OR INDIVIDUAL TEACHING AND LEARNING?

Group Teaching and Learning **Individual Teaching and Learning**

Instruction focuses on classes, not individuals. Working with students in groups of 25 within periods of an hour or less, teachers have little opportunity to address the needs of individual learners.

TRADITIONAL TEACHING VS. DIGITAL LEARNING

Teacher, Text **Digital**

Instruction is primarily teacher and text based. Although there may be some technology in classrooms, labs, or libraries, most students do not have meaningful access to computers every day within the school. Remove the technology and the school's instructional programs could continue with little change. Students often have access to considerably more technology at home than in their school.

21ST-CENTURY THINKING SKILLS

Knowledge Skills **Content + Problem-Solving Skills**

The focus of instruction is knowledge skills that can be measured by standardized written exams.

ASSESSMENT

Content Skills **Content + Problem-Solving Skills**

Standardized tests are used to monitor and confirm content skills. Instruction is geared to enhance success on tests such as those associated with district, state, or provincial standards and the No Child Left Behind Act.

LEARNING FOCUS

Traditional Content **21st-Century Literacies**

Even with the integration of technology into teaching and learning, the focus is primarily on traditional content. Students have little opportunity to develop 21st-century literacy skills within the school setting.

INSTRUCTIONAL ORGANIZATION

Departments and Disciplines **Interdisciplinary**

Administratively and spatially, the school is organized around disciplines and departments. There is little or no interdisciplinary instruction.

APPLICATION OF LEARNING

Classroom Theory **Real-World Relevance**

With the focus on theoretical content and knowledge skills within the campus context, students struggle to see the relevance of school to their futures in the real world; grades alone may be insufficient to motivate students to work hard and succeed.

RESPONSIBILITY FOR LEARNING

Teacher **Student**

Teachers determine what is to be learned, how and when it will be learned, and how that learning will be assessed. Students have little opportunity to assume or exercise any responsibility for their own learning.

TIME—SCHOOL YEAR

Fixed, Traditional **Flexible**

The school operates approximately 9–10 months a year, 180–200 days. The school day is approximately 6.5 hours. Instruction is typically available to students only during these times. Students and parents accommodate the school's schedule.

TIME—SCHOOL DAY

Fixed, Traditional **Flexible**

Like the length of the school year, time within the school day is fixed in periods defined by bells. Generally, the same amount of time is allotted every day for every subject, regardless of complexity, for every instructional method or activity for every student. Time is fixed, and learning is variable. Core instructional schedules may be structured around increments of time set aside for extracurricular activities.

STUDENT SUPPORT

Counselor **Teacher-Advisor**

Students have little opportunity to develop close relationships with any adult over their four years in high school. Students may be assigned a counselor who is responsible for several hundred students. Students' academic, social, and personal struggles may go unnoticed.

STUDENT LEARNING SPACES

Teachers' Rooms **Personal Workspaces**

Students may be assigned lockers, but otherwise they have no individual place to call their own.

SPATIAL FLEXIBILITY

Durable, Permanent **Responsive, Flexible**

Planned around departments and individual classrooms, Industrial Age schools are typically built of durable materials with the intent that they will last for decades. That permanence can constrain changes in curriculum, technology, teaching, and learning.

SCALABILITY—SCHOOL SIZE

Large Enrollment **Small Enrollment**

The Industrial Age school needs to be large to offer comprehensive instructional and extracurricular programs. Schools with 2,000–3,000 students are common, but much larger high schools exist.

COURSE OFFERINGS

Core + Broad Elective Subjects **Core Subjects**

Industrial Age schools are termed "comprehensive" because they may offer a broad range of core and elective subjects.

EXTRACURRICULAR ACTIVITIES

Extensive **Minimal**

With their large enrollments, Industrial Age schools can support extensive extracurricular programs including athletics.

COSTS—STAFF

High Cost per Student **Low Cost per Student**

Industrial Age schools typically have large administrative, instructional, extracurricular, and support (food services, maintenance, technology, police) staff. Despite the large number of total staff, the ratio of students to teachers in core subjects may be high.

COSTS—FACILITIES

High Cost per Student **Low Cost per Student**

To be comprehensive in their offerings, Industrial Age schools require large facilities with extensive specialized spaces for career, performing arts, and athletic programs. Despite the large number of students, the building area per student may be high.

Reflect on the Industrial Age High School and Consider Your Own High School(s)

1. How is instruction in your school student centered?
2. How does instruction in your school develop problem-solving and higher order thinking skills? How do your assessment methods measure those skills?
3. How have teaching and learning in your school achieved graduation and dropout rates that are viable for the future for your students, parents, and community?
4. How is your school using technology to address the needs of 21st-century students?
5. How has your school made time flexible to facilitate individual learning styles?
6. How are your students succeeding in the real world? In college? Do they need remedial courses to succeed in college?
7. How does your school's facility support teaching and learning?

6

Academies

Academy schools integrate core and elective or career studies in small learning communities to make schoolwork relevant and engaging for students. Their characteristics generally include the following:

- The schools is organized instructionally and spatially into academies or small learning communities, each serving 400–600 students in grades 9–12.
- Although each academy includes all the core subjects, it is identified by and organized around one or more disciplines, businesses, or subjects drawn from the real world.
- Students choose an academy on the basis of their personal interests.
- The school draws on resources in the surrounding community to enrich studies and to provide mentors on and off campus.
- The school uses flexible scheduling each day to accommodate varied instructional methods and learning styles. It also provides instructional services up to 12 months per year.
- Every student and teacher has his or her own digital device.

Academies

Instructional/Spatial Organization
Both instruction and facilities are organized around real-world strands of study. Each academy may serve 400–600 students in multiple grades. Instruction seeks to balance content/knowledge skills with higher order thinking and real-world skills

Academy Commons

Specialized Spaces

Technology, Engineering Academy

inars,
Classrooms

Admin

Academy Comm s

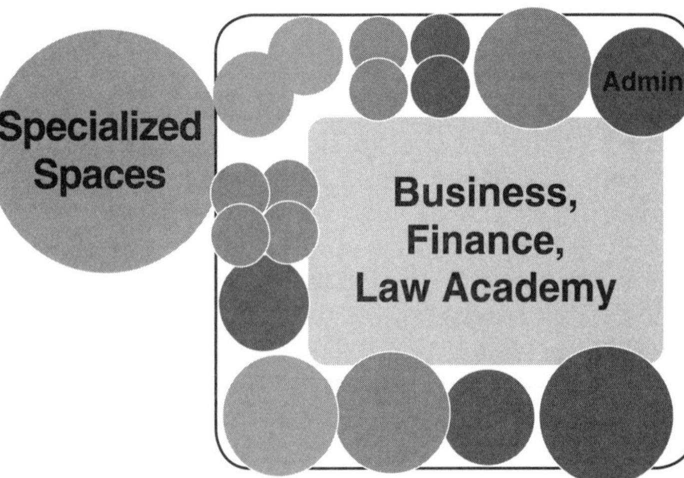

PE

Real-World Resources

Students, Teachers
Students and teachers work primarily within their academ but within that context draw each day on a wide variety o instructional spaces includin small lecture and seminar rooms, speciality labs, and project/work spaces.

School Size, Scalability

For teachers and students, the school is their academy. With both core and elective subjects and multiple grades in each academy, students and teachers work together for several years. The overall size of the school may vary with the number of academies.

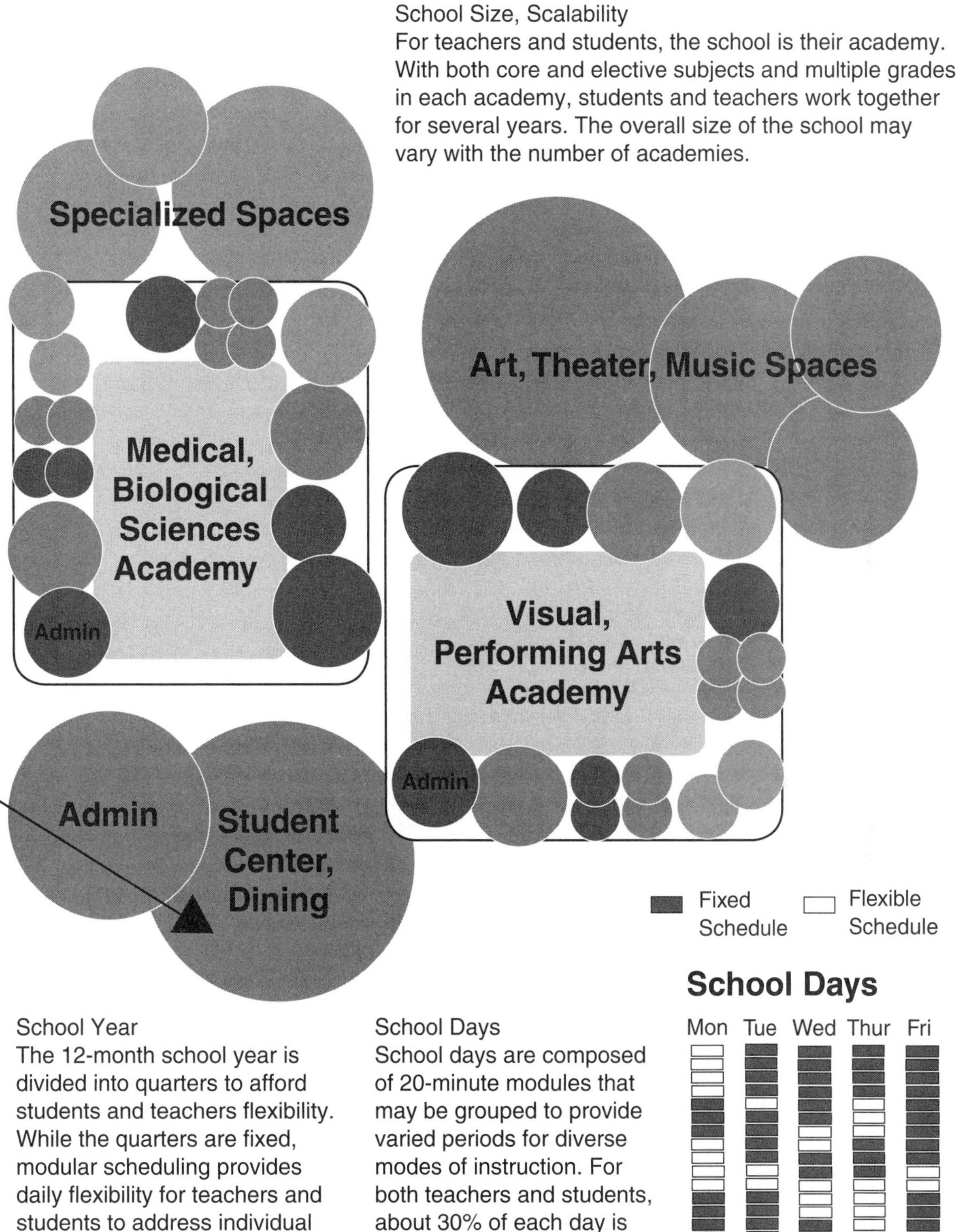

School Year

The 12-month school year is divided into quarters to afford students and teachers flexibility. While the quarters are fixed, modular scheduling provides daily flexibility for teachers and students to address individual learning styles.

School Days

School days are composed of 20-minute modules that may be grouped to provide varied periods for diverse modes of instruction. For both teachers and students, about 30% of each day is unscheduled.

School Year

J	F	M	A	M	J	J	A	S	O	N	D
1st Quarter			2nd Quarter			3rd Quarter			4th Quarter		

Because high school students do not perceive core subjects to be relevant to their future, they are often neither motivated by nor engaged in their studies. They therefore often struggle to learn. The academy school is composed of small learning communities in which core studies are integrated with career, elective, and personal interest themes that allow students the opportunity to choose a real-world learning context that is relevant and engaging to them.

Academy Schools Are Characterized by the Following:

- The school is organized into **academies** (small learning communities) that integrate core studies with real-world themes or strands. Students select an academy on the basis of their individual preferences, and all their studies are linked to that special interest. The following are examples of academy themes.
  - Business, Finance, and Law Academy
  - Technology and Engineering Academy
  - Medical and Biological Sciences Academy
  - Architecture, Engineering, and Construction Academy
  - Visual and Performing Arts Academy
  - Sports Academy

The number and type of academies may vary with the size of the school and from school to school within a district as required to serve all the community's students. Over time, the academy themes may change in response to student preferences and real-world conditions.

- Each academy includes a full complement of **core academic studies** including English, math, science, social studies, and foreign languages plus the **theme-related subjects**. Each academy is a school-within-the-school largely independent of the others. All the students and teachers share some functions, such as a central administration, cafeteria, and physical education areas.
- Because academy schools are specific rather than comprehensive in their course offerings and methods of instruction, they are **"schools of choice"** that students elect to attend. Their student body is not determined by an attendance zone or catchment area.
- Each academy may house **400–600 students** to support the diversity of core and theme-related elective courses. Students select an academy on the basis of their interests, and some may change from one academy to another as their interests evolve.
- Each academy serves a **vertical cross-section of students** in all the grade levels in the school, with some graduating and others beginning each year. This assures the development of long-term working relationships between students and teachers.
- Core subjects may be taught individually or in an interdisciplinary manner, but all are within the **context of the academy's theme** and

its elective real-world courses. Teachers within each academy work together to assure that courses are closely related.

- Instruction in the academies depends on every student and teacher having a **personal digital device**. The academies can offer the diversity of subjects inherent in the themes and meet the varied needs of students in four grades in such small learning communities only if the students have access to course offerings via technology.
- The academy school may not have a conventional **library**. The school's librarian is a research resource who helps students and teachers find materials via the Internet. Individual academies have collections of digital and printed resources specific to their themes.
- For both teachers and students, **their academy is the "school."** Both groups work within their academy most of each school day, leaving only for internships within the community and access to food services, the library, and other shared functions.
- **Spatially, academies are clearly defined**, distinctly different areas of the campus. Each academy includes classrooms and specialized spaces related to its theme. These are clustered around an open commons space housing teacher workstations, student work areas, and also instructional spaces for those career studies most likely to evolve over time. The use and configuration of the commons are highly flexible, changing frequently in response to instructional activities and projects. Areas within the commons are defined by movable partitions, furnishings, and equipment—not by fixed walls. The commons are reconfigured as needed by the teachers and students. Extensive areas of glass make all instructional spaces visually accessible so that everyone can see the interesting work being done in the academy.
- **Teachers have individual workstations** in the commons, but do not have their own classrooms. This ensures that teachers are readily accessible to the students. Teachers have access to small lecture halls, seminar rooms, labs, and theme-related specialty spaces as needed for instruction.
- To complement academy offerings, faculty, and facilities, some students go off campus for **internships** with businesses and individuals within the community. Although most of the academies are typically housed on a single campus, some may be located in the community near real-world resources related to their theme—such as a hospital or medical center, industrial plant, financial institution, art museum, or hotel. Conversely, some businesses may locate operations on the campus that are staffed primarily by students to serve the school community.
- Each academy has its own **administration** area with an assistant principal and counselor. With the close, ongoing, and long-term contact between teachers and students in each academy, students also look to those teachers who know them best to serve as advisors or counselors.

- Although **physical education** is provided to meet graduation requirements, extracurricular athletics may not be included at academy schools in order to accommodate extensive career programs. If some students wish to participate in athletics or other extracurricular activities, they may join teams at another district high school or programs in the community. Extracurricular activities are scheduled outside school hours.
- The academy **school year** is 12 months divided into quarters. Because of theme-related specialized staff, spaces, and equipment, instruction is synchronous. However, the **school day** is divided into 20-minute modules that may be grouped to provide varied periods of time for varied modes of instruction and subjects. No more than 70% of each student's or teacher's day is scheduled. The remaining flexible time may be used for teachers and students to work together individually as needed, and for students to undertake projects and independent studies. Each day's schedule is different for each student as instructional modes and modules of time vary from subject to subject. Teachers and administrators in each academy develop schedules to suit their teaching and learning processes and transmit them to the students digitally.
- The academy school may function on a conventional school year (approximately nine months) with terms or semesters and with less flexible daily schedules. However, the longer school year outlined above would significantly increase the efficiency with which the facilities are used and thereby decrease annual facilities costs per student. Flexible daily schedules would enhance the school's ability to address individual student interests and learning styles and provide opportunities for students to pursue internships off campus.
- Given the flexible schedule, the **student center** is open throughout the school day, providing a place for students to work and socialize, as well as food services. The space has both lounge furniture, tables, and chairs that the students may rearrange as appropriate to their needs.

For **teachers**, the academy school poses several challenges. First, they must realize the instructional objectives of individual disciplines within the context of each academy's theme. Each course must relate to and support work in other courses. Second, they must balance and integrate theoretical instruction essential to standardized tests with the academy's real-world theme and the development of problem-solving skills. This means teachers must be broadly knowledgeable in their field and work in collaboration with others. Third, given the enrollment and multiple grade levels in each academy, they must work with students in all of the school's grade levels concurrently. This assures long-term working relationships between teachers and students.

Academy high school **students** have the opportunity to make two important decisions about their schooling. First, they must choose to attend the academy school instead of another type of high school. Second, they must choose the academy within the school that truly interests them—the one that will engage and motivate them. Students should not come to the academy school unless they find such an area of interest. As their studies progress, students need to assess their own learning and interests and, when appropriate, recognize the need to change from one academy to another. The close and continuous working relationship with teachers is helpful in this regard. For the academy environment to work, students must be passionate about the theme within which they study. Academy students need to be focused on their academy studies because the school offers minimal extracurricular activities.

Academy administrators must focus on scheduling within their academy. The modular scheduling provides enormous flexibility to make time work in support of teaching and learning, but it can be quite complex. However, with much content delivery via technology, and with students and teachers having 30% of their time for independent work, scheduling only needs to address those activities where students and teachers work together in groups, such as seminars and labs.

For **campus administrators**, the greatest long-term challenge of the academy school is keeping its themes current. Administrators need to be knowledgeable about and responsive to real-world trends to ensure that academy programs remain relevant to the future. Administrators need to think like entrepreneurs by constantly rethinking their school to serve evolving needs.

Architects need to devise ways to make the academies and their specialized spaces highly flexible so that they may be substantially modified repeatedly over the life of the building. This is a major shift for architects, facilities, and maintenance staff, who have traditionally tried to make schools as durable and unchangeable as possible. Architects and teachers need to find ways to exhibit the interesting work happening in each academy. Each academy's commons should be visually open to the school's primary circulation space and lined with displays of student work. Each academy should "sell" the good things it is doing to everyone in the school.

Construction costs for the academy school's instructional areas are relatively high because of the specialized spaces and equipment required to support the academy themes. The building must also have an exceptional degree of long-term flexibility, which will affect structural and mechanical systems and interior lighting and finishes. However, these costs are substantially mitigated by the absence of facilities and site improvements for extracurricular activities and by use of the facility all year.

PRECEDENTS

- The Carl Wunsche Senior High School, a Career Academy in the Spring ISD near Houston, Texas (http://academy.springisd.org).

FOCUS ON TEACHING OR LEARNING?

Teacher Centered **Student Centered**

Academies integrate core subjects with career and elective strands to engage and motivate students and to provide a real-world context for their studies. The school affords students the opportunity to choose an academy on the basis of their own interests.

GROUP OR INDIVIDUAL TEACHING AND LEARNING?

Group Teaching and Learning **Individual Teaching and Learning**

Instruction occurs primarily in classrooms with groups of students, but flexible scheduling and personal technology accommodate some individual learning needs.

TRADITIONAL TEACHING VS. DIGITAL LEARNING

Teacher, Text **Digital**

All students and teachers have their own digital device. Instruction draws on teachers on campus in classrooms and virtual resources outside the school.

21ST-CENTURY THINKING SKILLS

Knowledge Skills **Content + Problem-Solving Skills**

With the mix of core and career and elective studies, there is an opportunity to develop both content and real-world problem-solving skills. The challenge is to integrate core and career studies so that they support and complement each other.

ASSESSMENT

Content Skills **Content + Problem-Solving Skills**

Assessment mixes standardized tests for core subjects with presentations and exhibitions for career subjects and projects.

LEARNING FOCUS

Traditional Content **21st-Century Literacies**

With personal technology and the integration of core and career studies, 21st-century literacy skills are developed and utilized across the curriculum.

INSTRUCTIONAL ORGANIZATION

Departments and Disciplines **Interdisciplinary**

By integrating core and career subjects, academies are highly interdisciplinary. The challenge is for all teachers, in both core and career subjects, to integrate elements of other subjects into their own instruction.

APPLICATION OF LEARNING

Classroom Theory **Real-World Relevance**

The objective of integrating core and real-world career subjects is to ensure that students find their work relevant, engaging, and motivating.

RESPONSIBILITY FOR LEARNING

Teacher **Student**

Teaching and learning are balanced between close teacher direction and support and the choices afforded students by the diverse career programs, personal technology, and the flexible schedule.

TIME—SCHOOL YEAR

Fixed, Traditional **Flexible**

The 12-month school year with quarters provides flexibility for students and teachers with regard to when and how long they are in school.

TIME—SCHOOL DAY

Fixed, Traditional **Flexible**

The school day is divided into 20-minute modules that teachers may assemble to create varied periods of time appropriate to the subject and the instructional method. Although approximately 30% of each school day is unscheduled for both teachers and students, much work is synchronous to assure students access to specialized real-world context, spaces, and equipment. Independent study time provides students with flexibility to accommodate individual interests and learning styles.

STUDENT SUPPORT

Counselor **Teacher-Advisor**

Counselors and assistant principals are located in each academy to be close to the students they serve. With each academy serving multiple grades, students and teachers have an opportunity to work together for four years. Each student is well known by numerous adults in his or her academy.

STUDENT LEARNING SPACES

Teachers' Rooms **Personal Workspaces**

Students do not have individual workstations. During their flexible time, students may go to the student center or work independently in classrooms or specialized career program spaces.

SPATIAL FLEXIBILITY

Durable, Permanent **Responsive, Flexible**

Those areas of each academy related to career studies are highly flexible to permit substantial changes to be made by teachers and students. Other areas, planned as more conventional classrooms, are less flexible. The use of personal technology affords instructional instead of spatial flexibility.

SCALABILITY—SCHOOL SIZE

Large Enrollment **Small Enrollment**

The size of the school is a function of the number of academies. The teaching and learning environment for students and teachers is determined primarily by their individual academy, not the overall enrollment of the campus. However, a small enrollment limits the number of academies and the choices provided to students.

COURSE OFFERINGS

Core + Broad Elective Subjects **Core Subjects**

Within each academy, broad elective offerings are paired with core subjects, but the school does not seek to be comprehensive. Instruction is focused on specific areas of study.

EXTRACURRICULAR ACTIVITIES

Extensive **Minimal**

With its focus on career strands in the academies, the school provides few extracurricular activities. Students may be able to participate in these programs at other schools or in community programs.

COSTS—STAFF

High Cost per Student **Low Cost per Student**

Extra administrative staff may be required to create and maintain links to community business resources, but the school has minimal staff related to extracurricular programs.

COSTS—FACILITIES

High Cost per Student **Low Cost per Student**

The career spaces within the academies substantially increase the building area, but without athletic programs the total area per student is comparable to that of a traditional high school. Costs for both staff and facilities in the academy school are more focused on instruction than on extracurricular activities.

Reflect on the Academies School and Consider Your Own High School(s)

- How do teaching and learning in your school engage and motivate students? How do you make your courses relevant to your students and their futures?
- How are your students' engagement and motivation reflected in their attendance, test scores, and graduation rates?
- How do you integrate instruction across disciplines in your school? Between your core and career programs?
- How is your school using digital technology to enhance teaching and learning and to accommodate the learning styles of individual students? How would teaching and learning in your school be affected if you no longer had digital technology?
- How does your school day work? What is included in the school day and what is scheduled after the school day? When are extracurricular activities scheduled?

7

Instructional Centers

Instructional center schools utilize different modes of instruction and different periods of time to serve varied subjects and diverse student needs. Their characteristics generally include the following:

- There is no classroom instruction.
- Four modes of instruction are used as appropriate to the subject and students: digital delivery of content, small group discussion or seminars, hands-on individual and group work, and independent studies.
- The school day is divided into small increments of time that are assembled to create varied periods as needed. Each day is different for each student and teacher.
- About half of each day for students and teachers is unscheduled time for independent work.
- Instructional centers provide workspaces for students and teachers and opportunities for close collaboration as appropriate to individual student learning.

Instructional Centers

Instructional Modes/Spaces

- **Content Delivery**—Individually via technology where/when the student elects.
- **Small Group Instruction**—10–15 students—focus on discussion of content, interaction of teachers/ students.
- **Hands-On**—Group and individual work in subjects that require special rooms and equipment (projects, science, art, some Career Technology Education (CTE), visual/performing arts)
- **Independent Study**—Individual work by both teachers and students. Opportunity for teachers and students to work 1:1 or in small groups as needed.

Students

Students are based in their instructional center. They may access primary content/instruction via technology from their center or anywhere, anytime. They go outside their center for seminars and hands-on work as required by their coursework. A substantial part (approximately 50%) of each student's and each teacher's day is unscheduled. Students are responsible for managing their time effectively. There are no bells. The campus is open for qualified junior and senior students.

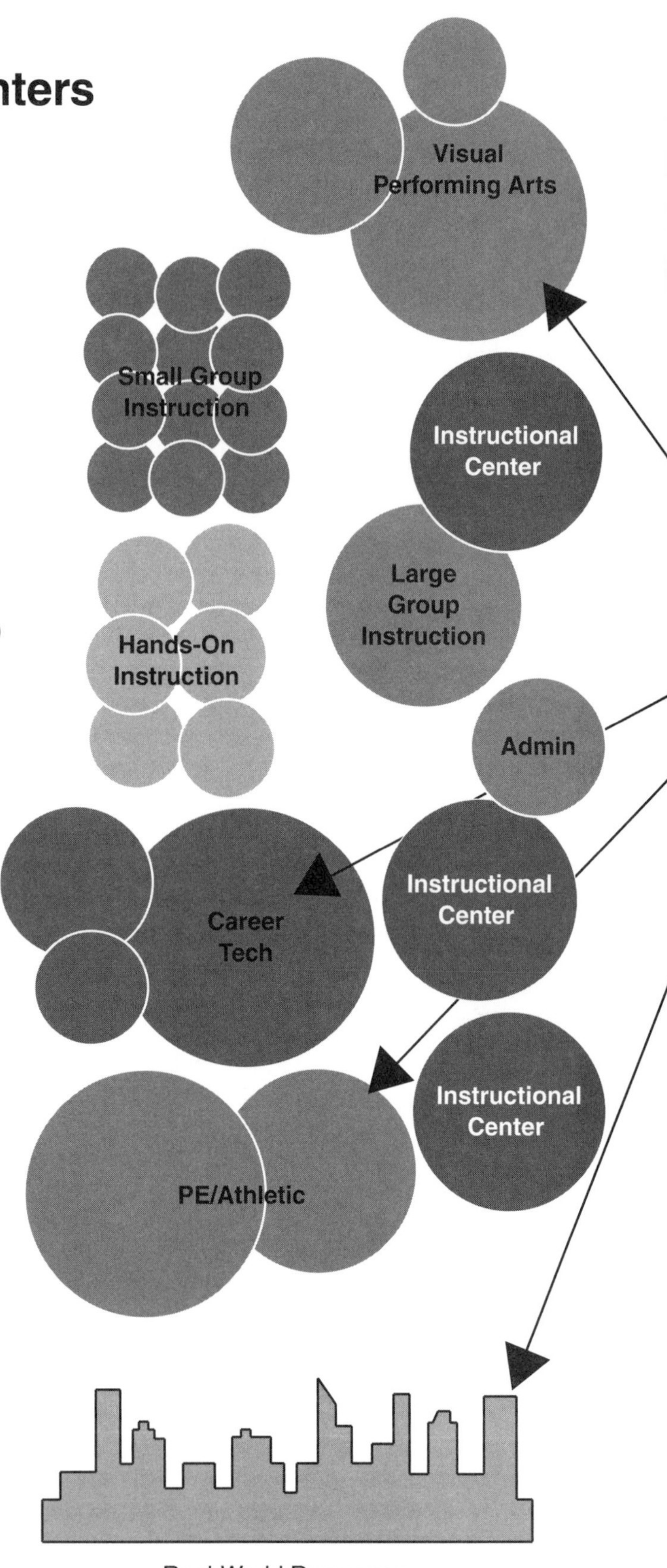

School Size, Scalability
For students and teachers, the school is their instructional center. They will meet and work with others, but their center is their base. The size of the school is a function of the number of centers.

Small Group Instruction

Instructional Center

Hands-On Instruction

Instructional/Spatial Organization
The school is organized around multidisciplinary instructional centers, each with workstations for a group of core teachers (English, math, science, social studies, and foreign language) and work areas for students. Both students and teachers work in the centers during their flexible time, then go out for seminars, hands-on instruction, and extracurricular activities. Within the centers, teachers may provide direction and monitoring, and students may seek support as needed. Each center accommodates grades 9–12 with students and teachers working together for the full 4 years.

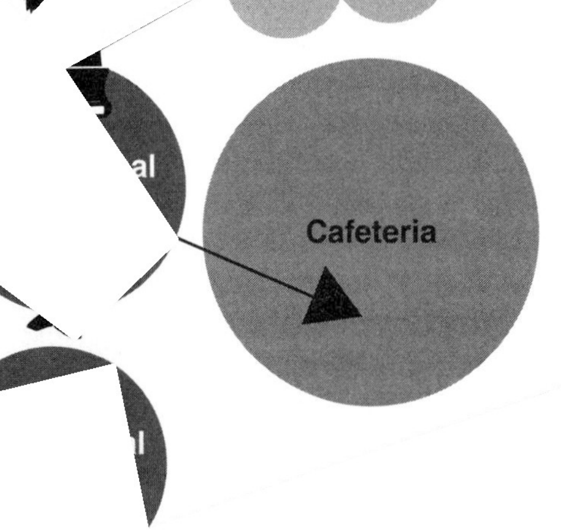

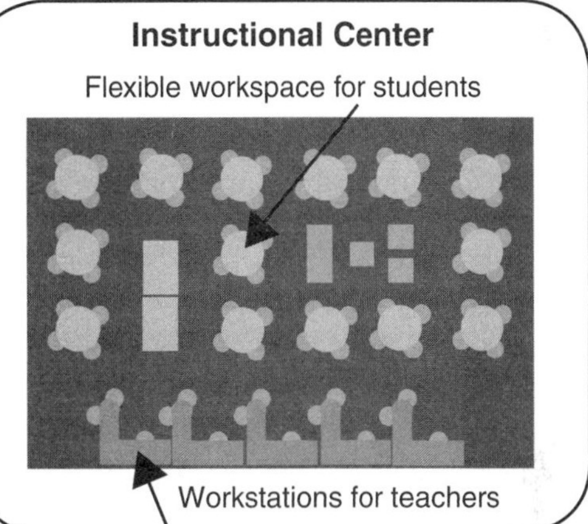

Time—School Days
The school day is divided into 20-minute modules, which may be grouped to provide different amounts of time for different instructional modes and subjects. To provide flexibility and support individualized study, about half of each day is unscheduled for both teachers and students.

Time—School Year
The school operates 12-months/year divided into quarters. Study is synchronous within the quarters, but independent study time accommodates individual learning styles. Time, not learning, is the variable.

Scheduled Study
Independent Study

School Days

Mon Tue Wed Thur Fri

School Year

Synchronous study with 12-month school year organized in quarters.

J	F	M	A	M	J	J	A	S	O	N	D
1st Quarter			2nd Quarter			3rd Quarter			4th Quarter		

Concepts for instructional center schools evolved from J. Lloyd Trump's remarkable book *Images of the Future,* published in 1959 by the National Association of Secondary School Principals. Trump argued that classrooms are too small because they force teachers to repeat instruction multiple times per day, leaving insufficient time for preparation and for individual work with students. Conversely, he argued that classrooms are too big for effective student participation in discussions and activities. In lieu of classrooms, he proposed several different modes of instruction coupled with flexible scheduling, the use of different types of teaching staff, links between the school and the community, and authentic assessment, and he even outlined uses for electronic learning devices (20 years before the PC). The model described below reflects much of Trump's original thinking, but it has evolved in response to new opportunities as well.

Instructional Center Schools Are Characterized by the Following:

- All teachers and students have **personal digital devices** for their use anytime, anywhere. Ubiquitous technology is an essential element of the school.
- In lieu of classrooms, instructional center schools use **four modes of instruction**.

   1. **Content delivery** is provided directly to students via technology—when and where they choose. Teachers generate some of the digital materials, whereas the school draws on outside resources for others. The digital materials focus on a single discipline or integrate issues across disciplines. The digital materials take many forms, but all actively engage the students, giving them real responsibility for and a measure of control over their studies, and monitor and reward them as they progress. The delivery of content via technology frees time for teachers to work with students individually and to collaborate with other teachers to prepare instructional materials. In *Images of the Future,* Trump envisioned large group lectures for the primary, initial delivery of content. Technology as envisioned by Mark Prensky in *Don't Bother Me Mom—I'm Learning* offers a far more powerful and flexible learning tool (Prensky, 2006).

   2. **Small group instruction** with groups of 10–15 teachers and students provides opportunities to explore and discuss course content, its links to other areas of study, and its relevance to the real world. The small groups allow every student to participate and contribute. It also allows teachers to guide students to additional resources and activities. Teachers schedule seminars based on the nature of the coursework. In some subjects, seminars are frequent and play a major role in instruction, whereas in other

subjects, seminars are infrequent. Content delivery is asynchronous, whereas small group instruction is synchronous.

3. **Hands-on instruction** allows students to work individually and collectively with teachers in specialized spaces or with specialized equipment, such as science labs, visual art studios, performing arts music or theatrical spaces, some career and technology subjects, and project work related to core subjects. Drawing on expertise outside the campus, some students pursue hands-on instruction in the much broader array of specialized facilities within the community. Although some hands-on instruction requires groups of students and is inherently synchronous, students work in other areas independently and set their own schedules.
4. **Independent study** makes up approximately half of each student and teacher's day.

Students Use the Time To:

- Access course content via technology.
- Work individually and with others on their studies.
- Pursue studies off campus with outside resources.
- Work independently in specialized hands-on spaces.
- Work individually with teachers as needed.

Teachers Use the Time To:

- Prepare digital course materials.
- Monitor students' progress in their digital studies.
- Work individually with students and provide support for them in their studies.

Independent study provides variable times for individualized instruction within a fixed school year. Independent study requires students to assume responsibility for the effective **management of their time**. As they begin their high school years, students' use of independent time is monitored, but as they progress and learn to use their time responsibly, the monitoring diminishes. Students who have been responsible for the management of their time may (with parental permission) come and go from the campus as they wish. Others are more closely supported and monitored in their studies. The independent study time provides the flexibility to accommodate both synchronous and asynchronous modes of study.

- With varied modes of instruction, there are **varied types of instructional personnel** with different skills and roles, as is typical in universities. The most highly trained and experienced, professional teachers are supported by instruction assistants, clerks, and general aides. All are complemented by community consultants and staff specialists.

- The school provides instructional services **12 months per year** divided into four equal quarters. Both students and teachers determine which and how many quarters (three or four) to be in school and the course load to carry or teach per quarter. The school seeks to make teaching and learning schedules flexible to serve varied individual needs.
- Different subjects and modes of instruction require different amounts of time. In lieu of fixed periods, the school day is divided into **20-minute modules** that are grouped to allot the time appropriate to different subjects and instructional methods. Given the diversity of subjects, the four modes of instruction, and the varied studies of each student, the schedule for every student is different every day. The substantial percentage of asynchronous independent study time provides the flexibility to schedule synchronous small group and hands-on work. There are no bells, hall monitors, or hall passes in the instructional center school. Students and teachers are expected to assume responsibility for managing their time—for being where they need to be when they need to be there.
- Instructional centers serve both **academic and social functions**. Each houses a group of core teachers (English, math, social studies, science, and foreign languages) and approximately 100 students from all the grades served in the school. Students remain in the same instructional center throughout their years at the high school. Instructional centers are flexible spaces, much like the reading room in a library. Teachers have open workstations including a conference table. Students have a storage cabinet for personal items and instructional materials plus tables and seating areas in which to study and collaborate. Within the instructional centers, teachers serve as advisors and counselors, guiding and supporting students in their studies and developing close working relationships. With the time allotted for content delivery and independent study, both teachers and students spend almost half of their school time in the instructional centers, with teachers providing assistance to students as they need it.
- Although each instructional center includes a **teacher in each core subject**, students typically take most of their courses from other teachers.
- **Teachers do not have dedicated classrooms**. Each teacher has a workstation in an instructional center and uses varied teaching spaces appropriate to her discipline and modes of instruction.
- **To use the school's facilities efficiently** and to provide teachers with access to diverse spaces, the instructional centers and supporting areas such as seminar rooms and specialized spaces (science labs, art studios, etc.) are independent of each other in the building. Teachers schedule these supporting spaces as needed.
- The manner in which teachers use the **modes of instruction** varies widely from course to course. Some may use a mix of all the modes, whereas others may have numerous seminars, and still others may

have extensive hands-on lab and group work. Every course can vary depending on the content and teacher.

- The instructional center school balances independent studies with those that develop **students' communication and interpersonal skills**. The four modes of instruction, modular scheduling, and 12-month school year raise conflicts for which the instructional center school is a compromise. Digital access to content and independent study time suggest that all students could work independently at their own pace. Yet the seminars, hands-on instruction, and the four quarters suggest a more synchronous group approach. Although the length of the quarter is fixed, independent study time allows students to receive different levels of support from their teachers as needed. If a student is struggling in a course, the teacher can provide substantial special help. Conversely, if a student quickly masters the content, the teacher can use the independent study time to provide enrichment opportunities.
- **Departments** exist spatially only for those disciplines (such as science, art, and some career technology subjects) that require highly specialized spaces or equipment. Others such as English, math, social studies, and foreign languages exist only as a group of teachers with particular expertise and are not articulated architecturally. Although core discipline teachers have their workstations in the instructional centers, they share expertise, experiences, and materials with colleagues in their discipline via conference and storage spaces located in the school's administration area.
- The school's **administration** is centrally located. Working closely with students throughout their high school years, teacher-advisors in the instructional centers perform the role of counselors.
- The school's faculty is complemented by **experts drawn from the community** to help with specific courses. Where appropriate, students work with businesses and individuals in the community for internships or to access specialized facilities and equipment.
- The size of the **enrollment** is not constrained by the instructional approach. However, although students and teachers will have a small-scale learning environment in their instructional center, their sense of the school will be shaped as they move about the much larger campus each day. As in the traditional school, the larger the scale, the more diverse and specialized offerings are feasible, but the more impersonal the total environment.
- The instructional center school may have **athletics and other extracurricular activities** that are scheduled outside the school day. The instructional schedule, including independent study time, is neither arranged around nor diminished by extracurricular activities.
- Although **assessment** at the instructional center school may include standardized tests per state or federal mandates, these are complemented by presentations, exhibitions, portfolios, and written

narratives for individual courses or across disciplines at critical junctures in each student's progress.

For **teachers**, the instructional center school requires a different set of skills from those in the teacher-focused classroom. With independent study time and content delivered largely by technology, the teacher's primary role is working with individual students to monitor, guide, and support their studies. In lieu of each teacher working on individual lesson plans, teachers work together to locate or create digital materials for all the students in each course. Teachers must also develop skills in facilitating discussions in seminar settings to help students explore and debate concepts and facts presented in their digital studies. Within the instructional centers, teachers function as advisors and counselors supporting students in their studies, in making college and career decisions, and in addressing personal issues. In the instructional center school, teachers have less responsibility for content instruction and more responsibility for helping the students find meaning and relevance in their studies.

For **students**, the instructional center school offers both freedoms and responsibilities. Independent study time gives students the opportunity to determine what they do and when they do it, but also the responsibility to manage their time effectively to succeed in all their studies. But, for those students up to the challenge, there are real rewards in terms of freedom in their schedules and movements. When students have the opportunity to be responsible participants, teachers can focus more on instruction and less on supervision.

For **campus administrators**, the challenge is scheduling the group activity aspects of the school day for teachers, students, and facilities. Teachers must define the schedule and instructional modes to be used for every course well before the start of each quarter. The flexibility inherent in the 50% of the day devoted to independent study for both teachers and students allows the scheduling of the seminars and hands-on work.

For **architects**, administrators, and teachers, the challenge is to compute the areas required for the instructional centers (that is, the numbers of students they are to serve at any one time) and the numbers of support spaces such as seminar rooms and labs that will be required to support the enrollment and instructional programs. Too many spaces will waste construction and operating costs, whereas too few will constrain scheduling flexibility and instruction.

Construction costs are comparable to those of the traditional industrial model, but the allocation of spaces is quite different. The area required for the instructional centers is offset by the absence of dedicated classrooms (all teachers "float" to instructional spaces as needed), extensive independent study time, and personal digital studies. However, relative to the traditional school, facility costs are substantially mitigated by operating the school 12 instead of only 9 months per year. Either fewer facilities are required to educate the same number of students, or the same size building has increased enrollment capacity.

PRECEDENTS

- J. Lloyd Trump, *Images of the Future: A New Approach to the Secondary School* (1959).
- Westside High School, Westside 66 School District, Omaha, Nebraska (http://www.westside66.org/westsidehs/site/default.asp).

FOCUS ON TEACHING OR LEARNING?

Teacher Centered **Student Centered**

With four modes of instruction (digital, small group, hands-on, and independent study) and a flexible schedule, the instructional center school focuses on the work that students do.

GROUP OR INDIVIDUAL TEACHING AND LEARNING?

Group Teaching and Learning **Individual Teaching and Learning**

Teachers work with groups of students for seminars and hands-on classes (science labs, arts, and some career programs that require specialized spaces and equipment), which make up about 50% of each school day. In the remaining independent study time, students work individually with teachers and digital learning resources.

TRADITIONAL TEACHING VS. DIGITAL LEARNING

Teacher, Text **Digital**

Digital (instead of teacher-based) instruction is one of the school's four modes of instruction. Every student and teacher has a personal digital device (currently a laptop). Teachers focus on helping students find resources and understand and explore the meaning of content.

21ST-CENTURY THINKING SKILLS

Knowledge Skills **Content + Problem-Solving Skills**

Although problem solving is not an integral part of the school's structure, it is a byproduct of the digital instruction and independent study that constitute approximately half of each student's day.

ASSESSMENT

Content Skills **Content + Problem-Solving Skills**

Students maintain portfolios, present and exhibit their work, and meet with their teacher-advisors. Assessment of both content and problem-solving skills is integral to the digital materials.

LEARNING FOCUS

Traditional Content **21st-Century Literacies**

In 1959, Trump proposed to deliver basic content via large group instruction. In this 21st-century reincarnation of his concept, basic content and digital literacy are realized through personal technology and independent study. This school could not function without its technology and without the students being fully conversant with the tools it affords.

INSTRUCTIONAL ORGANIZATION

Departments and Disciplines **Interdisciplinary**

The organization of the school permits instruction by discipline and across disciplines. Through the digital materials, some courses focus on a single subject, whereas others integrate work across multiple disciplines. The interdisciplinary instructional centers provide students with close support from teachers in all the core subjects.

APPLICATION OF LEARNING

Classroom Management **Real-World Relevance**

There is no stand-and-deliver classroom instruction with passive students. The digital courses, seminars, and hands-on work integrate real-world content and engage the students.

RESPONSIBILITY FOR LEARNING

Teacher **Student**

Students have the primary responsibility for managing their independent study time and for working with the digital learning materials. Teacher-advisors monitor and support students as they progress. Varying degrees of independence and flexibility are afforded students depending on the success of their studies and the maturity of their conduct. The campus may be open for junior and senior students succeeding in their work, whereas others may be more closely monitored and supported in the instructional centers.

TIME—SCHOOL YEAR

Fixed **Flexible**

Digital schooling is available 24/7/365. The school as a place is open 12 months per year divided into quarters with conventional 6.5-hour days.

TIME—SCHOOL DAY

Fixed **Flexible**

Although semesters and days are fixed to provide a social and academic context for students and teachers, all of them have 50% of their time unscheduled, which affords substantial flexibility for individualization.

STUDENT SUPPORT

Counselor **Teacher-Advisor**

Each instructional center serves students in grades 9–12. Students remain with the same group of teacher-advisors for their four years on the campus. Each student is well known by several adults.

STUDENT LEARNING SPACES

Teachers' Rooms **Personal Workspaces**

There are flexible areas for individual and group student study in the instructional centers, and each student has a storage cabinet for personal items. Students do not have dedicated individual workstations.

SPATIAL FLEXIBILITY

Durable, Permanent **Responsive, Flexible**

With varied modes of instruction, floating teachers, digital learning, modular scheduling, and instructional centers, the school is very flexible spatially. The school could accommodate significant changes in instructional programs without requiring modifications to the facility.

SCALABILITY—SCHOOL SIZE

Large Enrollment **Small Enrollment**

The digital instruction programs and therefore the potential course offerings are not significantly affected by the size of the school. The environment for students and teachers is largely defined by the instructional centers instead of the overall enrollment of the school.

COURSE OFFERINGS

Core + Broad Elective Subjects **Core Subjects**

Digital instruction provides access to a broad range of both core and elective subjects.

EXTRACURRICULAR ACTIVITIES

Extensive **Minimal**

The instructional center school may have conventional extracurricular activities after the end of the school day.

COSTS—STAFF

High Cost per Student **Low Cost per Student**

The ratio of total staff to students is similar to that in an industrial model school.

COSTS—FACILITIES

High Cost per Student **Low Cost per Student**

The total building area per student is comparable to that of an industrial model school, but the allocation of spaces is different. Areas for the instructional centers are offset by much smaller areas for seminar rooms instead of classrooms.

Reflect on the Instructional Center School and Consider Your Own High School(s)

- What methods of instruction are used in your school? How do these methods vary from subject to subject, teacher to teacher?
- How do your instructional methods accommodate our students' varied learning styles?
- How does your daily schedule accommodate different modes of instruction, different subjects, and different learning styles?
- How do your instructional methods and schedules afford students and teachers opportunities to work together individually?

8

Academic Focus

Academic focus schools have one clear priority—graduate every student ready for college. Their characteristics generally include the following:

- The schools are small with a low ratio of students to teachers.
- Schools are organized around advisories and families that house workstations for students and teachers.
- School days provide large segments of flexible time controlled by teachers and students.
- The 12-month school year has quarters separated by intercessions for special programs. School days extend from 8 to 5. Special support is provided as needed to students on Saturday mornings.
- Every student is supported in seeking college admission and is prepared for success in postsecondary studies.
- The school does not offer competitive athletics or elective programs that might distract from the academic focus.

Academic Focus

Instructional/Spatial Organization
Instructionally and spatially, the school is organized around academic houses, each serving approximately 150 students. Each house is composed of 10–11 advisories, each with about 15 students. Students/teachers work at specialized workstations within their advisories, which also contain seminar rooms that accommodate both discussion and project work. Specialty labs are provided for art, sciences, engineering, or other subjects requiring specific equipment and spaces. Usable for dining, meeting, and performance, the commons is the social heart of the campus. All the spaces are linked by the gallery, in which student projects are displayed. Many of the interior walls are glass to allow everyone to see the work underway.

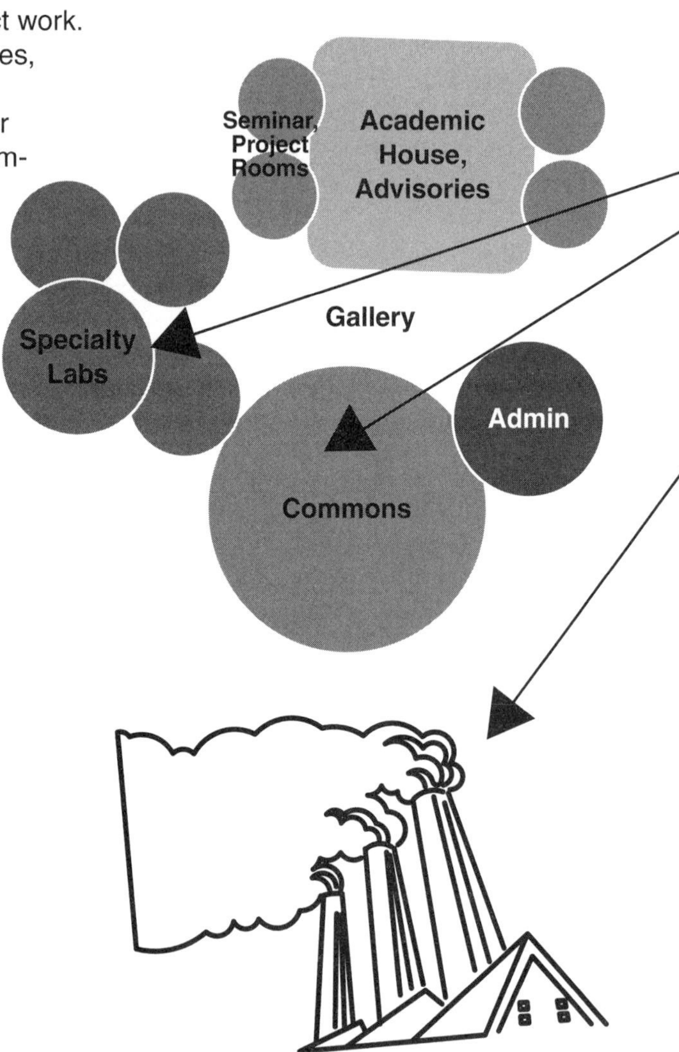

Students
Students work primarily with the advisors/teachers in their advisory and with off-campus mentors addressing specific areas of personal interest. Advisors guide and assess progress in project work and provide support in specific subjects where appropriate. Studies are highly individualized within a small scale supportive social environment.

School Size, Scalability

The school's maximum enrollment should not exceed 450 to assure close student-teacher working relationships. For students and teachers, the school consists of both their advisory and the spaces they share with those in other houses. The intent is that everyone in the school should know each other.

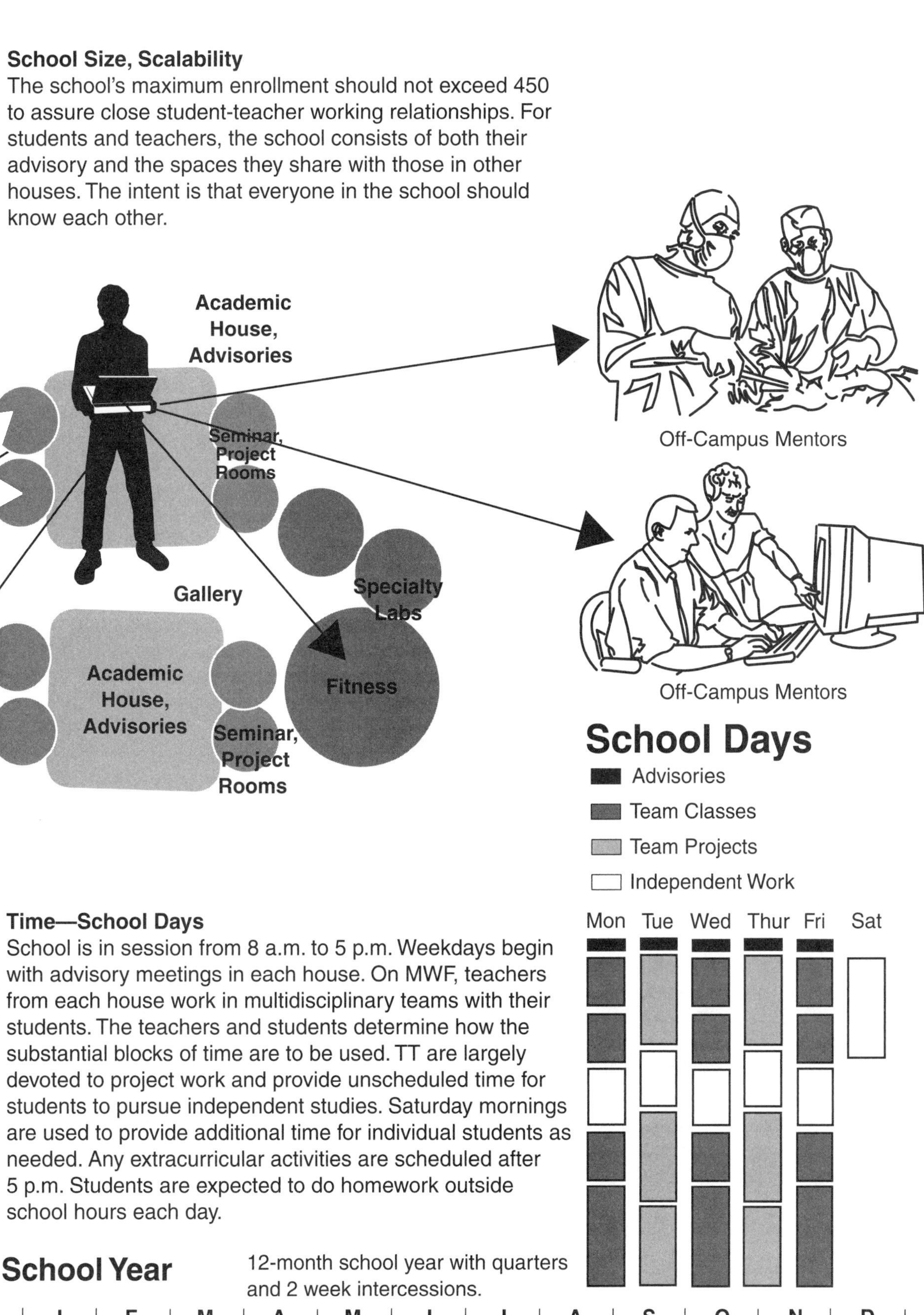

Time—School Days

School is in session from 8 a.m. to 5 p.m. Weekdays begin with advisory meetings in each house. On MWF, teachers from each house work in multidisciplinary teams with their students. The teachers and students determine how the substantial blocks of time are to be used. TT are largely devoted to project work and provide unscheduled time for students to pursue independent studies. Saturday mornings are used to provide additional time for individual students as needed. Any extracurricular activities are scheduled after 5 p.m. Students are expected to do homework outside school hours each day.

School Year

12-month school year with quarters and 2 week intercessions.

Readers should not be misled by the apparent simplicity of this model. The simplicity is not the product of an unsophisticated instructional program, but the clarity of its priorities—to help students succeed in "core academics" at a "high level." "Students" means a very high percentage of a diverse group of learners—not a select few culled from a big mass. "Core" means college preparatory basics, and "high level" means that graduates are ready to pursue and to succeed in postsecondary studies.

This academic focus model grew from a diverse group of public charter and private schools characterized by the following.

- **College preparatory core academics** (English, math, social studies, science, and languages) are *the* priority of the academic focus school. The school offers minimal electives and performing arts. It offers few if any career programs on campus, but other programs might be offered in the community via mentors. It provides physical education, but has little or no competitive athletics. The academic focus school gives students very few choices and focuses on success. Failure is not an option.
- **The school's teachers believe that students are capable of succeeding in challenging academic programs.** They believe that students who perceive their work as relevant and interesting will take responsibility for their own learning and that teachers for such students should be primarily advisors, mentors, guides, and coaches. Neither the vocabulary nor the attitude of administrators and teachers is focused on supervision and classroom management.
- **The total school is small**—no more than 400–500 students. It is no larger than one of the small learning communities proposed in *Breaking Ranks* for traditional high schools (National Association of Secondary School Principals, 1996). The school is divided into still smaller houses of approximately 150 students. Primarily social instead of academic, the houses are sufficiently small that students and teachers can grow to know each other well and provide a supportive environment. Teachers and students in each house gather several times per week to make announcements, celebrate successes, address problems, hear special presentations, and attend special events.
- The school enrolls and engages both **students and their parents**. Parents must sign an agreement with the school to support their child's studies and to participate in assessment and presentations.
- Houses comprise approximately 10–11 **advisories**, each with a teacher and no more than 15 students in a single grade level. The advisory groups work together for the full four years of high school study. The houses contain a vertical mix of grades, with some students entering and others graduating during a single school year. Advisors help students with goal setting, studies, and interpersonal relationships. They ensure that each student is well known by a caring adult on the campus and part of a small supportive group of

fellow students. The advisor is the school's primary contact with each student's parents and regularly engages them on the campus and in their home in assessing and planning for their child's studies.

- Students work hard and long. Absent most of the extracurricular programs and electives of the traditional high school, students spend more time on core studies with fewer distractions. A survey of 41 states and the District of Columbia cited in *Prisoners of Time* (National Education Commission on Time and Learning, 1994) indicated that "only 41 percent of secondary school time must be spent on core academic subjects" (p. 5). These were not students at an academic focus high school.
- The **school day** starts at 8 a.m. and extends to 5 p.m. Any extracurricular activities occur *outside* the school day. Homework is an integral part of the program. The school provides some services on Saturdays for those students needing extra help in specific areas. Each weekday begins with advisories during which advisors and students plan their day. At times, a single teacher will work with a group of students. More often, teachers will work in teams to explore concepts across disciplines.
- Each morning and afternoon **blocks of time** are allocated to groups of related subjects—English, history, and languages or math and science. Within these blocks, teachers and students determine how to use their time effectively. Each day, time may be allocated to each subject as appropriate to the work at hand. The makeup of the blocks evolves during each quarter. An extended lunch period allows students time to eat and to reflect on their studies. On Tuesdays and Thursdays, a block of time is set aside for individual study as determined by each student. These flexible periods allow some students to pursue enrichment studies beyond the content of their courses and others to receive additional help and time with subjects in which they are struggling.
- The **12-month school year** is divided into 11-week quarters separated by two-week intercessions. Students and teachers may elect to be in school three or four quarters each year. Although the intercessions include holiday or vacation time, their primary purpose is not time off, but a change of pace from typical studies. They may include travel by groups of students to see university campuses, visits to sites of interest, community service, or work to address deficiencies encountered during the previous grading period. When students return to the school from intercession ventures, they are expected to share what they have seen or learned with others via presentations and exhibitions.
- A minimum of **26 credits** including at least four years of math and science are required for graduation. The four years of high school study are fully utilized to build solid transcripts for university admissions or success in some form of postsecondary studies.

- Seeking to maximize learning opportunities, the academic focus high school does not offer **AP** (Advanced Placement) or **dual-credit classes** to supplant college instruction. Students are fully challenged and engaged in every course from their freshman through their senior year.
- The school does not offer **GT** (gifted and talented) or **special education** classes. Because the school individualizes instruction to a high degree, the needs of all students are met within the same learning environment.
- The school has a **low student-to-teacher ratio** of approximately 15:1. The total adult-to-student ratio is not exceptional because of the clear focus on core academic studies and the absence of extracurricular and elective programs. Each of the school's administrators teaches at least one course.
- Every student and teacher in the school has one or more **personal digital devices** (laptop, handheld, cell phone) for use anytime, anywhere. The school has a high-speed wireless network. Students, parents, and teachers can access instructional materials and school data from inside or outside the school at anytime.
- **Digital course materials** are prepared by the teachers or drawn from outside resources and provided online. These materials frame the content and relevance of each course, offer varied ways to learn, provide links to other resources, and show how the subject matter is relevant to the real world. Class time in the morning and afternoon blocks is devoted to dialogues with the teacher and students and to project-based work that knits together the various disciplines. The digital materials, seminars, and projects provide students with opportunities to work both individually and in groups.
- The school does not have a library, but does have a digital research specialist to help students access online resources effectively. With personal technology, teachers and students have access to the Internet and research opportunities anytime, anywhere.
- There is a strong emphasis in the school on **project-based learning** that helps students explore individual interests and develop problem-solving skills in conjunction with their core studies. Freshmen and sophomores (grades 9–10) work primarily on the campus and are largely focused on the development of core subject knowledge skills. These studies are supplemented by individual and group projects that help students develop problem-solving skills across disciplines. On the basis of their individual interests, junior and senior students (grades 11–12) select an adult mentor in the community with whom they will work for their last two years via shadowing, community service, field studies, internships, and independent projects. Seniors work with their chosen mentor to create an independent project integrating academic content and real-world issues.
- The school provides numerical or letter grades to students solely for the purposes of college admissions. The school does not compute and

publish GPA or class rankings. **Assessments** that enhance learning include formal verbal and graphic presentations of projects to fellow students, teachers, and parents and exhibitions of those presentation materials for everyone in the school to see. Students maintain portfolios in both paper and digital formats. The intent of the presentations is for students to demonstrate not only their communication skills and knowledge, but also their ability to apply what they've learned to solve real-world problems. The digital materials include queries and challenges by which students evaluate their own work as they progress. Projects require that students define objectives against which the students ultimately measure themselves. Several times per year, students lead conferences with their advisor and parents to present their portfolio, to assess progress and growth, and to define goals for the work to come. In addition to grades, the final assessment at the end of each grading period includes a written narrative of the student's work from their advisor.

- The **facilities** for the academic focus school are modest compared to those of traditional high schools. Absent spaces for a library, athletics, performing arts, and career-related electives, the school provides substantially less building area per student and requires less site area. Although the academic focus school is ideally located in a specially designed school district facility, it could also function in a commercial office or retail structure.
- The school facility is organized about **several types of spaces**.
  - The primary workspace for teacher-advisors and students is the **academic house,** which serves a family and its advisories. The house provides workspaces for each teacher-advisor and student, plus conference and meeting areas. With flexible furnishings, teachers and students frequently rearrange their advisory area to accommodate varying needs.
  - Adjacent to the houses are **seminar rooms** in which small groups meet to discuss materials presented in the digital course materials.
  - **Project rooms** are workspaces housing equipment and furnishings students use to prepare projects for presentations and exhibitions. Both of these spaces open to the advisory area and are highly flexible.
  - **Specialty labs** house equipment required for science, art, and other specific areas of study.
  - The **commons** is both the school's dining area and its major meeting and social space. It is highly flexible and is adapted to meet activity needs constantly. Theatrical lighting and sound systems accommodate presentations and performances.
  - All of these spaces are linked together by the school's primary circulation, which functions as a **gallery** for the display of student work. Most walls between the gallery and houses are glass so that every activity can be seen and shared.

- The school works very hard to ensure that every student succeeds in his or her studies and graduates. Advisors know each student well, monitor progress constantly, and provide the academic and personal support required for success. The school wants all students to have the **opportunity to go to college**, and takes them to visit and experience college campuses. The school supports each student in identifying colleges of interest and requires, as a condition of graduation, that each student apply to more than one four-year college. Almost all academic focus students graduate from high school and continue with postsecondary studies. The school tracks its graduates through their postsecondary years to measure the merits of its own programs.
- The school clearly demonstrates the **power of success** to motivate students. The school provides none of the extracurricular activities often touted as attracting students to or retaining them in traditional comprehensive schools. Rather, it offers students the opportunity to succeed in their studies, to see the relevance of their efforts, and to imagine the implications for their future. That motivation makes pleasurable the hard work required.

For **teachers**, the academic focus school entails the assumption of an additional and equally important role as an advisor. Working within their own disciplines, teachers provide direct instruction to students through digital learning materials, seminars, and projects. Working as advisors, they guide and support a small group of students in every aspect of their multiple-year experience at the school. The challenge for teacher-advisors is to help students integrate their studies across all the disciplines.

For **students**, the academic focus school requires a real commitment to learning motivated by the heightened prospect of success in high school and admission to college. Students must attend this school for the rewards of learning, not for ancillary interests in sports, arts, or career programs. Students must be willing to work longer hours and do more homework. But, the school helps students understand the relevance of their studies for their futures and helps them to succeed day by day. Learning is its own reward.

For **administrators**, the challenge is to find teachers who can thrive in the dual role of teacher and advisor, and to find people in the community who will serve as mentors. Much of the responsibility in the school for scheduling is assumed by teacher-advisors within their house. The spirit of the school is important as a supportive context for teaching and learning. Administrators must encourage and support this within each house and across the school.

For the **architect**, both the gallery and the houses are important challenges. The gallery is the primary circulation space, physically and visually linking every area of the school together. It must also be a social gathering place and a display area for student projects. The advisory area is the primary space in each house. It must provide identity for the house and a good working environment for both teacher-advisors and students.

Costs for academic focus schools for both staff and facilities are different from those for the traditional school. With the emphasis on academic studies and low student-to-teacher ratio, the cost for instructional staff is relatively high, but costs for other staff including administrators and teachers in other fields (athletics, Career Technology Education, and performing arts) is low. The total student-to-staff ratio is not exceptional. The school provides considerably less building area per student than a traditional high school because of its minimal offerings in career, performing arts, and athletic programs.

PRECEDENTS

- KIPP High School, a public charter school in Houston (http://www.kipphouston.org).
- YES (Youth Engaged in Service) College Preparatory Charter School, Houston (http://www.yesprep.org).
- School of the Woods, a private Montessori high school in Houston (http://schoolofthewoods.org).
- Gary & Jerri-Ann Jacobs High Tech High, a public charter school in San Diego (http://www.hightechhigh.org).

Beyond the general characteristics delineated above, it should be noted that each of these widely different schools share other traits.

1. **Students elect to attend** them in lieu of the traditional comprehensive high school to which they are zoned by virtue of where they live. Academic focus schools must attract students with their instructional programs to survive.
2. These schools typically have far more applicants than they can accommodate.
3. Although each of the public charter schools seeks a broadly representative student body and uses lotteries to select students, the quality of students and the success they achieve reflect the fact that they chose schools with a demanding academic focus.
4. With the exception of the Montessori School of the Woods, all of these are public charter schools that operate with the same or greater financial constraints as the typical public schools in their area. Measured by the outcomes for their students, they use their funds very well.

FOCUS ON TEACHING OR LEARNING?

Teacher Centered **Student Centered**

The academic focus school measures its success in terms of outcomes realized by its students.

GROUP OR INDIVIDUAL TEACHING AND LEARNING?

Group Teaching and Learning **Individual Teaching and Learning**

The school balances direct instruction and small group work with independent digital study and individual student-teacher discussions.

TRADITIONAL TEACHING VS. DIGITAL LEARNING

Teacher, Text **Digital**

The focus is on digital instruction with very strong teacher support.

21ST-CENTURY THINKING SKILLS

Knowledge Skills **Content + Problem-Solving Skills**

The combination of interdisciplinary instructional methods and project-based learning is designed to ensure both content and problem-solving skills.

ASSESSMENT

Content Skills **Content + Problem-Solving Skills**

The school employs multiple types of assessment (presentations, exhibitions, portfolios) to help students learn and to measure outcomes.

LEARNING FOCUS

Traditional Content **21st-Century Literacies**

Twenty-first-century literacy is inherent in the school's extensive use of digital instruction.

INSTRUCTIONAL ORGANIZATION

Departments and Disciplines **Interdisciplinary**

The school's instruction, time, and spaces are organized around interdisciplinary studies.

APPLICATION OF LEARNING

Classroom Theory **Real-World Relevance**

For students, the realization that they can succeed in high school and continue to college is powerful motivation.

RESPONSIBILITY FOR LEARNING

Teacher **Student**

Students have real responsibility for pursuing their digital learning and for managing their own time, but they work in close contact with their teacher-advisors.

TIME—SCHOOL YEAR

Fixed **Flexible**

The school operates 12 months per year. Students and teachers have flexibility as to when and how long they are in school.

TIME—SCHOOL DAY

Fixed **Flexible**

School days are organized in large blocks, but teachers and students define the use of time within the blocks. There is substantial flexibility to accommodate varied activities.

STUDENT SUPPORT

Counselor **Teacher-Advisor**

All students are well known by their advisor and by all the teachers in their house. Students work with this same group of adults throughout their years in the school.

STUDENT LEARNING SPACES

Teachers' Rooms **Personal Workspaces**

Each student has an individual workstation.

SPATIAL FLEXIBILITY

Durable, Permanent **Responsive, Flexible**

Spatial flexibility is enhanced by the open house and by the use of digital instruction.

SCALABILITY—SCHOOL SIZE

Large Enrollment **Small Enrollment**

A small enrollment (400–500 students) is essential to the school environment. To accommodate more students, multiple campuses should be created.

COURSE OFFERINGS

Core + Broad Elective Subjects **Core Subjects**

The school focuses on core subjects. It offers minimal elective subjects.

EXTRACURRICULAR ACTIVITIES

Extensive **Minimal**

With its strong focus on academics, the school offers minimal extracurricular activities.

COSTS—STAFF

High Cost per Student **Low Cost per Student**

Staff costs per student are comparable to those for a traditional industrial model school, but with fewer administrative and extracurricular personnel, there is a much lower ratio of students to teachers.

COSTS—FACILITIES

High Cost per Student **Low Cost per Student**

Without performing arts, career, or athletic spaces, the building area per student is significantly lower than in a comprehensive traditional high school. The facility cost per student is relatively low.

Reflect on the Academic Focus School and Consider Your Own High School(s)

- What is the focus of your school's instructional program?
- Which students does your school seek to serve? All students? A particular group of students?
- What percentage of your students graduate, and how do they fare in college or work after graduation?
- How well do your teachers know their students and their families? Do your teachers also serve as advisors to our students?
- What is your ratio of students to teachers? Do your campus administrators also teach and have daily contact with students?

9

Learning Labs

Learning lab schools use projects to integrate disciplines, to develop higher order thinking skills, and to create a relevant, motivating, real-world context for the student's studies. Their characteristics generally include the following:

- The school is organized into learning labs in which both teachers and students (approximately 100) have workstations.
- The school integrates direct instruction in core subjects with multidisciplinary project work.
- The school draws on outside resources for support with projects.
- School days are flexible to accommodate both individual courses and projects. The 12-month school year is divided into quarters.
- All students and teachers have personal digital devices.
- The school has minimal elective and extracurricular programs. The focus is on academics and projects.

Learning Labs

Instructional/Spatial Organization Both instruction and facilities are organized around learning labs, each of which accommodates workstations for 5 core teachers (English, math, science, social studies, foreign language) and approximately 100 students plus project work areas. Learning labs share adjacent clusters of seminar and lab spaces.

Students
Both knowledge and problem-solving skills are taught in each learning lab. Core instruction is provided via digital technology, seminars, and labs. The disciplines are integrated, and problem-solving higher order thinking skills are developed via multidisciplinary projects. The students and teachers in each learning lab work together through grades 9–12 to develop both skills. Students leave their learning labs only for electives, arts, food service, and athletic programs.

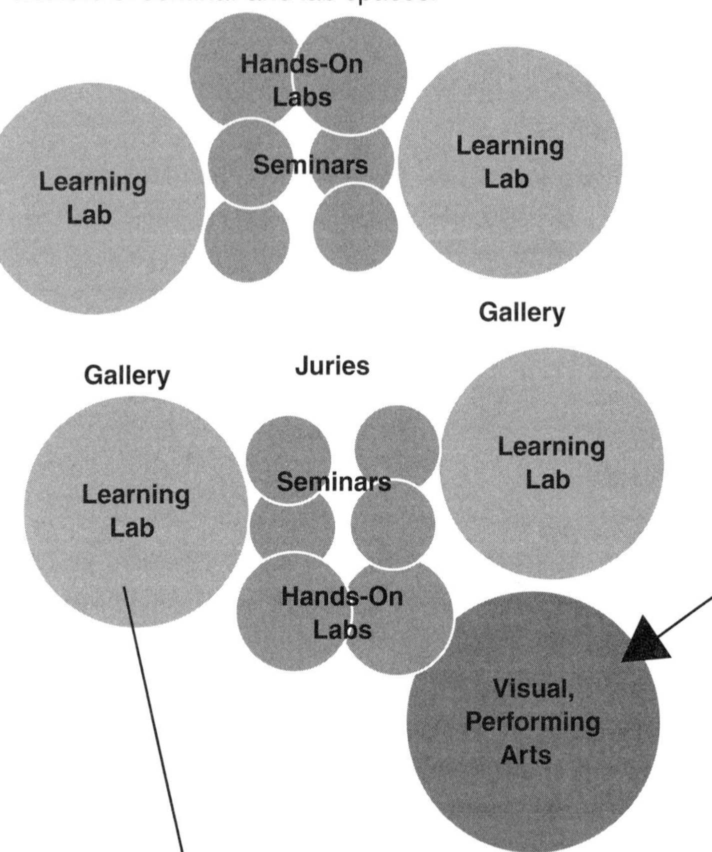

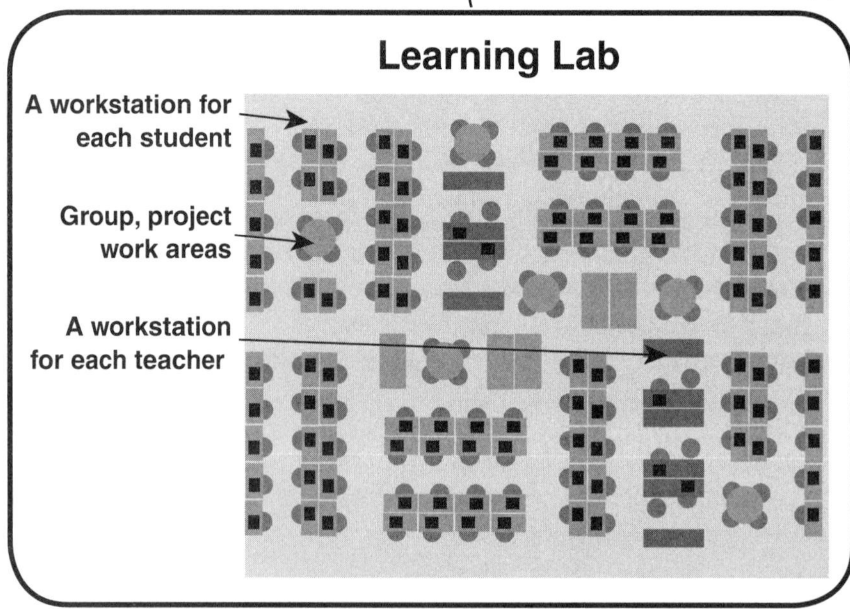

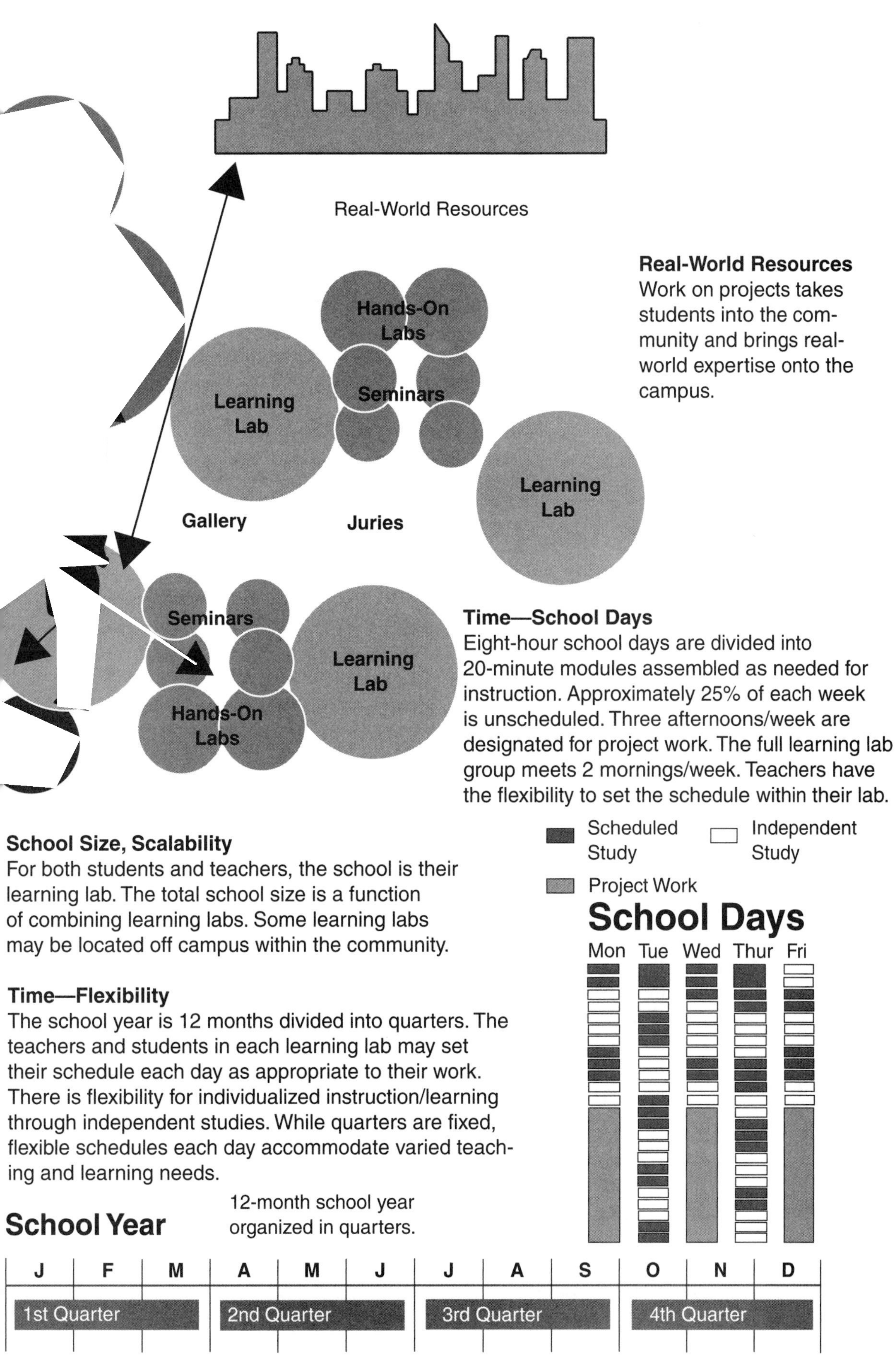

Real-World Resources
Work on projects takes students into the community and brings real-world expertise onto the campus.

Time—School Days
Eight-hour school days are divided into 20-minute modules assembled as needed for instruction. Approximately 25% of each week is unscheduled. Three afternoons/week are designated for project work. The full learning lab group meets 2 mornings/week. Teachers have the flexibility to set the schedule within their lab.

School Size, Scalability
For both students and teachers, the school is their learning lab. The total school size is a function of combining learning labs. Some learning labs may be located off campus within the community.

Time—Flexibility
The school year is 12 months divided into quarters. The teachers and students in each learning lab may set their schedule each day as appropriate to their work. There is flexibility for individualized instruction/learning through independent studies. While quarters are fixed, flexible schedules each day accommodate varied teaching and learning needs.

Although project-based instruction is a relatively new and emergent idea for high schools, it has distinguished architectural education at universities since the 19th century. Concepts for learning lab schools are substantially drawn from architectural education.

But why are the methods used to teach architects relevant to high school students?

Architects are problem solvers. They design buildings to meet specific functional requirements on particular sites within budgets and schedules using a palette of construction materials. In the process, they draw on a very wide range of skills. They analyze and document their clients' needs to define the problem to be solved by their design. The design process requires creative, visual, and artistic skills to explore and illustrate concepts and communication skills to explain those concepts to clients. Knowledge of art and architectural history and the context for the building is important. The design must comply with zoning and life-safety codes; have workable construction details and materials, a sound structural system, and functioning mechanical, electrical, and plumbing systems; and be completed on schedule and within the budget.

In short, **the practice of architecture requires both knowledge and real-world problem-solving skills across a spectrum of disciplines**—and architectural education has evolved for over a century to develop those skills. Today, this balance of left- and right-brain skills seems no less critical for high school than for architectural students.

Learning lab schools are designed in much the same way and are characterized by the following:

- **Knowledge skills and problem-solving skills** are taught through two different but closely coordinated methods of instruction.
  1. **Knowledge skills** are developed by courses in individual disciplines focused on essential concepts and facts. Teachers guide students to digital course materials and then bring students together for seminars or hands-on labs to discuss and explore the materials.
  2. **Problem-solving skills** are developed through real-world projects that require knowledge from multiple disciplines. By providing context and relevance for the content of other coursework, problems require and encourage students to expand on and link together their studies in different disciplines. Each method of instruction makes the other more effective and the entire process engaging and motivating for students and for teachers.

All teachers work with students via courses in individual disciplines and projects that draw on multiple disciplines.

- **Learning labs** are the heart of the school. Each lab includes individual workstations for approximately 100 students and five teachers

(English, math, science, social studies, foreign language) plus meeting and work areas. Spaces and workstations within the learning labs are defined by highly flexible furnishings that students and teachers may rearrange as they choose. Each learning lab serves students from a single grade level. These students remain together with the same teachers throughout their years at the high school.

- **Seminar rooms** and **science** and **project labs** for hands-on work are located separate from, but adjacent to, the learning labs in order to be accessible to teachers and students. Each science lab is equipped to serve instruction in biology, chemistry, and physics.
- **Teachers use both methods of instruction** concurrently to teach knowledge skill classes within their discipline and problem-solving skills involving multiple disciplines. Students work primarily with the teachers within their learning lab, but they also have access to other teachers as needed for specialized coursework and particular expertise.
- The key steps of the **problem-solving process** were outlined by Ted McCain in *Teaching for Tomorrow* (2005, p. 50). Students are taught the four Ds.
    1. **Define** engages students in the definition of the problem to be solved. The teacher needs to frame the objectives but leave details for the student to explore and develop.
    2. **Design** is the process of solving the problem the students have defined and mapping out how the solution will be achieved.
    3. **Do** is the realization of the solution to the problem—the students' production within the time budgeted of a product that meets the requirements.
    4. **Debrief** involves the students, teacher, and others in presenting their projects and reviewing how well they solved the problem defined and how they were realized within the time allotted.
- There are two critical requirements for **project topics**:
    1. Students must perceive the project as personally relevant and interesting. Solving the problem must be engaging and motivating for the student.
    2. The topics must require students to draw on knowledge and skills from their other classes and disciplines to solve the problem. The project must cultivate the development of both knowledge and problem-solving skills.
- Students may **work in groups or individually** on projects.
    1. Teachers may assign the same project to individual students or to groups. As the students work concurrently to solve the same problem, the dialogue between students becomes an important part of the learning experience.

2. More advanced individual students may select their own projects based on personal interests and work independently with the support of teachers in the learning lab. Where resources are available in the community, students may work off campus with individuals or businesses related to their projects.

- The learning labs serve **diverse academic interests**—they are not focused on specific topics or areas of study. The interests of individual students and teachers are served by the selection of project topics, flexible time, and the use of resources from the community.
- Within the learning labs, teachers serve as advisors and counselors to groups of approximately 20 students. They work together as a group through their years at the school. Teachers guide and monitor the students and get to know them and their families well. The full learning lab complement of five teachers and approximately 100 students is a learning community that provides a supportive, caring environment.
- The typical **school day** is divided into 20-minute modules, which are grouped as needed by the teachers in each learning lab for various subjects and methods of instruction. Seminars, hands-on and lab work, and project time are scheduled, but approximately 25% of each school week is designated for unscheduled independent study time. The full lab community meets at least once a week as well as on special occasions to share celebrations and challenges. Three afternoons per week are set aside for project work. To provide time for projects and independent work, the typical school day extends from 8 to 5.
- The **school year** is 12 months divided into quarters. Students and teachers may elect to be in school 9 or 12 months per year and, provided space is available, may select the quarters they wish to attend. Because all disciplines are closely integrated through the projects, students must carry a full course load every quarter. This school cannot offer students the option of attending school all year with less than a full class load each quarter.
- **Personal technology** is an integral part of the school. Guided by the teacher-advisors in the learning labs, students access content anytime and anywhere primarily through technology. Students and teachers work together in seminars, labs, and project spaces to discuss content and develop knowledge and higher order thinking skills.
- **Specialized spaces** for the visual and performing arts, physical education and fitness, and food services are separate from the learning labs. All students in the school share these spaces.
- The school includes **visual and performing arts** programs to complement project-based instruction. Wherever possible, work in these areas is integrated with projects in the learning labs.

- The school provides **career programs** based on the individual interests of students by drawing on resources within the community. Students may go off campus to work with mentors at their site, or experts may come to the campus to work with students. Work in career programs is integrated with projects in the learning labs.
- The school provides **physical education and fitness** programs, but its eight-hour school days and reliance on work with mentors off campus preclude competitive athletic programs. The facility includes a gym and fitness/weight room.
- There is much to be learned about **assessment** from Ted's fourth D (debrief) and from architectural schools. Both engage students in reviewing their own work against their own definition of the problem. Both have the students present and defend their work. In architectural schools, these presentations are called "juries." Other faculty and students, as well as experts from outside the school with backgrounds related to the projects, attend these presentations. Students present their work, and all those in attendance ask questions and offer observations and critiques. The ensuing dialogues are learning opportunities for students and teachers. After the presentations, projects are displayed for other students to see. "Debriefing" and "juries" make assessment a valuable part of the learning process.
- Given that each of the learning labs is a semi-autonomous community, the total **enrollment** of a learning lab school is flexible. However, if the school is very small, there will not be sufficient students to support diverse arts programs, and if it is very large, communications between teachers and students in different labs becomes more difficult. The diagram at the beginning of the chapter suggests eight labs that provide approximately 800 students with two labs per grade level.
- Because the individual learning labs are semi-autonomous, it is possible to locate some **labs within the community** separate from the main campus. Locating portions of the school within the community would reduce the size of the central campus and enhance the school's relationship to the community. Given that the spatial requirements of the learning labs are not large or complex, labs could easily be located in leased space in office or retail buildings in the community.
- The school does not have a **library**. Students access the Internet via their personal wireless digital devices and have access to printers on the campus as needed. Students may also use public libraries or other schools' libraries.
- With the school's **flexible schedule**, there are no bells or lunch periods. Throughout the school day, the student center serves as a dining room, meeting area, lounge, and study space for both students and teachers.

The learning lab school substantially broadens and enriches the role of the **teacher**. Although much of the content is delivered through technology, teachers are responsible for the development of both knowledge and problem-solving skills. Teachers provide instruction in their individual disciplines and problem-solving project-based instruction that entails multiple disciplines. The teachers in each learning lab work as a team to schedule instruction and define and coordinate projects. Defining projects to address specific learning goals across disciplines is a challenge for teachers. Because students and teachers of each learning lab stay together for four years, teachers must be able to provide instruction within their disciplines for students in all of the grades served by the school. Working closely with their students in the learning lab, teachers also serve as advisors and counselors. There are no specialized counselors in the central administrative offices. Students have contact with other teachers in the school, but those in their learning labs know them best. Each teacher has a workstation in the learning lab and access to seminar rooms, labs, and other specialized spaces as needed. Teachers do not have dedicated classrooms. With a larger role, longer days, and the potential for a longer more productive school year, teacher compensation is relatively high.

The learning lab school requires that **students** accept real responsibility for their learning and manage their time effectively. Although teachers can closely monitor students and direct much of their work, the school is most effective for those who use the flexible schedule responsibly.

For both **students and teachers**, project-based instruction requires a different mindset from that in the traditional high school, where the teachers pose questions for which the answers are generally known. In a learning lab school, when the problem is defined (the first D), neither the teacher nor the student knows what the answer or design (the second D) might be. The teacher has more expertise than the students in "finding" the design solution, but does not know in advance what it will be. In addition, virtually all real-world problems (as opposed to conventional school problems) have multiple potential solutions—some better, some worse than others, but all possibilities. Both teacher and students search together for solutions, and all have to be comfortable with the idea that there is no "right" answer. Good project work is a learning experience for both the student and the teacher.

For **campus administrators**, the challenge is to find extraordinary teachers and to fuse them into learning lab teams. Staff development and support and sharing between lab teams are exceptionally important.

For **architects,** the challenge is to make the learning labs stimulating working environments, filled with light and life. The furnishings, lighting, and power and data distribution must be highly flexible so that teachers and students can constantly change the configuration of the space as projects and studies require. Also, they must be durable workspaces in which students may create projects using all manner of media. In modest ways, both students and teachers should be able to personalize the workstations and areas that are their "home" for multiple years of work.

Construction costs for the building shell may be slightly less than those of a traditional school, whereas costs for the flexible furnishings may be higher. Relative to the traditional school, the area of the learning lab school is increased by the labs, but decreased by the reduction in classrooms and absence of athletic, library, and career technology spaces. Using the facility 12 instead of 9 months per year significantly increases the numbers of students it serves and thereby reduces the facility cost per student.

PRECEDENTS

- The best precedents for learning labs are the architectural schools at universities across the country. It is interesting to note that while *Breaking Ranks* (NASSP, 1996, dedicated to Ernest Boyer) was being written, Boyer was at work with Lee Mitgang on *Building Community: A New Future for Architecture Education and Practice,* both of which were published in 1996—both are good reads. High school educators would be well served by looking to schools that have been using project-based instruction for more than a century.
- Ted McCain's *Teaching for Tomorrow* (2005) provides concepts for project-based instruction in high schools.
- School of Environmental Studies at the Minneapolis Zoo—The Zoo School. Designed by the firm of Hammel Green (Bruce Jilk) (http://www.ISD196.K12.mn.us/schools/ses).
- New Technology Foundation (http://www.newtechfoundation.org/index.html).
- New Technology High School, Napa, California (http://www.newtechhigh.org/Website2007/index.html).
- Star Lane Center, Casper, Wyoming (http://starlane.1wyo.net), Mardie Robinson, *What Box? Creating a Problem-Based Learning Program. The Story of Star Lane Center* (2003).

FOCUS ON TEACHING OR LEARNING?

Teacher Centered **Student Centered**

Project-based instruction is inherently student centered. Although groups of students are given the same problem to solve, each student pursues her own solution. Teachers counsel each student individually as he works.

GROUP OR INDIVIDUAL TEACHING AND LEARNING?

Group Teaching and Learning **Individual Teaching and Learning**

				●		

To ensure that instruction via disciplines and projects fit together, all instruction occurs in classes on a synchronous schedule. While working on projects, the dialogue between students as they struggle to create their own solutions is a particularly important part of the learning process.

TRADITIONAL TEACHING VS. DIGITAL LEARNING

Teacher, Text **Digital**

					●	

Instruction by discipline is primarily digital with teachers in guiding, supporting roles.

21ST-CENTURY THINKING SKILLS

Knowledge Skills **Content + Problem-Solving Skills**

						●

The objective of integrating instruction by disciplines and through projects is to assure that students develop both content and problem-solving skills.

ASSESSMENT

Content Skills **Content + Problem-Solving Skills**

						●

Juries, presentations, and exhibitions of projects assess both content and problem-solving skills. They are a very important part of instruction.

LEARNING FOCUS

Traditional Content **21st-Century Literacies**

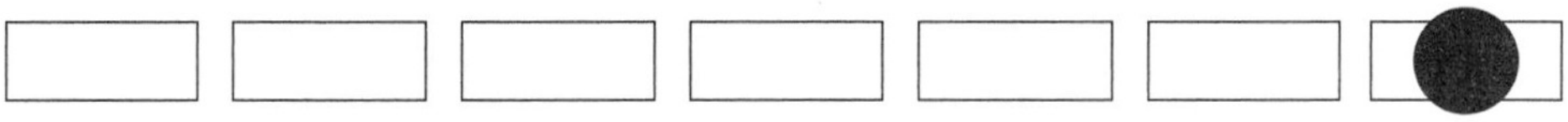

Twenty-first-century literacy skills are essential to digital instruction in individual disciplines and to the solution of interdisciplinary problems.

INSTRUCTIONAL ORGANIZATION

Departments and Disciplines **Interdisciplinary**

The school is organized around instruction by disciplines and interdisciplinary projects.

APPLICATION OF LEARNING

Classroom Theory **Real-World Relevance**

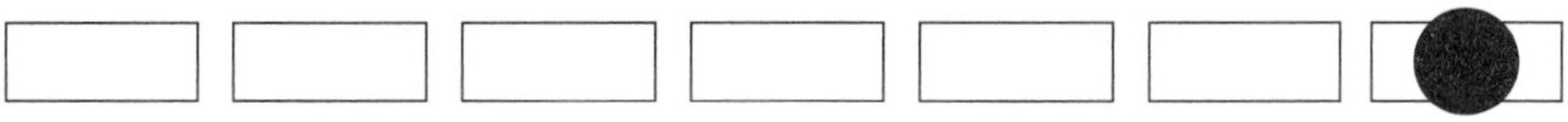

The project-based instruction addresses real-world problems relevant to the students.

RESPONSIBILITY FOR LEARNING

Teacher **Student**

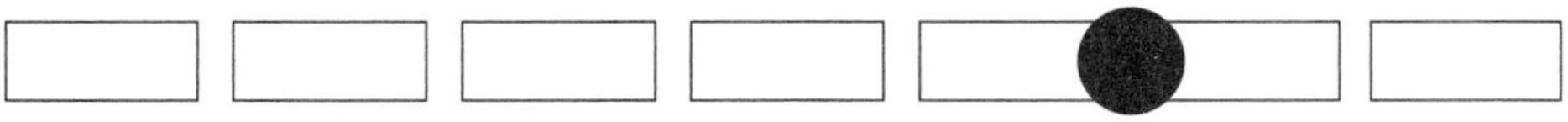

Although all of the work is done in classes with continuous teacher supervision and support, students have real responsibility for their digital learning and for the creation of projects. Because projects have stipulated completion dates, time management is particularly important.

TIME—SCHOOL YEAR

Fixed **Flexible**

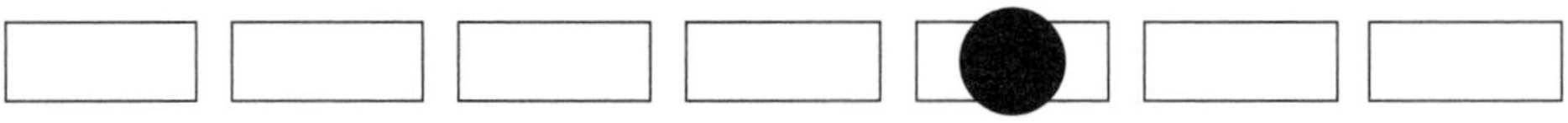

The 12-month school year is organized into quarters. Within each quarter, all courses are synchronous. Teachers and students may chose which quarters to attend over the year.

TIME—SCHOOL DAY

Fixed **Flexible**

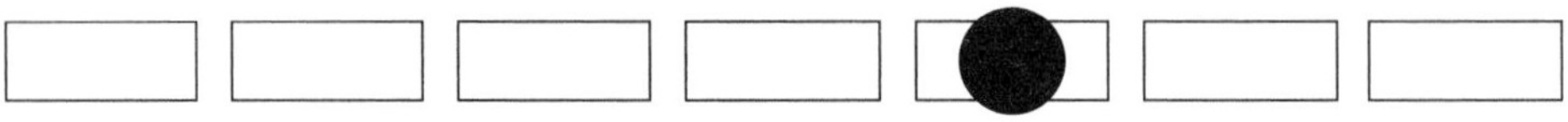

Modular scheduling and digital learning resources provide flexibility to accommodate subject and modes of instruction. However, the problem-based instruction is scheduled three afternoons per week to ensure dialogue between students and teacher and among the students.

STUDENT SUPPORT

Counselor **Teacher-Advisor**

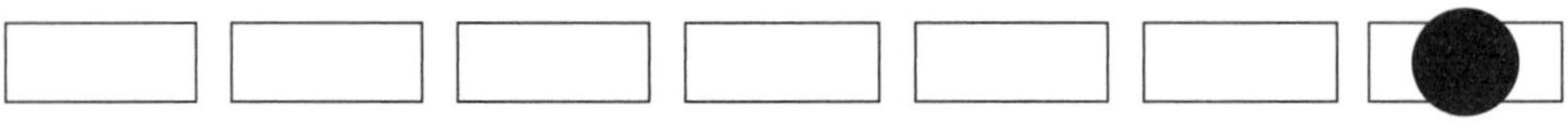

Groups of about 20 students work with a teacher-advisor throughout their years at the school. Students are also well known by the other teachers in their learning lab.

STUDENT LEARNING SPACES

Teachers' Rooms **Personal Workspaces**

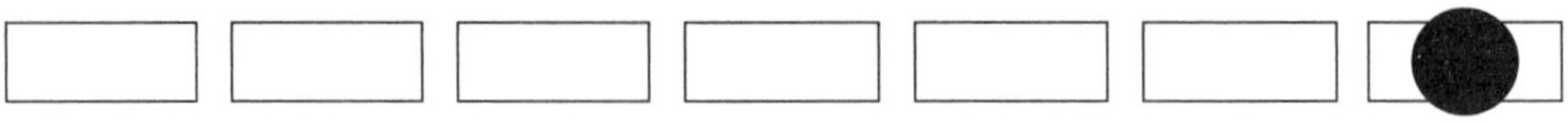

All students have their own workstations for the duration of their time on the campus.

SPATIAL FLEXIBILITY

Durable, Permanent **Responsive, Flexible**

The learning labs are open spaces with flexible furnishings that teachers and students may rearrange as needed. Other instructional spaces are generic in nature and may be adapted to serve widely varied purposes.

SCALABILITY—SCHOOL SIZE

Large Enrollment **Small Enrollment**

The enrollment capacity is a function of the number of learning labs, each with approximately 100 students. School size does not significantly affect the teaching and learning environment, but it does affect the school's ability to support visual and performing arts programs.

COURSE OFFERINGS

Core + Broad Elective Subjects **Core Subjects**

The school offers visual and performing arts. Some elective subjects are available via digital resources. Students may pursue some career interests via mentors outside the school.

EXTRACURRICULAR ACTIVITIES

Extensive **Minimal**

The learning lab school offers visual and performing arts, but not competitive athletics because of scheduling conflicts.

COSTS—STAFF

High Cost per Student **Low Cost per Student**

The ratio of students to teachers is lower than in traditional comprehensive high schools, but the overall ratio of students to total staff is higher given that the school has no athletic programs.

COSTS—FACILITIES

High Cost per Student **Low Cost per Student**

The learning labs require considerable area for each teacher and student, but this is substantially offset by the absence of competitive athletic facilities.

Reflect on the Learning Lab School and Consider Your Own High School(s)

- Phillip Schlechty (1997) suggests that the most important work done in schools is the work teachers get the students to do. If this is the case, where do the students in your school do that important work? Do they have a place of their own in which to work and to store their stuff?
- How is your school developing both knowledge and problem-solving skills?
- How does your school make assessment a teaching and learning tool?

10

Self-Directed Learning

Self-directed learning schools provide individualized instruction within a campus context. Their characteristics generally include the following:

- Under the direction of teacher-advisors, students work at their own pace using digital learning guides.
- Teachers support and monitor progress, gathering students for group discussions or work when appropriate.
- Students have access to teachers as needed.
- Both students and teachers have places to work in advisories and learning halls.
- There are no periods during the school day nor semesters during the 12-month year. Learning is self-paced. Schooling is a continuous process.

Self-Directed Learning

Instructional/Spatial Organization

Students work independently and asynchronously, but look to the campus for support and guidance, for group activities, and for specialized spaces and equipment. Instructionally and spatially, the school is organized around learning halls that house approximately 200 students in families and advisories. Each advisory is composed of a teacher-advisor and 20 students while each family includes 5 advisories and 100 Students. Around the learning halls, students and teachers have access to seminar rooms, labs, and other specialized spaces.

Career Tech
Admin
Seminar Rooms
Student Center
Digital Learning Guides
Seminar Rooms
Lab

Students Work With Teacher-Advisors

Students pursue their studies independently and at their own pace under the direction of their teacher-advisors, via digital learning guides. Teachers in specific disciplines provide support/supervision. Students work with advisors in the same family for the duration of their studies at the school. While graduation typically occurs within 4 years, students working at their own pace may complete requirements in more or less time. Students and their teacher-advisors work together to create individual study plans and schedules for each day/week. Typically students work on 3–4 courses simultaneously. Learning guides are usually composed of approximately 20 sections, each typically requiring 5–6 hours. Students advance from section to section with their teacher's approval.

When the student and teacher believe studies are sufficiently advanced, the student may, depending on what is appropriate, make a presentation/exhibition, write a paper, present a portfolio, or take a test to demonstrate command of the subject and to complete the course. Students are responsible for managing much of their own time. Learning guides may focus on individual disciplines/content/knowledge skills or may pose problems and develop skills across disciplines. Teaching/learning may happen within the school or draw upon real-world resources in the home and community.

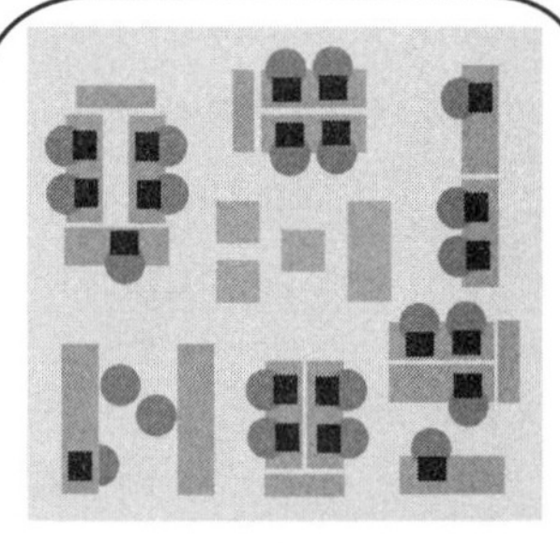

Advisory with workstations for a teacher-advisor and 20 students.

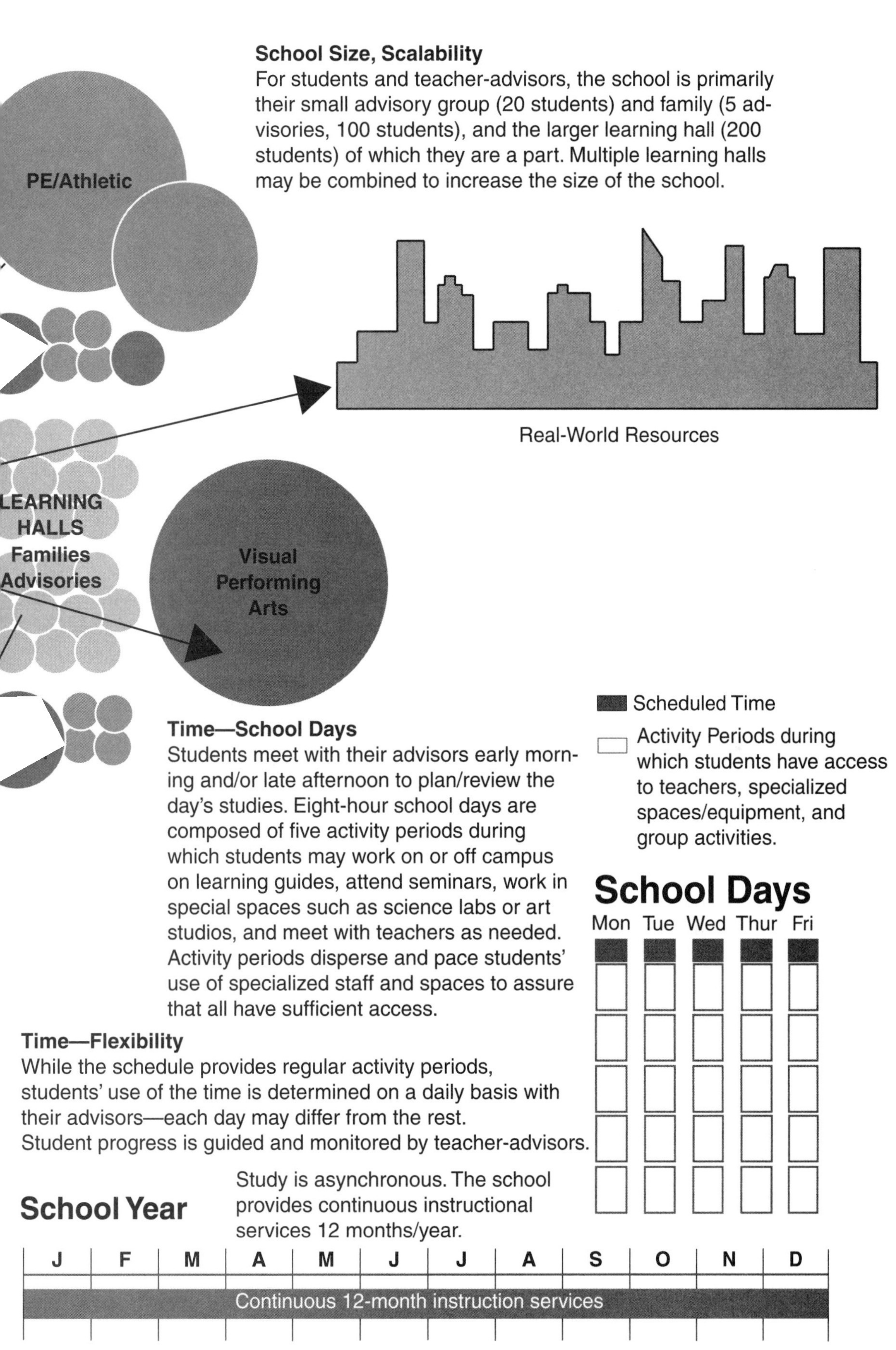

School Size, Scalability

For students and teacher-advisors, the school is primarily their small advisory group (20 students) and family (5 advisories, 100 students), and the larger learning hall (200 students) of which they are a part. Multiple learning halls may be combined to increase the size of the school.

Time—School Days

Students meet with their advisors early morning and/or late afternoon to plan/review the day's studies. Eight-hour school days are composed of five activity periods during which students may work on or off campus on learning guides, attend seminars, work in special spaces such as science labs or art studios, and meet with teachers as needed. Activity periods disperse and pace students' use of specialized staff and spaces to assure that all have sufficient access.

Time—Flexibility

While the schedule provides regular activity periods, students' use of the time is determined on a daily basis with their advisors—each day may differ from the rest. Student progress is guided and monitored by teacher-advisors.

Study is asynchronous. The school provides continuous instructional services 12 months/year.

Chapter 7, "Instructional Centers," was partially based on thinking from Trump's *Images of the Future* (1959), and this chapter reflects and expands on Trump's more recent *A School for Everyone* (1977), which is now 30 years old. Whereas *Images of the Future* proposed varied modes of instruction and flexible modular scheduling that offers some opportunities to accommodate diverse learning styles, *A School for Everyone* called for fully individualized, year-round, asynchronous learning that could take place simultaneously on the campus, in the home, and in the community. It was a remarkable proposal that educators still struggle to realize.

Self-directed learning schools are characterized by the following:

- **Personalization** for both students and teachers is the school's primary focus. It seeks to provide real choices for both.
- **Teachers serve dual roles**. As subject-area teachers, they develop learning guides and provide academic advice, feedback, coaching, monitoring, seminars, large group presentations, and assessment to students. Teachers typically meet face to face with students twice a week or as needed by the student.
  1. As advisors, teachers work with a group of approximately 20 students (from each of the grades served in the school) in an advisory. The teacher-advisor and students in the advisory meet several times per week as a group as well as individually to review schedules, monitor progress, and address personal issues. The advisory structure ensures that each student is well known by, and has a close personal working relationship with, at least one adult on the campus. Advisors function as counselors on day-to-day academic matters, but the school also has some specialized staff to provide additional expertise in career and college matters.
- Spatially, each **advisory** consists of a teacher workstation and flexible tables, comfortable seating, and storage units for students and the teacher. The teacher-advisor and students rearrange and personalize their space to suit their work and interests. Over time, each advisory develops its own personality. Students may change their space to work individually or in small groups as needed.
- Advisories are grouped in **families** (five teacher-advisors and approximately 100 students) with one teacher from each of the core disciplines (English, math, science, social studies, and languages). Through the families, students have immediate access to a teacher in each core subject. All of the students and faculty in each family come to know and to support each other as they work together over time. Ideally, students remain within the same advisory and family during their time on the campus, but changes may be necessary as students progress at different rates and may attend school during different parts of the year. Families typically meet twice a week to

celebrate events and achievements, discuss common issues, and bond as a group.

- Families are grouped in **learning halls** that house up to two families or 200 students and 10 teacher-advisors. The high school campus may consist of one or several learning halls. The learning halls are the instructional, social, and spatial core of the school for students and teacher-advisors.
- The learning halls are ringed by **seminar rooms** and **support areas**. The seminar rooms provide opportunities for teachers and small groups of students (10–15) to discuss materials from the learning guides and issues raised in projects. The support areas provide specialized spaces and equipment related to science, career technology, visual and performing arts, and physical education and athletics for use as needed by students and teachers.
- Because students and teacher-advisors pursue their **work asynchronously**, there are no scheduled lunch periods. The school provides food services throughout the school day ranging from breakfast to lunch to snacks and beverages in between. The school does not have a cafeteria, but a student center includes spaces for both eating and relaxation. Students and faculty may go there when they wish.
- Although teacher-advisors are grouped in multidisciplinary families, in larger schools with several families, **departmental conference and material storage areas** are appropriate to encourage dialogue among teachers in their areas of expertise. These spaces are located around the learning halls, where they may also serve as conference seminar rooms.
- Every student and teacher-advisor has a personal digital device and may access digital resources wirelessly anywhere, anytime. Students work from **digital learning guides** written by teachers or drawn from other sources outside the school. With multiple sources for coursework, individual students may, with the assistance and approval of their teacher-advisor, select those learning guides best suited to their personal learning styles. Under the direction of their teacher-advisor, students often work on several guides (typically four) simultaneously. Learning guides are road maps to sources (digital links), activities, experiments, and projects. The guides typically are organized in sections (approximately 20), each requiring 5–6 hours of work. Each guide includes an introduction that outlines for the student the scope and relevance of the course. Working together, students and teacher-advisors may go beyond the learning guides to create projects across disciplines and to draw on resources in the community. The guides define learning outcomes and suggest opportunities for additional in-depth work and creative activities. Reviews with teacher-advisors and pretests within the learning guides help students know when they have realized learning goals

and are ready for formal evaluation and completion of the course. The learning guide software allows teacher-advisors to monitor each student's progress and to assemble small groups for seminars to discuss course content. Students informally assemble such groups within their advisories and families as they work.

- The teacher-advisors work together to prepare and update **learning guides** or to select them from digital resources outside the campus. The school provides digital expertise to help teachers develop learning guides that incorporate text, images and graphics, videos, and sound. The guides include interactive materials that require students to work through materials in order to progress from level to level and that permit teacher-advisors to monitor the students' studies. In this regard, teachers may learn much from digital games. Long-term instructional flexibility in the school is a function of modifying digital learning guides instead of rearranging spaces.
- Through the learning guides, most of each student's **core studies are self-paced**. Students begin and complete courses at different times. Students work with their teacher-advisor to build their schedules on a daily or weekly basis. Each student's schedule differs from that of other students, and each student's schedule typically varies from day to day. Helping students learn to manage their time effectively is an important part of the school's program.
- Wherever possible, studies are self-paced. However, some elective, career, performing arts, and athletic programs require that students work together or utilize costly and potentially dangerous equipment. These programs are **conventionally scheduled** and may only be offered seasonally. Students must sustain their self-paced studies while participating in these programs with fixed schedules.
- **The typical day is 8–5**. Working with their teacher-advisor, students determine when to work on what. The day begins with a brief advisory period during which the teacher-advisor and students discuss general and individual issues and progress as well as individual schedules for the day. The remainder of the day is for independent study and is divided into activity periods during which students may work in their advisory area, attend seminars, meet with teachers related to their learning guide studies, work independently, or go to specialized work areas. The sole purpose of activity periods is to distribute students across the school day to facilitate access to teachers and specialized spaces. There are no bells to fix or announce the periods.
- **The school operates year-round,** providing continuous instructional services for its students without fixed time periods such as semesters or quarters. Teachers work year-round to provide instructional support for students pursuing self-paced studies. With students beginning and completing courses throughout the year, it

is important that they have continuous access to teacher-advisors. Students join with their teacher-advisor to define their course load and to assure the availability of school resources. Students may take less or more than four years to graduate as determined by their own learning capabilities and personal needs.

- With the focus on **independent study** based on digital learning guides accessible anytime, anywhere, "school" extends beyond the campus to include the student's home and community. With the approval of the school and parents, students may do portions of their work off campus or wherever they learn most effectively. For those juniors and seniors with sufficient academic standing and the approval of their parents, the campus is open. These students need to be on campus only as needed to interact with teacher-advisors and other students and to draw on the school's resources.
- Trump noted in ***A School for Everyone*** (1977, p. 129), "A school that stresses independent study recognizes that students have to do the learning and that there is no effective substitute for more personal experiences in school, home and community." The objective of independent study is for students to assume and to demonstrate responsibility for their own learning, for self-evaluation of their learning and progress, for persistence in their studies, and for satisfaction in their own successes. Trump said that every teacher's goal "is to become increasingly dispensable" (p. 137).
- Students are initially assigned to a **teacher-advisor**, but may change to another provided a space is available in their advisory. The students select the teachers with whom to work during their activity periods. The objective is to provide maximum choice and opportunity for each student and to find the learning environment best suited to their personal needs and interests. Providing students with choices encourages teacher-advisors to conduct their advisory such that they attract and retain students.
- **Assessment** occurs for students as an integral and continuous part of each course of study, but a final evaluation marks their successful completion of the learning objectives. The students and their teacher-advisors decide together when the individual students are ready to complete a course. The final assessment may take several forms including tests, papers, presentations and exhibitions of projects, or portfolios. The subject area teacher with whom the students worked reviews the results face to face with the students, who then may have the opportunity to revise their work until the learning objectives are realized. The grade and credit a student receives are based on the learning outcome, not the time spent. There are no failures, but there are no credits for learning that has not been completed.
- Students' **opportunity for choice**, independent study, and flexible time is a function of their ability to assume responsibility for their

own learning. If a student is not doing well, the teacher-advisor may stipulate that the student adhere to a defined schedule, work in the advisory space, or work with a specific teacher to remedy the problem. If students are doing well, the school environment offers them great flexibility to make choices.
- As delineated above, the self-directed learning school is an **intermediate concept** between a traditional campus-based Industrial Age school and a cyber school. It is a physical place at which teachers and students work together, yet instruction is digital, largely self-paced, and substantially independent of the school as a place. The self-directed learning school recognizes the campus as both an academic and a social context for students and preserves the traditional custodial role of school campuses.

In some ways, the self-directed learning school both expands and contracts the roles of the **teachers**. They function as advisors to a small group of students and as teachers in their area of expertise. Through the advisories, teachers develop a close, personal working rapport with a small group of students over an extended period of time. Within the family and learning hall structure, the teacher may work with a large number of students as they progress through their learning guides. With the learning guides, there is no repetitive stand-and-deliver within a classroom setting. This allows teachers time to work with students in small groups or individually. Each teacher has a workstation in an advisory instead of a classroom. Teachers, typically working in teams, prepare digital learning guides for complete courses for all students instead of lectures for their own classes. Teachers have access to seminar rooms and specialized workspaces (for example, science labs) as they are needed. Based on feedback from software related to the learning guides, teachers assemble students when appropriate for seminars to discuss the materials. Assessment takes many forms, engaging both the teacher and the student. With the exception of advisories, there is no regular daily schedule for teachers or students.

For **students**, the self-directed learning school provides new opportunities and requires the assumption of new responsibilities. Working with their teacher-advisor and the learning guides, students have the opportunity to pursue their studies in varying venues (on campus, at home, or in the community), on varying schedules, and with varied resources. Through the learning guides, the school sets the basics, but students have the opportunity to consider these within their own context. Studies framed in this manner are more relevant for the students, who are motivated to assume more responsibility for their own learning. This is a profoundly different environment from that in the traditional high school. It demands more of, but offers more to, each student.

For **administrators**, the challenge of asynchronous studies on campus, in homes, and in the community will be to gauge the demand for faculty and facilities. They will have to determine the need for faculty or the capacity of a school facility with students carrying varying loads on varying schedules throughout the year. The prospect may be daunting, but it is one community colleges and many businesses face daily in serving diverse and numerous customers.

For the **architect**, the learning halls are the focal point of the school—the base for teacher-advisors and students. Other spaces are important, but secondary and supporting. The learning halls must be large, filled with natural light, and highly flexible—much like the reading rooms in great libraries. Surfaces and furnishings must be soft to dampen sounds in the open space. Furnishings and equipment must allow teacher-advisors and students to rearrange and personalize their advisories easily.

Both the staffing and facility **costs** for the school will be quite different from those in traditional high schools. Because both teachers and facilities will be needed 12 months per year, the total number of teachers and quantity of facilities required for a given number of students will be reduced in proportion to the longer school year over which they serve. Teachers' annual compensation will increase to reflect the additional time they work.

PRECEDENTS

While substantially modified in this proposal for the self-directed learning school, many of the concepts were drawn from Trump's *A School for Everyone* and are related to schools reflecting his thinking, including the following, all members of the Canadian Coalition for Self-Directed Learning (http://www.bchs.calgary.ab.ca/ccsdl):

- Banff Community High School (Banff, Alberta)
- Bishop Carroll High School (Calgary, Alberta)
- Bishop O'Bryne High School (Calgary, Alberta)
- Frances Kelsey Secondary School (Mill Bay, British Columbia)
- Mary Ward Catholic Secondary School (Scarborough, Ontario)
- St. Joseph High School (Edmonton, Alberta)

FOCUS ON TEACHING OR LEARNING?

Teacher Centered **Student Centered**

					●	

Students are provided a selection of digital learning guides and the opportunity to work at their own pace.

GROUP OR INDIVIDUAL TEACHING AND LEARNING?

Group Teaching and Learning | **Individual Teaching and Learning**

Each student works independently.

TRADITIONAL TEACHING VS. DIGITAL LEARNING

Teacher, Text | **Digital**

The learning guides are digital.

21ST-CENTURY THINKING SKILLS

Knowledge Skills | **Content + Problem-Solving Skills**

The digital learning guides teach both content and problem-solving skills.

ASSESSMENT

Content Skills | **Content + Problem-Solving Skills**

The digital learning guides include continuous assessment as the students progress through them. The software tracks each student's progress, which her teacher-advisor may monitor.

LEARNING FOCUS

Traditional Content | **21st-Century Literacies**

Use of the digital learning guides assures the development of 21st-century literacy skills.

INSTRUCTIONAL ORGANIZATION

Departments and Disciplines **Interdisciplinary**

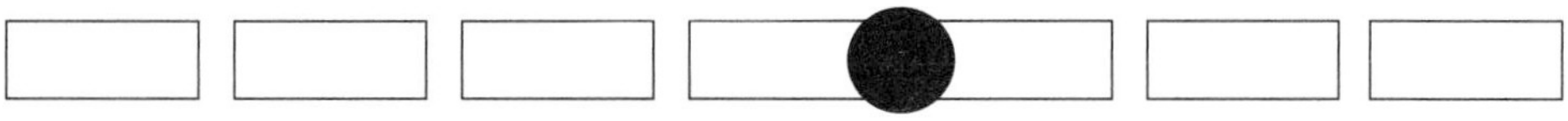

The school is organized around families and learning halls, but interdisciplinary studies are dependent on the digital learning guides. The challenge is to create guides that span multiple disciplines.

APPLICATION OF LEARNING

Classroom Theory **Real-World Relevance**

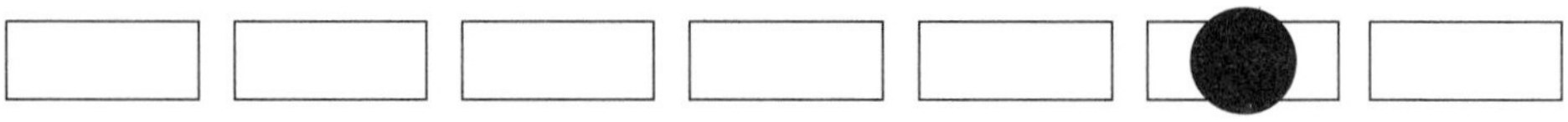

The digital learning guides provide links to resources from around the world. They provide the digital environment to which high school students are particularly attuned.

RESPONSIBILITY FOR LEARNING

Teacher **Student**

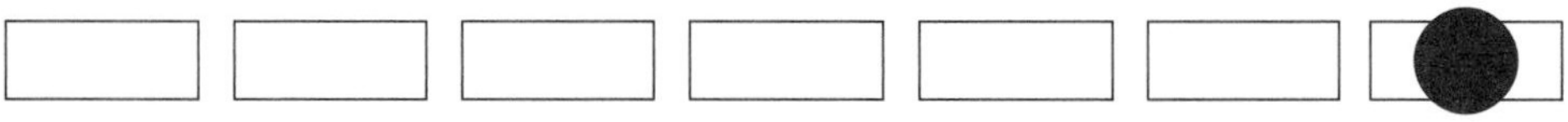

Students have the primary responsibility for their learning. Teacher-advisors monitor and support students, but students must assume real responsibility for the management of their time and studies.

TIME—SCHOOL YEAR

Fixed **Flexible**

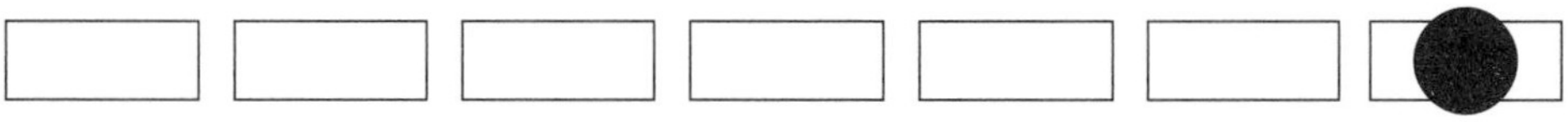

The school provides services all year to allow students to work at their own pace. Only seasonal extracurricular activities are scheduled.

TIME—SCHOOL DAY

Fixed **Flexible**

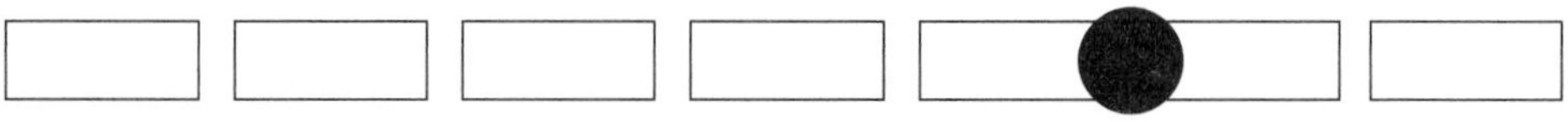

Although the school day is divided into activity periods to assure students access to teachers and specialized spaces, their studies are self-paced. Students join with their teacher-advisors to plan their studies and use of time. Group activities such as performing arts, some career programs, and athletics have fixed schedules.

STUDENT SUPPORT

Counselor **Teacher-Advisor**

The school is organized into advisories, each with a teacher-advisor and approximately 20 students.

STUDENT LEARNING SPACES

Teachers' Rooms **Personal Workspace**

Advisories include flexible student work areas, but not individual workstations.

SPATIAL FLEXIBILITY

Durable, Permanent **Responsive, Flexible**

Although the learning halls provide substantial spatial flexibility, the school's real flexibility is based in its digital learning guides, which may be updated and modified continuously.

SCALABILITY—SCHOOL SIZE

Large Enrollment **Small Enrollment**

The size of the school may vary considerably without affecting the learning environment, but a small enrollment will limit some career, arts, and athletic programs.

COURSE OFFERINGS

Core + Broad Elective Subjects **Core Subjects**

The school offers both core and broad electives via its digital learning guides and specialized spaces on the campus.

EXTRACURRICULAR ACTIVITIES

Extensive **Minimal**

The school has performing arts and athletic programs.

COSTS—STAFF

High Cost per Student **Low Cost per Student**

The ratio of students to staff is comparable to a traditional industrial model high school.

COSTS—FACILITIES

High Cost per Student **Low Cost per Student**

The building area per student is comparable to that of a traditional industrial model high school.

Reflect on the Self-Directed Learning School and Consider Your Own High School(s)

- How does your school serve the learning style of each student?
- How do you allow students to work at their own pace to succeed in their studies?
- How does your school year accommodate the varied needs of families and learning styles of students?
- How are you making digital technology and learning materials available to every student anytime, anywhere? How would your school function if the technology was not there?
- How do you provide for each student direct individual access to teachers as needed to support learning?

11

Time—Less + More

The time—less + more school reflects the earlier onset of puberty for 21st- versus 19th-century students. The length and nature of both primary and secondary schooling are changed.

- Students begin elementary schools (K–6) at ages 4–5 and graduate from secondary schools (grades 7–11) at age 16–17.
- Less time is allotted for primary and secondary schooling. Students graduate from high school at the end of grade 11 instead of grade 12 ready for college or work.
- More instructional time is provided via eight-hour school days and a 210-day school year.
- Studies for grade 7–8 students are organized into multidisciplinary pods, whereas grade 9–11 students work with advisors in learning labs.

Time— Less + More

Less Time + More Time
The secondary school is intended to serve 21st-century students, who mature several years earlier than the 19th-century students for whom the traditional model high school was designed. Students now start kindergarten at 4–5 years of age and graduate in 12 years, whereas in the past they attended school for 13 years and graduated from the 12th grade at 17–18 years of age. This secondary school serves grades 7–11. The school year is of 210 days long and organized in quarters. Each school day is 8 hours long.

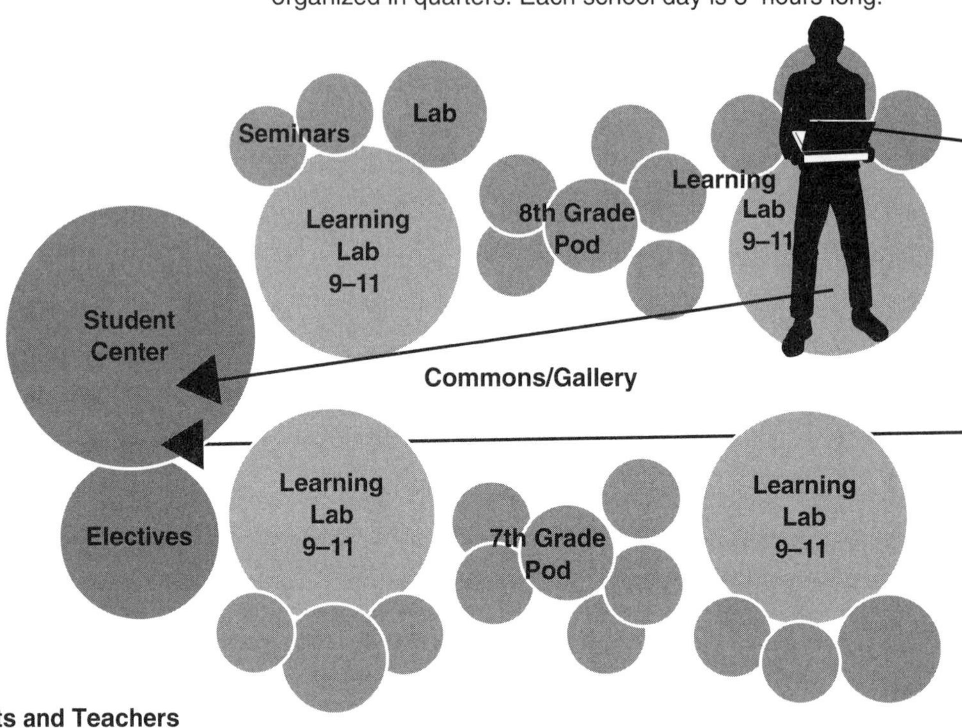

Grade 7–8 Students and Teachers
Five teachers and 100 students work together in a 'pod'. Within that context, the teachers work together to define schedules and to integrate disciplines. The pod has a central common space surrounded by flexible instructional areas that may be opened and combined as needed.

Grade 9–11 Students and Teachers
Five teachers and "100" students work together in a learning lab—a highly flexible space with individual workstations. Seminar and supporting spaces are adjacent to the lab.

For both students and teachers, the school consists primarily of the pod or lab. They go out only for dining, arts, CTE, and physical education activities.

GRADES

Age	Before WWII	After WWII	Current	Time-Less+More	
4–5				K	Start K at age 4 vs. 5
5–6	K	K	K	1	Self-contained classrooms
6–7	1	1	1	2	
7–8	2	2	2	3	
8–9	3	3	3	4	
9–10	4	4	4	5	
10–11	5	5	5	6	
11–12	6	6	6	7	Pods—structured environment
12–13	7	7	7	8	
13–14	8	8	8	9	Labs—individualized, self-paced, technology based
14–15	9	9	9	10	
15–16	10	10	10	11	
16–17	11	11	11	Students graduate at grade 11 to pursue college or work	
17–18	12	12	12		

Primary | Jr High | Secondary

7th Grade Pod

Learning Lab 9–11

Visual, Performing Arts

Commons/Gallery

Learning Lab 9–11

Physical Education

8th Gra
Pod

School Size, Scalability

For students and teachers, school is organized around small communities (each for approximately 100 students) composed of pods for grade 7–8 students and learning labs for grade 9–11 students. The size of the school is a function of combining pods and labs. With the focus on digital instruction, there are few advantages to a large enrollment. With students ranging from ages 11–16, a relatively small enrollment is advantageous.

9–11 School Days

Eight-hour school days begin with advisories. Seminars and group work are organized in the mornings while the afternoons are used for individual studies and project work. Teachers within each lab serve as advisors and provide support/supervision as needed. Students have significant responsibility for the management of their own time and studies.

Grade 7–8 School Days

Grade 9–11 School Days

Advisory

Projects, Independent Study

Group, Seminar Study

Mon Tue Wed Thur Fri

rade 7–8 School Days

hour days (8–4) are organized to morning and afternoon ocks for core studies with a exible period in the middle for nch and the pursuit of individual udies/interests. Shorter periods the start and end of the day commodate advisories, ectives, arts, and PE. Extracurricular tivities occur after 4:00 PM.

School Year

The 210-day school year with four 11-week quarters and four 2-week breaks provides 8,400 hours of instruction in 5 years vs. 7,020 hours in the traditional 180-day school year with 6.5-hour days.

J F M A M J J A S O N D

Although each model in the preceding chapters has explored concepts for the school day and year, we have not yet addressed the full duration of K–12 schooling and related grade alignments. Some publications (*Prisoners of Time,* National Education Commission on Time and Learning, 1994) and statistics describing the success of high school graduates in college and the related need for remedial studies suggest that more time is needed for high school teaching and learning. Other publications (*Jefferson's Children,* Leon Botstein, 1996, and *Tough Choices or Tough Times,* New Commission on the Skills of the American Workforce, 2006) contend the 12th/senior year and possibly even the 11th/junior year are poorly used, and the growing interest in altering the relationship between high school and college suggests that less time is needed. This chapter explores the implications of this debate and outlines a model that provides both less and more time for high school studies.

In *Jefferson's Children,* Botstein argued that when high schools were originally designed in the 19th century, students matured at a later age. He noted that in 1840, the average age of girls at the onset of menstruation was 16.5 years; it was between 15 and 16 at the start of the 20th century and 13 in the late 1990s. He concluded, "The blunt fact is that the American high school was designed for 15–18 year olds who were children only beginning their journey to adulthood. It is now filled with young adults of the same age" (Botstein, 1997, pp. 79–80).

Exploring the failure of high schools, Botstein observed that

> The old core courses—general education and the sort of basic training we associate with the college of yesteryear—are therefore much more appropriate for high school-age youngsters now in the 11th and 12th grades. Colleges are no longer able to pick up the pieces of what is broken or left unfinished during the high school years. And because of the clash between the high school and maturity, the last two years of high school, particularly the senior year, are a waste of time. (Botstein, 1997, pp. 95–96)

He noted that students can complete minimum graduation requirements in 3 to 3 ½ years and that their senior year may be both wasteful and boring. As an alternative, he proposed that students should finish high school earlier and go on to college, work, or other endeavors—and that is the premise of the model that follows.

However, Botstein's assessment and the remedies he proposed also raise difficult and important questions. If today's students are more mature than those in the past, and if they have more than enough time for their high school studies, it would seem that a very high percentage should graduate and those graduates should be well prepared for college work—which is clearly not the case. Are our high schools so weak that they have converted the advantages of heightened maturity and generous time into mediocrity? If high school lasts too long, is filling the "unused time" by bringing college work into high schools via AP, dual credit, and early college high school programs a valid remedy?

What are the characteristics of these programs, and why are they not a sound solution to the genuine problems Botstein identified? According to the Web site of the Early College High School Initiative (http://www.earlycolleges.org, as of July 2006), these schools are intended to do the following:

- **"Permit high school students to earn high school and college credits concurrently so that students graduate from high school with enough college credits to enter a 4 year college program as a junior."**

  The effect for students is to eliminate two of the eight years of study typically required to earn both high school and four-year Bachelor of Arts degrees. Although this efficiency is admirable, it is difficult to imagine, all else being equal, that learning opportunities are not significantly reduced by deleting two years or 25% of teaching and learning time. Could we take advantage of the excess time Botstein identifies to address the shortcomings noted in *Prisoners of Time* and the difficulties ill-prepared high school graduates face in college? Will eliminating two years of study improve either high school or college graduation rates or the ability of those graduates to compete in the global economy?

- **"Provide guidance and support from adults to students (while still in high school) during their first two years of college."**

  This has been one of the primary failures of high schools and was discussed at length in *Breaking Ranks* and *Breaking Ranks II* (National Association of Secondary School Principals, 1996, 2004). The problem needs to be addressed, but introducing college courses to high school will not ensure any change in this regard. Some undergraduate college programs are even less successful with regard to student-teacher rapport than those in high schools—and the college freshman dropout rate is no improvement over the ninth-grade high school dropout rate.

- **"Increase the number of 1st generation, low-income, English language learners and students of color attaining post secondary degrees."**

  This has been accomplished with remarkable success in existing high schools such as the MET in Providence, the KIPP and YES Academies in Houston, and High Tech High in San Diego. The keys are academics that provide sufficient preparation for college success, contextualized learning, awareness of the possibilities and opportunities of attending college, hard work, and a very high level of support for each student. College classes in high school are not the issue.

- **"Ease the transition from high school to college."**

  The transition from high school to college is difficult for students because many high school instructional programs are insufficient. If we take full advantage of the four years of high school, students will have fewer problems adjusting to college work. Beyond their academics, the KIPP and YES high schools assist students in learning about colleges and college life and in applying for admission. Both are sufficiently successful to require acceptance at a four-year college as a condition of high school graduation.

- **"Save money (for families and tax payers) and time by integrating high school and college level work."**

  Savings will be realized only if students are more successful in both their high school and college work, and are thereby better prepared for life in the 21st century. Costs and savings must be measured against outcomes, not time alone.

- **"Provide the rigor, depth, and intensity of college-level work in high school."**

  There are no existing constraints whatsoever to realizing this aspiration in high schools now. Great high schools have done this for years. We lack only the will to elevate the rigor of teaching and learning.

Botstein outlined some aspects of a school to resolve the problems he raised. We have taken the liberty of fleshing out a complete model. The time—less + more high school model is characterized by the following:

- To address the fact that students develop and mature earlier than they did a century ago, school starts with kindergarten students when they are 4 instead of 5 years of age and they graduate from high school after the 11th grade at the age of 15 or 16. **Less time, 12 instead of 13 years,** is allowed for students to achieve a high school diploma—and they graduate two years earlier, ready to go to college, work, or other endeavors.
- Reconfiguration of the school day and year provides **more time**. The school year, comprising four 11-week quarters with four 2-week breaks plus national holidays, includes 210 days of instruction. The school day is 8 hours. Extracurricular activities are extracurricular—that is, they occur outside the school day. The total instructional time for 5 years (Grades 7–11) with 210 eight-hour days of instruction is 8,400 hours. (The current agrarian calendar with 180 six-and-a-half-hour days per school year provides 7,020 hours over six years.) Teachers and students are in school all four quarters each school year.

- Reflecting on **grade alignment**, Botstein observed:

> In the postwar (WWII) period, in part influenced by the novel psychological literature on the special nature of adolescence, elementary school was reduced to encompass kindergarten through grade 6. An invention that has proved to be a disaster came into being, the junior high, spanning grades 7–9. The junior high segregates out the most vulnerable age group in human development, thereby separating them from older and younger peers. By so doing, the young adolescent loses an older, more adult model for the setting of goals, and by being cut off from younger children is robbed of any reminder within the daily life of school of the positive dimensions of incipient adulthood vis-à-vis childhood. (Botstein, 1997, p. 114)

The time—less + more school serves Grades 7–11 in conjunction with K–6 primary schools. There are no junior, middle, or intermediate schools. The table below describes former and existing grade alignments and that proposed.

GRADES

Age	Before WWII	After WWII	Current	Time—Less + More	Time—Less + More Modes of Instruction
4–5				K	Start K at age 4 vs. 5
5–6	K	K	K	1	Self-contained classrooms
6–7	1	1	1	2	
7–8	2	2	2	3	
8–9	3	3	3	4	
9–10	4	4	4	5	
10–11	5	5	5	6	
11–12	6	6	6	7	Pods—structured environment
12–13	7	7	7	8	
13–14	8	8	8	9	Labs—individualized, self paced, technology based
14–15	9	9	9	10	
15–16	10	10	10	11	
16–17	11	11	11	Students graduate at Grade 11 to pursue college or work	
17–18	12	12	12		

Primary   Jr High   Secondary

- The time—less + more school serves students in **grades 7–11** in a single structure. All of the students and teachers share the central commons, dining, arts, career, and physical education spaces. There is the expectation that older students will serve as mentors for those just beginning their studies.
- Teachers and students at all secondary grade levels have **personal digital devices** and wireless access to the school's network and the Internet; personal technology is essential to teaching and learning in this school.
- Although there is no junior or middle school, **varied approaches to both time and instruction are used for secondary school students in grades 7–8 and 9–11**. A more contained and structured environment is provided for the younger, grade 7–8 students. Teachers work in teams of five with approximately 100 students. Each group of teachers and students works together through grades 7 and 8. Instructional spaces are grouped in pods around a shared common area. The pods are both academic and social "homes" for the students. Rooms are paired or separated by movable walls so that teachers are able to work in teams (math and science, language arts and social studies, for example) across disciplines.
- The **school day** for grade 7 and 8 students begins and ends with one-hour periods for advisories and electives, arts, and physical education. Before and after lunch, major blocks of time (approximately 2¼ hours) are allotted for core subjects. The teachers within each pod work together to determine how to use these blocks. Teachers have real flexibility to use varied instructional methods, to integrate studies in different disciplines, and to address the individual needs of students. In the middle of the day, 1½ hours are allotted for lunch and for independent reflection and study time for the students. Students may use this time to work on their own or to meet with teachers as needed. Students and teachers spend most of each day in the small environment of their pod, but they have contact with individuals from other parts of the school as they share spaces for dining, electives, arts, and physical education. Although both spaces and time are generally defined for the younger grade 7–8 students, they and their teachers have real flexibility to address individual needs.
- For the older **grade 9–11 students**, the school environment is less structured and time is more flexible. Instruction is primarily digital and self-paced in core subjects. Students work independently with the guidance of their teachers, but come together for advisories, seminars, and group work where appropriate. School days begin with advisories during which teacher-advisors work with students as a group and individually to review the status of their studies and to plan the day ahead. Seminars and other group activities (such as performing arts and some career courses) are scheduled in the mornings. Afternoons are reserved for project work and independent studies.

- Similar to the grade 7–8 students, **the grade 9–11 students** are organized in groups of approximately 100, each with five teachers. Including students in grades 9–11 (some begin and others graduate every year), the groups function as academic and social "families" for students and teachers.
- Each group is housed in a learning lab consisting of an open space with highly flexible **individual workstations for every teacher and student**. Although students work independently at their own pace, the open environment assures contact and communications with other students and with the teachers. Around the perimeter of the lab are seminar and other support rooms that teachers and students may use as needed. Projects focused on real-world problems provide context and meaning for core studies. Wherever possible, teachers bring individuals from the community into the school to assist with projects, and some students may visit resources off-campus pertinent to their projects.
- Although the instructional process for grade 9–11 students allows them great **flexibility**, it also requires that they assume real **responsibility** for their studies and for the management of their time—skills essential to succeeding in the real world beyond high school, including college.
- The time—less + more school curriculum gives each graduate the **option of attending college** if they wish. Coursework is rigorous for *every* student. Instruction is individualized and time is flexible to assure that every student can succeed. AP and dual-credit courses are unnecessary to allow the most capable students opportunities to excel or to shorten the total time required for high school and college. The reduction in total school years (from K–12 to K–11) is not reflected in a diminished curriculum or lower graduation requirements.
- **Credits are earned for outcomes instead of seat time**. Treated as individuals, students study at the pace best suited to their abilities and circumstances—time, not learning, is the variable. Absent Carnegie Units, many of the concerns Botstein raised in *Jefferson's Children* vanish. Although the design of the school is predicated on five years of study, some students require less time and others more.
- Teachers have, as a minimum, a four-year degree in their field. The school provides **teacher training** on campus.
- Although the school may offer **athletics** via intramural after-school activities, the ages of its students and alignment of its grades do not match those of traditional schools and the opportunity to compete in University Interscholastic League sports may be severely limited absent other comparable schools.

For **grade 7–8 teachers**, the time—less + more school provides a much broader context within which to teach. Both teachers and students are part of a more diverse group. Both have the opportunity to work together within the same school for five years. Teachers in each pod stay with their students through grades 7 and 8 and must therefore be able to teach both grade levels. Teachers work closely together to integrate instruction and to make decisions about the allocation of time. Because they work as a team, the teachers in each pod get to know all of the students, and they share their observations to help each student succeed. There are few opportunities for students to "fall through the cracks."

For **grade 9–11 teachers**, the challenge is to relinquish their traditional role at the front of the classroom and become advisors, guides, and facilitators for the students. Teachers assemble students from time to time for seminars that provide the opportunity for dialogue about important topics, but most of their time is spent working with individual students. Because each student works at her own pace, every student is truly different. Although teachers work in their own area of expertise with students, they also work on projects with the specific objective of integrating disciplines. Both teachers and students are challenged to consider their work within a real-world context.

For **students**, the challenge of the school is completing a more rigorous curriculum through longer school days and a longer school year and at a younger age in fewer years. However, the rewards are clear. Flexible time accommodates each student's learning style. Students learn to manage their own time and studies. Their schoolwork is relevant and engaging. And by finishing two years earlier, far better use is made of the precious years of youth. Students can pursue college or other interests earlier. Students in grades 9–11 have the opportunity and obligation to serve as role models for their younger classmates in grades 7 and 8. No longer isolated in middle or junior high schools, the younger grade 7–8 students have the opportunity to learn within a context that includes older students and adults.

For **administrators**, the challenge is that the school does not fit within the current K–16 context. Relative to the time—less + more school, conventional seventh graders arrive behind in their development and 11th graders may graduate too young for today's colleges. Certainly, therein lies the rationale behind the compromises represented by AP, dual-credit, and early college high school programs—but those are huge compromises that fail to address the real issues Botstein identified. At the very least, this school requires administrators to rethink the grade alignment of their entire school district—and then they must cope with No Child Left Behind and state-mandated tests.

For **architects**, the challenge is to integrate the open grade 9–11 learning labs with the relatively contained grade 7–8 pods and to juxtapose the two to create an overall environment that encourages the younger and older students to intermingle. The layout of the building, selection of building systems, and furnishings must provide a very high level of adaptability so that teachers and students may rearrange their spaces constantly.

The architecture of the school must focus on flexibility rather than permanence and durability.

Operating and construction **costs** are very different for time—less + more schools than for conventional K–12 schools. Teachers' salaries will increase because of the longer school days and year, but students will go to school 12 instead of 13 years and therefore fewer teachers will be required.

PRECEDENTS

The time—less + more school grew out of Botstein's *Jefferson's Children,* and it reflects some of the recommendations in *Tough Choices or Tough Times* (New Commission on the Skills of the American Workforce, 2006), but at this date we are unaware of any precedents or examples that truly realize Botstein's aspirations. However, compromise solutions abound in the form of AP, dual-credit, and early college high school programs—including the Bard High School Early College (http://www.bard.edu/bhsec) in New York, a joint creation of the New York Board of Education and Bard College, of which Leon Botstein is president.

FOCUS ON TEACHING OR LEARNING?

Teacher Centered **Student Centered**

With its flexible school day and year, multidisciplinary instruction, and personal technology, the school is strongly student centered.

GROUP OR INDIVIDUAL TEACHING AND LEARNING?

Group Teaching and Learning **Individual Teaching and Learning**

In grades 7 and 8, students and teachers work together in five classroom pods. Flexibility to serve individual needs is provided by the highly flexible daily schedule. In grades 9–11, students work individually at their own pace with digital instructional programs.

TRADITIONAL TEACHING VS. DIGITAL LEARNING

Teacher, Text **Digital**

Every teacher and student has a digital device. Instruction for both grade 7–8 and grade 9–11 students exploits the capabilities of the available technology.

21ST-CENTURY THINKING SKILLS

Knowledge Skills **Content + Problem-Solving Skills**

The more structured pod environment for the grade 7–8 students focuses on content, but it does provide flexible time for independent work. For the grade 9–11 students, the combination of digital access to learning materials and project-based instruction balances content and knowledge skills with problem-solving skills.

ASSESSMENT

Content Skills **Content + Problem-Solving Skills**

With the use of flexible scheduling, personal technology, and project-based instruction, varied modes of assessment are employed for students in both grades 7–8 and 9–12. Portfolios, presentations, and exhibitions are important to both groups.

LEARNING FOCUS

Traditional Content **21st-Century Literacies**

With the extensive use of digital instruction, 21st-century literacy is integral to the learning experience.

INSTRUCTIONAL ORGANIZATION

Departments and Disciplines **Interdisciplinary**

The school is organized into multidisciplinary, multigrade groups for both grade 7–8 and grade 9–11 students. Departments exist organizationally instead of spatially to facilitate staff development and communications between teachers within each discipline.

APPLICATION OF LEARNING

Classroom Theory **Real-World Relevance**

Both parts of the school draw on digital learning resources that students perceive as relevant to themselves.

RESPONSIBILITY FOR LEARNING

Teacher **Student**

Teachers provide close support and guidance for the younger students in grades 7–8. In grades 9–11, students are expected to assume real responsibility for the pursuit of their studies and management of their time.

TIME—SCHOOL YEAR

Fixed **Flexible**

Organized in quarters, the 210-day school year (with eight-hour days) provides more teaching and learning time in five years than the traditional calendar with six years each with 180 6.5-hour days. Although the longer school year provides eight instead of 16 weeks of vacation or holiday time, students graduate a full year earlier at the end of grade 11 rather than at the end of grade 12.

TIME—SCHOOL DAY

Fixed **Flexible**

Although schedules for the eight-hour school days are substantially different for grade 7–8 and 9–11 students, both provide considerable periods for flexible independent study and project work.

STUDENT SUPPORT

Counselor **Teacher-Advisor**

Students work with the same teachers through grades 7–8 in the pods and with the same teacher-advisor through grades 9–11 in the learning labs. Every student is well known by several adults at the school.

STUDENT LEARNING SPACES

Teachers' Rooms **Personal Workpace**

Teachers and students work together in classroom pods in grades 7–8. In grades 9–11, teachers and students have individual workstations.

SPATIAL FLEXIBILITY

Durable, Permanent **Responsive, Flexible**

The learning labs for grades 9–11 are open spaces with modular furnishings that teachers and students may rearrange as needed. Pods for grades 7–8 consist of classrooms around a common area. Movable walls allow teachers to combine spaces when appropriate.

SCALABILITY—SCHOOL SIZE

Large Enrollment **Small Enrollment**

Given the grade alignment within the school, two grade 7–8 pods (each with 100 students) feed into three grade 9–11 learning labs (each with 100 students). Given the varied ages of the students and configuration of teaching and learning spaces, the optimum size for the school is approximately 1000 students.

COURSE OFFERINGS

Core + Broad Elective Subjects **Core Subjects**

Through digital resources, the school offers both core and elective subjects. Specialized spaces are provided for visual and performing arts and some electives.

EXTRACURRICULAR ACTIVITIES

Extensive **Minimal**

With the intensity of the school schedule and atypical grade alignment, there are minimal extracurricular activities.

COSTS—STAFF

High Cost per Student **Low Cost per Student**

Compared to a traditional comprehensive high school, the ratio of students to teachers is low, whereas the overall ratio of students to total staff is higher because the school has no athletic programs. The cost for teachers is increased by the longer school year but reduced by the elimination of the 12th grade.

COSTS—FACILITIES

High Cost per Student **Low Cost per Student**

The building area per student is comparable to or less than that at a traditional school because of the limited spaces required for elective and extracurricular activities. The 12-month, four-quarter school year does not offer economies because the facility is used by the same group of students for the full 12-month year instead of the traditional nine-month year. However, considerable facility economies are realized by the completion of high school at the 11th instead of 12th grade.

Reflect on the Time—Less + More School and Consider Your Own High School(s)

- How do you challenge and engage your students in their senior year?
- How are you preparing students for the rigors of the world of college or work they will face after high school graduation?
- How does your high school program help students to assume real responsibility for their own learning and for the management of their time?
- How do you prepare your students in high school so that they will not require remedial instruction to succeed in college or work?
- How do your advanced placement and dual-credit classes further the learning opportunities of your students as they progress through grades 9–16?

12

Individualized Instruction

In the individualized instruction school, each student has a learning plan based on his or her personal interests and needs.

- All students have an advisor on the campus and a mentor related to their interests in the community.
- With guidance from their advisor, students work individually with digital learning materials on campus to develop knowledge skills, and work with their mentors off campus on real-world projects to develop higher order thinking skills.
- Group meetings in advisories and families are scheduled to provide a supportive context for students who otherwise pursue self-paced independent studies each day. The 12-month school year is divided into quarters.

Individualized Instruction

Instructional/Spatial Organization
Instructionally/spatially, the school is organized around relationships between advisors, students, mentors, and the community, not subjects. Facilities reflect diverse working modes vs. disciplines/subjects.

Real-World Mentors

Real-World Mentors

Learning Families
Some of the school's learning communities may be grouped together to form a campus, but others may be separated and located at a distance within the surrounding community. Some may be in school district structures and others in leased spaces in commercial structures.

Learning Through Interests
With guidance from the school, students select mentors based on their own interests. Mentors/internships are located throughout the community. Students spend 2 days/week working off campus at their mentor's place of work.

Students
Students work with their advisors to create individual learning plans and identify mentors. Advisors guide and assess progress in project work with mentors with a particular eye to learning objectives in core subjects.

Real-World Mentors

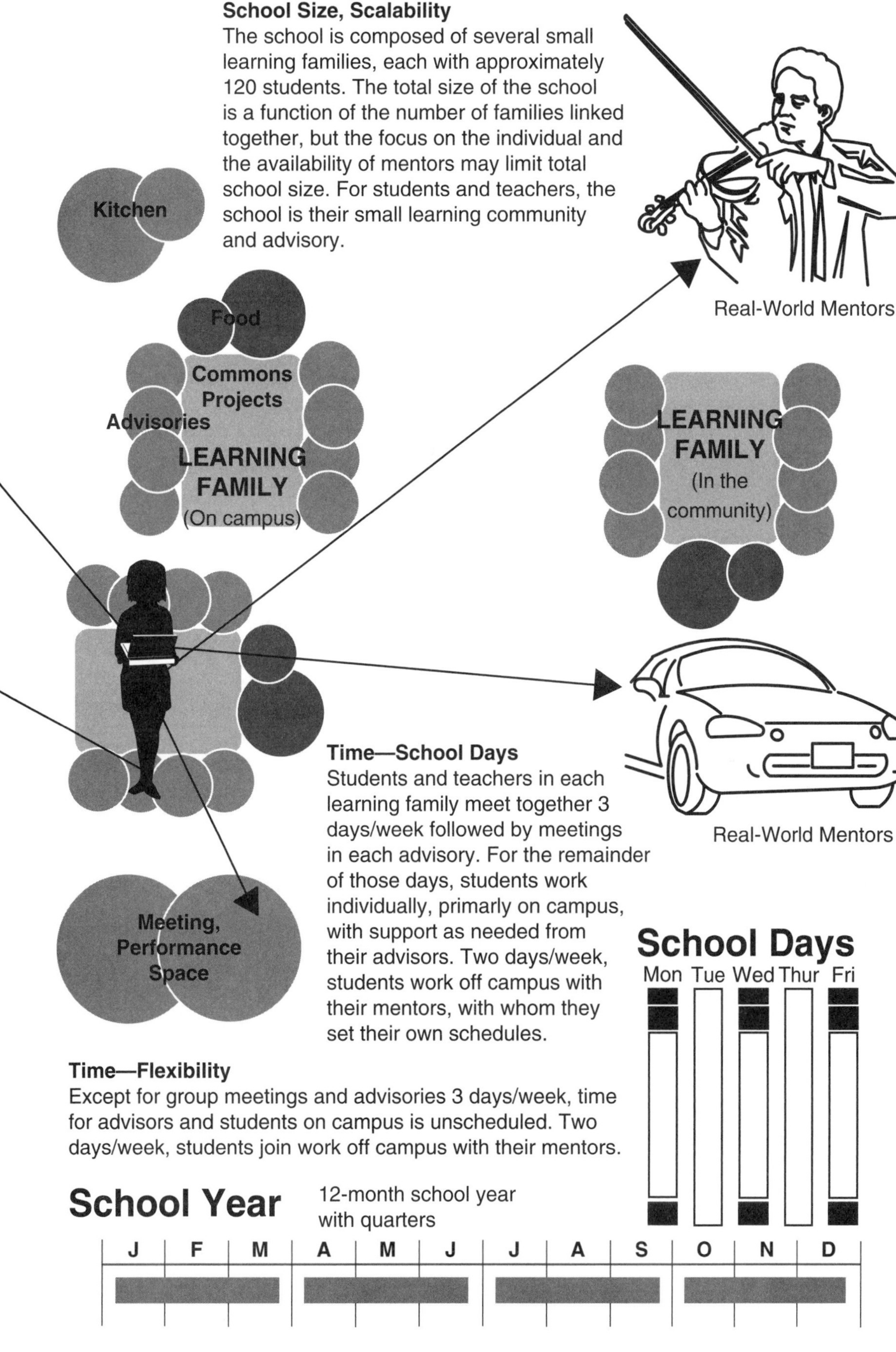

School Size, Scalability

The school is composed of several small learning families, each with approximately 120 students. The total size of the school is a function of the number of families linked together, but the focus on the individual and the availability of mentors may limit total school size. For students and teachers, the school is their small learning community and advisory.

Time—School Days

Students and teachers in each learning family meet together 3 days/week followed by meetings in each advisory. For the remainder of those days, students work individually, primarily on campus, with support as needed from their advisors. Two days/week, students work off campus with their mentors, with whom they set their own schedules.

Time—Flexibility

Except for group meetings and advisories 3 days/week, time for advisors and students on campus is unscheduled. Two days/week, students join work off campus with their mentors.

Of the 10 models delineated herein, none stands in greater contrast than the Industrial Age school (Chapter 5) and the individualized instruction school. The Industrial Age school is organized around the efficient delivery of instruction. Taught in groups in classrooms one discipline and one hour at a time, students are raw materials to be transformed. Traditional schools are strongly teacher centered. The individualized instruction school is organized around students with instructional methods and schedules adapted to the needs and interests of each individual. The individualized instruction school is a very different place for both students and teachers.

Although the self-directed learning and individualized instruction schools both focus on individual students, they are also quite different. Studies are self-paced in the self-directed learning school. Students work primarily on campus with a curriculum and coursework defined by the school. In the individualized instruction school, graduation requirements are defined in terms of knowledge and skills developed, not courses completed. The path to graduation for every student is different.

Although this model departs considerably from its precedent, it nonetheless reflects important aspects of the MET in Providence, Rhode Island. Opened in 1996, the MET was conceived by the Big Picture Company (Dennis Littky and Elliot Washor). It is an extraordinary departure from traditional thinking about high school instruction—even from the concepts for individualized instruction described by Trump in *A School for Everyone* (1977). Individualized instruction schools are characterized by the following:

> The school's organizing principle is that education must be personalized "one kid at a time" (the title of Eliot Levine's book about the MET, *One Kid at a Time: Big Lessons From a Small School,* 2002). The school has five learning goals (see the MET learning goals, www.bigpicture.org), but does not have standard graduation requirements defined by Carnegie Units in specific disciplines focused on stipulated content or knowledge skills.
>
> 1. **Communications:** "How do I take in and express ideas?"
>
> "This goal is to be a great communicator: to understand your audience, to write, to read, to speak and listen well, to use technology and artistic expression to communicate, and to be exposed to another language."
>
> 2. **Empirical Reasoning:** "How do I prove it?"
>
> "This goal is to think like a scientist: to use empirical evidence and a logical process to make decisions and to evaluate hypotheses. It does not reflect specific science content material, but instead can incorporate ideas from physics to sociology to art theory."

3. **Personal Qualities:** "What do I bring to this process?"

"This goal is to be the best you can be: to demonstrate respect, responsibility, organization, leadership, and to reflect on your abilities and strive for improvement."

4. **Quantitative Reasoning:** "How do I measure, compare, or represent it?"

"This goal is to think like a mathematician: to understand numbers, to analyze uncertainty, to comprehend the properties of shapes, and to study how things change over time."

5. **Social Reasoning:** "What are other people's perspectives on this?"

"This goal is to think like an historian or anthropologist: to see diverse perspectives, to understand social issues, to explore ethics, and to look at issues historically."

These learning goals are very different from those of schools focused on state-standard-driven content and No Child Left Behind testing. They seek to help students learn to learn and thrive in the real world on the assumption that within their lifetimes, the content or knowledge skills essential to their success will change constantly and significantly. The industrial school's curriculum and NCLB are based largely on the premise that there is a static body of knowledge every student needs to know, that the school knows what that is, and that most of this body of knowledge will remain valuable and relevant to students in the future.

- Each student has an **individual learning plan** that reflects her interests, talents, and needs. The individual plans are developed and maintained by the students and their advisors. Based on their own interests, each student is matched with a mentor from the community outside the school.
- Compared to enrollments in traditional comprehensive high schools, individualized instruction schools are small—**500–700 students**. Relationships between students, faculty, parents, and mentors are critical to achieving success for each individual. But the day-to-day environment students and faculty experience is still smaller. The high school is composed of learning families, each with approximately 120 students. The families are in turn composed of approximately eight advisories, each with one faculty member and about 15 students.
- As the primary organizational unit of the school, **advisories** are created as freshmen enter the school and remain together through graduation. Advisories are formed for maximum diversity of gender, ethnicity, race, and socioeconomic background. Advisors have the ultimate responsibility for the success of their students. They manage their students' individual learning plans and relationships with mentors. Although advisors are certified teachers, they do not

"teach" in their subject area within their advisory, but draw as needed on resources both within and beyond the campus to meet the needs of each student.

- Advisory groups meet each morning and afternoon (30–60 minutes) three days a week. Whereas the students pursue individual and very different learning plans, advisories are an opportunity to share experiences and problems, to expose students to new concepts and learning opportunities, and to build a sense of belonging and trust in each other and in the educational process. The interactions amongst the students and between the students and advisor are equally important. Like a family, the advisories are caring and supportive, but also set high expectations for achievement.
- **The school "enrolls" both students and their families.** Both are interviewed before school begins, and both sign agreements to participate in the educational process. Advisors maintain regular communications with the parents, who are required to participate in their student's exhibitions. Students and their studies are well known by their advisor, parents, and mentor. If a student begins to struggle in any way, adults know and provide support when it is most effective. Learning, not teaching, is the school's primary measure of success.
- All teaching and learning are **project based**. There are no departments, classrooms, bells, or direct instruction. Working with their advisors, students define projects related to their areas of interest through which they can realize the school's learning goals.
- Every year, each student is paired with a **mentor** from the community related to his or her own interests. Two days a week (a minimum of 10–12 hours), students work off campus with their mentor in an internship doing authentic projects of interest, relevance, and benefit to both the student and the mentor. The adult mentors provide real-world expertise and guidance and equip students with the experience of functioning in an adult environment.
- With the flexible schedule, and the need for students to work both on and off the campus, a **personal digital device** (a laptop computer at this date) is essential for every student. The computers provide access, as directed by the advisors, to instructional materials that complement project-based work, and they are an essential part of communications between teachers, parents, students, and mentors.
- On the campus, **students have access as needed to faculty members** with expertise in traditional academic disciplines. Advisors communicate frequently, often face to face, with their students. They work to monitor progress on student projects and to direct them to resources both on and off the campus as needed. To complement their project work as needed in specific areas, advisors may direct students to digital learning materials from a wide range of sources outside the campus, including digital, virtual schools. Students share their project experiences in the advisory meetings each week.

- The individualized instruction school does not rely on grades for **assessment**. Each quarter, students present and exhibit their projects for their peers, advisors, parents, and mentors. All join in dialogue about the merits of the projects. Students maintain portfolios throughout their years to the school to create a record of their accomplishments. They keep a journal of their experiences and write autobiographies before graduation. Each quarter, advisors provide written narrative assessments for each student and review them with the students and their parents.
- All students are required to make **postsecondary school plans**. The school requires and helps every student to gather information on and visit colleges, to take entrance exams, and to submit multiple applications for admittance and, if needed, financial aid. Students may or may not elect to attend college, but it is the school's objective to provide each student with the best possible opportunity to do so.
- The individualized instruction school provides services **12 months** of the year divided into quarters. In contrast to the exceptional individualization of other aspects of the school, it is important to the environment of the learning families, advisories, and mentors that all the students and teacher-advisors work concurrently. Students and teachers do have options with regard to the quarters they attend or work in the school.
- The **school day,** however, provides substantial flexibility within which to address individual needs. In the typical week, Mondays, Wednesdays, and Fridays begin and end with brief meetings of the entire small community to make announcements, celebrate special events, and build a sense of community. On these same days, advisories also meet mornings and afternoons. The remainder of these days is open and may be used by students and teacher-advisors as needed for their projects. On Tuesdays and Thursdays, students are typically off campus working with their mentors. For both students and teachers, their work over the majority of each week and day is self-paced.
- With its small size, individualized instruction, and flexible school day, the school focuses on **academics** and does not offer competitive sports or performing arts programs. It does not offer career programs, because students address these interests through the projects and mentors they select.
- **Facilities** for the individualized instruction school are organized around the families and their advisories. The campus is composed of four to six families that share some common facilities such as administrative and clinic spaces, a gym for physical education and fitness, a meeting and performance space, and a central kitchen. Each small learning community has its own meeting spaces (used for dining, group meetings, and exhibitions), advisory rooms, and

project areas. The advisory rooms are offices for the teacher-advisors and conference space for the advisory meetings. These are clustered around highly flexible project spaces where students work with their laptops and other resources on their studies and projects.

- The school does not have a **library**. Students use their laptops to access libraries and information sources via the Internet. They also have access to public libraries while off campus two days a week to work with their mentors. For the same reasons, the school does not have science labs or art studios. Students address these subjects and access the related specialized spaces and equipment via technology and off campus via their mentors and internships.
- Because the families are largely independent of each other and share functions that are not critical, some are located away from the campus in the **community** using leased office or retail spaces where they may be closer to both mentors and students.

For **teacher-advisors**, the challenge is orchestrating the work of each of the 15 students in their advisory so that each realizes the school's five learning goals and develops state- and NCLB-mandated content skills. Given that each student has different interests, capabilities, and learning styles, is working on different projects and mentors, requires different resources, works on different schedules, and has a general absence of direct instruction, this is no small task. Advisors also need to be able to support each student's project work in their own disciplines and to direct students to teachers in other fields as needed. For these reasons, teachers in the individualized instruction school need a real-world multidisciplinary perspective to be effective advisors. For teacher-advisors, every student and every day is different.

For **students**, the individualized instruction school provides the opportunity to have teaching and learning opportunities shaped to their personal interests and learning styles. And it provides through the teacher-advisors and mentors an exceptional level of individual guidance and support. At the same time, however, it requires that students assume much responsibility for their own learning, for the related management of their time, and for conducting themselves as adults in the real world off-site with their mentors. The individualized instruction school is structured on the premise that given the opportunity, students will find such engaging, motivating studies sufficiently compelling to exercise the requisite maturity.

For **administrators**, the challenge of the individualized instruction school is finding and developing great teacher-advisors and identifying mentors in the community. Continuous staff development is essential because much of what the school is about is entirely different from the experiences teachers may have had in their own education and in other schools.

For **architects**, the spatial challenge is to create fine working spaces in the advisories and related project areas, as well as in the meeting and exhibition spaces in the commons. Spaces and furnishings common to highly flexible corporate offices provide better precedents than the fixed and permanent construction that has typified school construction in the past.

Given the 1:15 ratio of teacher-advisors to students, the **costs** for instructional staff are high compared to that in traditional schools. However, given the multiple roles the teacher-advisors assume and the absence of performing arts, electives, and extracurricular programs, the total staff-to-student ratio is comparable to that of a traditional school. Similarly, the building area per student and related construction costs are considerably less.

PRECEDENTS

The MET (http://www.metcenter.org) is part of a group of 48 schools (in 2008) across the country created by the Big Picture Company (http://www.bigpicture.org). The MET and the Big Picture Company have been described in a number of books, including the following:

- *One Kid at a Time: Big Lessons From a Small School*, by Eliot Levine (2002).
- *High Schools on a Human Scale*, by Thomas Toch (2003).
- *The Big Picture: Education is Everyone's Business*, by Dennis Littky and Samantha Grabelle (2004).

FOCUS ON TEACHING OR LEARNING?

Teacher Centered **Student Centered**

						●

Each student has an individual learning plan built around her interests, capabilities, and learning style. Each student works individually with his teacher-advisor and mentor. Totally focused on individual students, the school is strongly student centered.

GROUP OR INDIVIDUAL TEACHING AND LEARNING?

Group Teaching and Learning **Individual Teaching and Learning**

						●

The school focuses on individuals. There is no group or class instruction.

TRADITIONAL TEACHING VS. DIGITAL LEARNING

Teacher, Text **Digital**

Every student has a personal digital device; direct instruction is minimal via either technology or teachers. Students learn primarily in real-world settings from their mentors and teacher-advisors with supplementary digital instruction.

21ST-CENTURY THINKING SKILLS

Knowledge Skills **Content + Problem-Solving Skills**

The school is strongly focused on the development of real-world problem solving and higher order thinking skills. Absent direct instruction, students gain content and knowledge skills only through the projects they pursue via their teacher-advisors and their mentors.

ASSESSMENT

Content Skills **Content + Problem-Solving Skills**

Without instruction in specific subjects, teacher-advisors review their students' progress through group advisory discussions and individual conferences with students, mentors, and parents. Students present and exhibit their projects and maintain portfolios. Quarterly, teacher-advisors provide each student with a written narrative assessment. Students also take state- and NCLB-mandated tests.

LEARNING FOCUS

Traditional Content **21st-Century Literacies**

With personal technology, 21st-century literacy is developed by creating projects, making presentations, maintaining portfolios, managing time, and communicating with mentors and teacher-advisors.

INSTRUCTIONAL ORGANIZATION

Departments and Disciplines **Interdisciplinary**

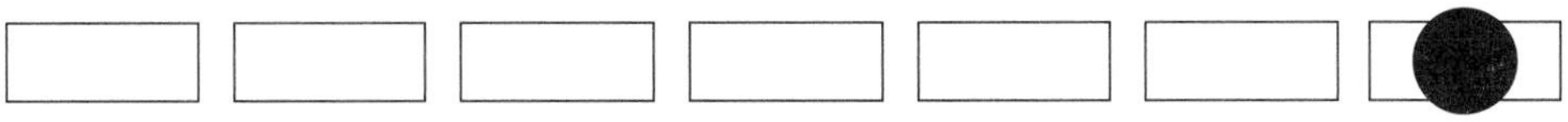

The school has no departments. It is organized into families and a visories focused on individualized instruction, which is inherently interdisciplinary.

APPLICATION OF LEARNING

Classroom Theory **Real-World Relevance**

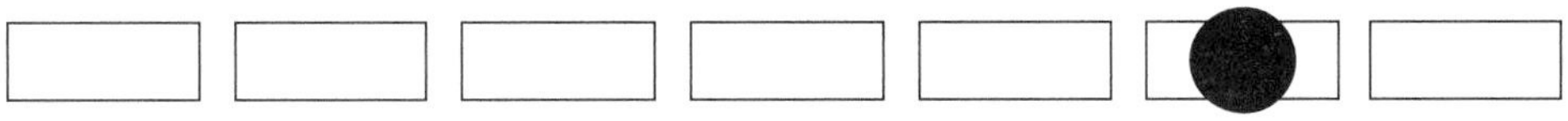

All students have mentors with whom they work at a site off campus in the community. There is no classroom instruction. Real-world connections are an integral part of the school's instruction.

RESPONSIBILITY FOR LEARNING

Teacher **Student**

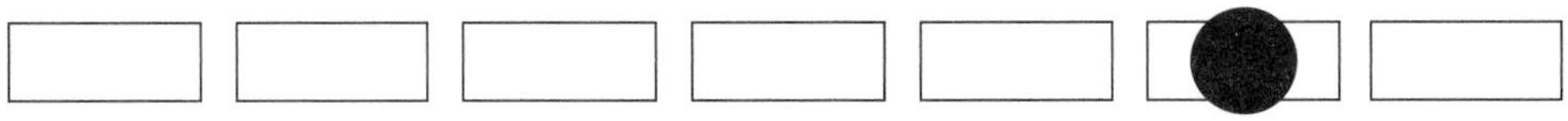

The school works only if students have clear interests that can guide the development of their individual learning plans, and if they are sufficiently engaged and motivated to assume responsibility for their work on and off campus. Although students have the guidance and support of their teacher-advisors, they must ultimately manage their own studies.

TIME—SCHOOL YEAR

Fixed **Flexible**

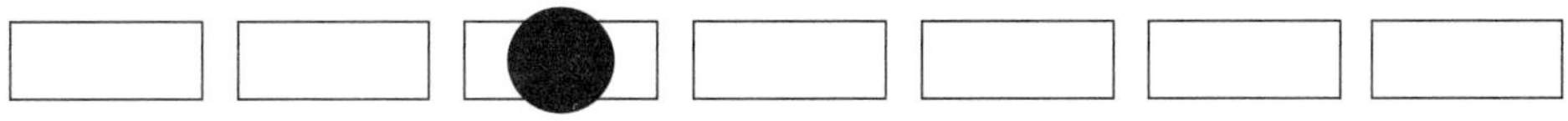

The school operates 12 months per year divided into quarters. Students and teachers have options about the quarters they attend or work. Within the quarters, it is critical that all students and teachers work concurrently through the learning families and advisories. The school day provides flexibility, but the length of the quarters is fixed.

TIME—SCHOOL DAY

Fixed **Flexible**

The school week and school days are highly flexible. Students are on campus three days a week. Parts of these days are devoted to group meetings, but most of the time is open for individual work to be scheduled by the student and teacher-advisor. On Tuesdays and Thursdays, students are off campus working with their mentors with whom they plan those days. Time on school days is very flexible.

STUDENT SUPPORT

Counselor **Teacher-Advisor**

Students work for their entire time at the school with their own teacher-advisor. Each student works closely (two days a week) with a mentor off campus in the community. The teacher-advisor knows both the students and their parents. Students have meaningful, long-term relationships with adults in the school and in the community.

STUDENT LEARNING SPACES

Teachers' Rooms **Individual Workstations**

Students work on the campus in their advisories, project rooms, and commons. Two days per week, they work off campus with their mentors.

SPATIAL FLEXIBILITY

Durable, Permanent **Responsive, Flexible**

The largest space in each learning family is the commons, which is open and flexible to serve many functions. However, the real flexibility in the school results from the use of numerous and diverse mentors in the community and personal technology.

SCALABILITY—SCHOOL SIZE

Large Enrollment **Small Enrollment**

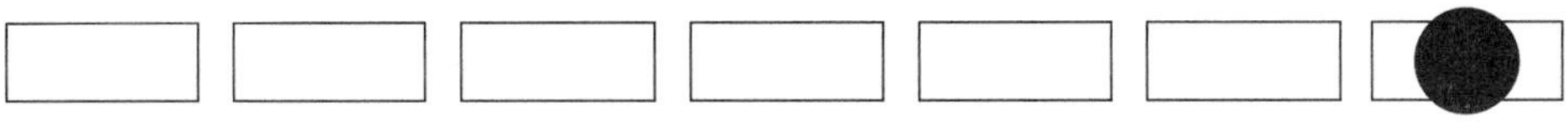

Although the size of the school is a function of the number of learning families (each with approximately 120 students), enrollment must remain small to ensure the close bond between teacher-advisors and students and the availability of sufficient mentors within the community.

COURSE OFFERINGS

Core + Broad Elective Subjects **Core Subjects**

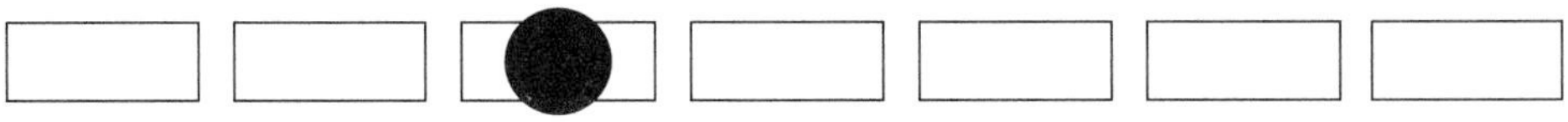

Although the school does not offer electives, students have access to "elective" subjects through their choice of mentors and individual learning plans.

EXTRACURRICULAR ACTIVITIES

Extensive **Minimal**

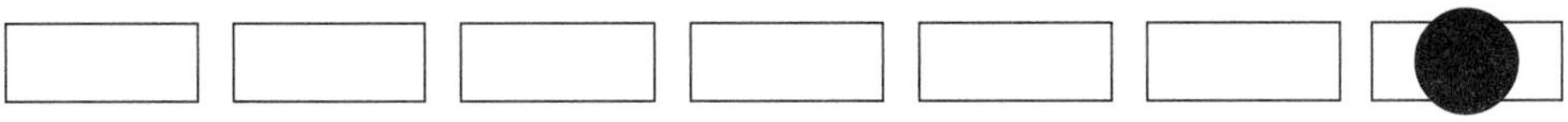

Given the school's small enrollment, individual learning plans, and off-campus work with mentors and flexible schedules, it offers minimal extracurricular activities.

COSTS—STAFF

High Cost per Student **Low Cost per Student**

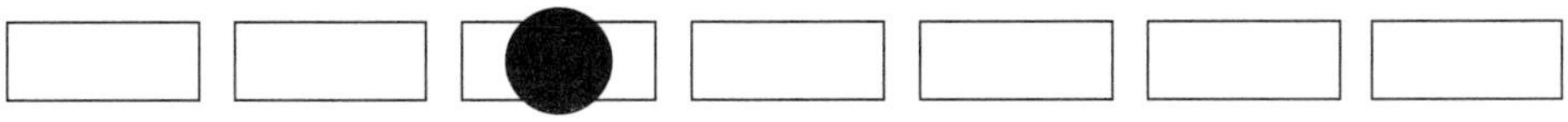

Although the ratio of academic teacher-advisor staff to students is relatively high, the total ratio is comparable to that in traditional schools given the absence of elective, performing arts, and athletic personnel.

COSTS—FACILITIES

High Cost per Student **Low Cost per Student**

Without electives, performing arts, and athletic programs, the building area per student is modest compared to traditional schools.

Reflect on the Individualized Instruction School and Consider Your Own High School(s)

- How does your school create an individual learning plan for all students tailored to their personal interests and learning style?
- How do your methods of instruction engage and motivate every student?
- How does your school complement its resources and capabilities by drawing on individuals and companies in the community?
- How does your school provide close guidance and support for all students by adults who know them well? How do you engage parents in their child's learning?
- How do your facilities relate to and draw on the community around our school? Do you provide every facility you need on your campus? Do you use some facilities jointly with the community?

13

Cyber Schools

The cyber school is not a physical place, but a service, available to students anytime, anywhere.

- Students may earn all of their high school credits at the cyber school or use it to complement studies at a local campus.
- Although instruction is entirely digital via the Internet, students are assigned a teacher for every course with whom they have digital and phone communications.
- Instruction is available around the clock all year. Students works at their own pace, starting and completing courses when they wish.
- The school offers a wide range of courses that are updated frequently. Highly qualified teachers are drawn from across the country and specifically trained for digital instruction.

Cyber School

Instructional/Spatial Organization
The school is the digital teaching/learning process. It is not a building. It has no district or attendance zone. Teachers and students may be located anywhere. It is funded on the basis of courses taught and credits earned in lieu of average daily attendance. Funds may come from states, districts, or individuals. It exists as a place only to house its servers, technical staff, and administrators, which may be housed in leased space anywhere.

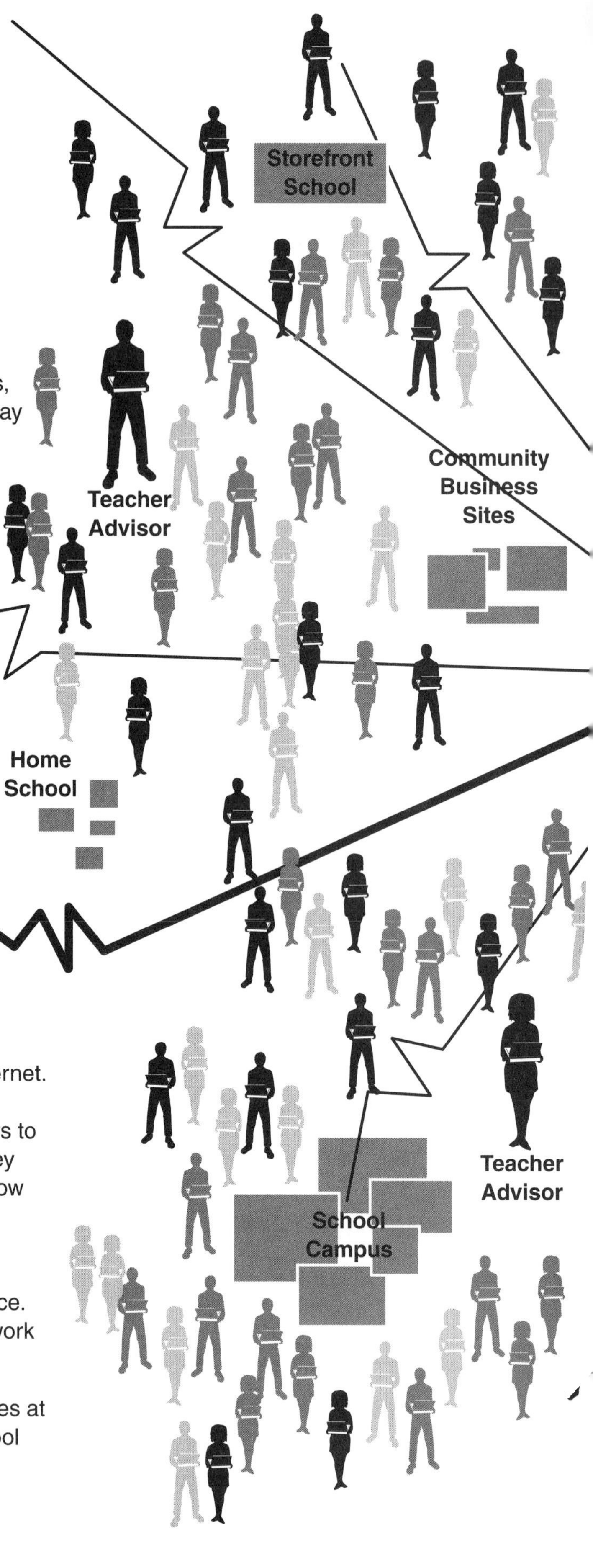

Instructional Resources
Although some digital course materials may be prepared by teachers within the school or district, much will come from sources with particular expertise (such as existing text book and game companies) that create sophisticated materials for use in many districts. Absent the limitations of individual teachers within classrooms, every student should have access to very high quality instructional materials.

Students
Students interface with their advisor and teachers and follow coursework via the Internet. Interactive instructional materials include assessment, allowing advisors and teachers to guide, monitor, and support students as they progress. E-mail, blogs, and chat rooms allow students and teachers to communicate continuously and informally as they work. Study is asynchronous—students may start and complete courses at their own pace. Coursework may include both knowledge work and project-based instruction.

Some students may supplement their studies at a sticks and bricks campus with cyber school courses taken online.

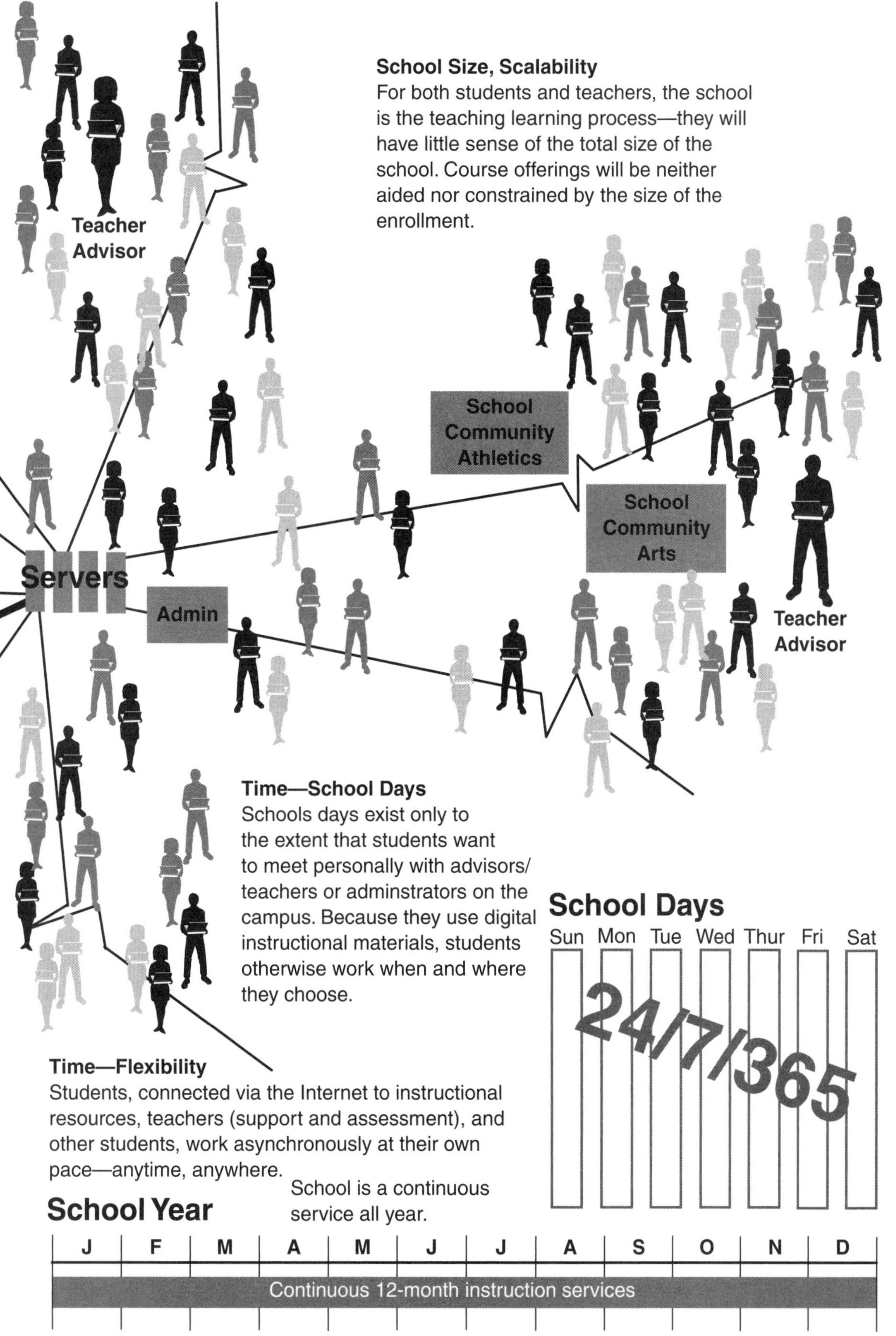
School Size, Scalability
For both students and teachers, the school is the teaching learning process—they will have little sense of the total size of the school. Course offerings will be neither aided nor constrained by the size of the enrollment.
Teacher Advisor
School Community Athletics
School Community Arts
Servers
Admin
Teacher Advisor
Time—School Days
Schools days exist only to the extent that students want to meet personally with advisors/ teachers or adminstrators on the campus. Because they use digital instructional materials, students otherwise work when and where they choose.
School Days
Sun
Mon
Tue
Wed
Thur
Fri
Sat
24/7/365
Time—Flexibility
Students, connected via the Internet to instructional resources, teachers (support and assessment), and other students, work asynchronously at their own pace—anytime, anywhere.
School Year
School is a continuous service all year.
J
F
M
A
M
J
J
A
S
O
N
D
Continuous 12-month instruction services

Cyber schools will use technology to communicate with students and parents, deliver instruction, and assist students with their learning. In the future, cyber learning will be an essential and everyday part of each student's education. Cyber schools will range from a physical school that uses technology to extend and enhance instruction to a completely virtual school that is accessed entirely online. Cyber schools will open up new options for choice in education. To ensure that the school can fulfill a custodial role, families may choose to have a student physically attend one of the "bricks and mortar" facilities. On the other hand, some families may decide to have a student attend a completely virtual cyber school from home.

HIGH TECH SCHOOLS TODAY—WE'RE NOT THERE YET

When a new technology is introduced into society, it is natural to try to make the new advance fit in with the old way of doing things. People's mindsets have not expanded to see the potential of the new technology, and so they just graft it onto the existing way of doing things. For example, when the automobile was first introduced in the early 1900s, it was called a horseless carriage. It was given this name because people still had a "horse mindset," and they really thought it was just a new way to do what a horse had always done. Their lack of experience with this new transportation tool meant they weren't able to grasp the significance of what it would do to the world. Today, we know that the automobile was a development of enormous importance. It has radically changed the world in a multitude of ways that the people in the early 1900s just could not see. Think about it for a moment—the automobile has greatly altered the way people and goods move around the countries of the world, and it has become an enormous force in the economy with a significant portion of the workforce devoted to manufacturing it, selling it, repairing it, insuring it, and regulating it. In addition, the automobile has caused a great change in the geographical landscape of cities—indeed, the whole world—and it has greatly affected the environment of the planet. Why couldn't the people in the early 1900s see this? It was because they had never seen this kind of technology before, and so they weren't able to appreciate the new and different things it could do. And so they naturally just incorporated it into the way things had been done when all they had were horses.

It is our observation that we are still very much in the horseless carriage stage in the use of electronic online technology in schools, even when referring to schools that claim to be "high tech." These new technological tools are still a novelty to many educators who haven't had enough experience with them to be able to see the truly innovative ways they could be used to enhance learning. Consequently, many teachers are still at the stage of grafting technology onto the traditional way they have always done things in their classrooms. Despite the "high tech" label, the basic instructional approach of the vast majority of these schools remains focused on 20th-century thinking. Even with online computers in every classroom, many teachers still teach content-focused lessons and students still sit and listen. The same traditional content is taught in a slightly more high-tech manner, but the traditional relationships between teacher, student, content, and assessment remain in place. Often the uses of technology in these schools are still not essential to achieving learning in the classroom. And sadly, many teachers think they have "arrived" as users of technology because they have their students do research on the Internet, or they prepare their lessons with PowerPoint, or they put assignments and learning resources on the school's Web site. But in many cases, the roles of the student and teacher have not changed significantly from other "low tech" high schools in the same school district. Often new technology is being used to support very traditional approaches to teaching. What we are seeing is electronic versions of traditional approaches to teaching. Unfortunately, there are still a great number of teachers who have not embraced the use of technology as a tool for instruction in any meaningful way. These teachers may use a computer as a personal tool for the production of teaching resources, but they do not see the real potential these new tools have for teaching and consequently they do not use technology as a central tool to extend and enhance learning experiences for students.

Also clouding our view of the potential that technology has to radically alter the learning process is the generally "underwhelming" effectiveness of many of the current applications of technology in education. A large proportion of current technological tools for learning are quite rudimentary. Most educational software still focuses on simple skill reinforcement and reflects the traditional mindset of schools today. There are some communication tools, simulations, planning tools, and reference resources that provide valuable aids to learning, but the vast majority of current educational applications of technology available to the K–12 school system do not live up to the promise of radically new and effective ways that could transform how students learn. Many of the online courses available today are nothing more than digitized correspondence materials put up on Web sites. Although there is great potential in distance learning, the course material and the means of interacting with others do not make for a very natural and rewarding learning experience for most students. In many cases, it's not really distance learning, it's just distance teaching.

One of the current major areas of focus for many schools and districts is the development of a Web portal. Web portals are electronic gateways that provide "one-stop shopping" access to information, communication systems, educational resources, and a variety of other electronic services for the district, schools, programs, students, teachers, and the community. The services provided might include the following:

- the publication of current, relevant, and essential district, program, school, and community information.
- direct links to school Web sites, blogs, and wikis that provide general information including school newsletters, schedules, learning goals, event calendars, school philosophy, codes of conduct, awards, scholarships, accomplishments, general program overviews, program profiles, teacher profiles, course outlines, and teacher developed and/or acquired course-related learning materials.
- a digital learning center accessible through the Web portal to students, parents, teachers, staff, and the community from anywhere including school, home, the library, and the community. The resources available could include the following:
    - a clearinghouse of exemplary grade level-, subject-, and topic-specific digital learning, instructional, and assessment resources for the use of teachers and aligned with the district's learning goals and state or province standards.
    - digital materials to support students with research, homework assistance, study, and exam preparation, and to communicate online.
    - learning materials and resources to support home school, at-risk, teen mom, and hospitalized- or homebound students, as well as students who might want to take an extra course that they can't fit into their schedule.
    - online professional development programs including undergraduate and graduate course credit.

The problem with the Web portals is, just like distance learning and Internet use in classrooms, that although it smacks of high tech, the development does not really change the way the majority of teachers teach, how they communicate with students, or how learning is assessed. But just like teachers who work in high-tech high schools, many educators and administrators think they have arrived in the 21st century just because they have a Web portal.

NOW LET'S TALK ABOUT REAL CYBER SCHOOLS

In the very near future, we will experience truly radical advances in how we use technology. These developments will greatly affect the way teaching, learning, and assessment take place. We see the emergence of cyber schools that are almost entirely based on technology for the delivery of instruction, communication with students, and the monitoring of student performance. We see schools based on a new 21st-century approach to education that customizes the learning experience to the learning preferences of each individual student. The focus of instruction in these schools will be on 21st-century fluency skills such as critical thinking, problem solving, information processing, and multimedia project design intended to provide a context to traditional content. We will see significant changes in the roles of both the students and the teachers in these new schools. And we will see a radically altered communication process that will be almost entirely based on digital information.

The Key to Understanding Where the Future Is Headed

Let's stop and ask a critical question. What is it about the world of technology that gives us these ideas about the future of schools and learning? To comprehend what inspires us to make such bold statements about 21st-century schools, it is critical that you grasp the information we are about to present. Without this understanding, the predictions we make will seem improbable, even silly. However, if you appreciate that what we are about to predict is based on the explosion of technological power that is taking place right now and certainly will continue to occur in the next few years, you will not only understand that these predictions are possible, you may also see that we really have not gone as far as we could have in predicting where technology will lead and what effect it will have. The key concept is that of the exponential growth in the power of technology. This is growth that doubles, triples, quadruples, or more every year. It is the kind of growth that electronic technology has consistently experienced since its inception.

In *The Singularity Is Near* (2005), Ray Kurzweil, a renowned inventor and thinker who has been consistently on the mark for more than 30 years in predicting where digital technology is taking us, makes a compelling case for the continued exponential growth of digital technology throughout the 21st century. He claims that as a result of this growth by the year 2045, "the nonbiological intelligence created in that year will be one billion times more powerful than all human intelligence today" (Kurzweil, 2005, p. 136). It is tremendously difficult to grasp exactly what that kind of power will mean for our daily lives. Many predictions will fall short of the reality that will emerge, but since education is very much a futures endeavor, we feel it is essential to at least try to envision what technology will do for education in the first part of the 21st century. So here are our unabashed predictions of where technology is leading and what it will mean for schools and cyber schools.

Amazing Interactivity With Online Technology

First, there will be incredible growth in the interactivity of electronic online experiences. Although there are hints today that suggest what this future will look like, it will be difficult for many of the people reading this book to appreciate the significance of what we are about to discuss. Most adults are at a huge disadvantage in seeing where technology is heading because they do not really participate in the current online technology-based interactive world and have had little or no experience with the examples we cite below. However, it is vitally important for you to realize that just because you aren't aware of the developments we describe or where they are leading, this doesn't mean that these trends are not happening—because they are.

Of the multitude of technological advancements occurring in the world today, there are three developments in technology that we feel are especially worth noting because they point to the powerful new digital experiences that will soon be available. The first is the development of electronic and online games known as Massively Multiplayer Online Role Play Games or MMORPGs, exemplified by EverQuest, Maple Story, World of Warcraft, and City of Heroes. These are interactive games in which literally millions of gamers may be playing simultaneously. Many adults are not aware of the remarkable sophistication that has already been achieved with MMORPGs because they just don't have the time to spend immersing themselves in digital games. But ask any youngsters and they will tell you that modern electronic games have some very sophisticated features and are so complex that it takes hours and hours of practice to master them. And they will tell you that the online, networked games are remarkably unpredictable because you can't just depend on yourself. Rather, you have to cooperate, compete, strategize, and interact with other players, as well as the characters created by the software as they work toward success in the task the game requires. Truly these are tools of mass collaboration.

But there is much more going on in these games than just the game itself. These games are also designed to teach gamers experientially as they play. They provide positive feedback every few seconds and have proven to be very effective vehicles for teaching and learning—and not just for simple skill development. Current games also allow for high-level interaction and collaboration among networked players. Many of these games have already become sufficiently sophisticated that higher level thinking and problem solving are absolutely required to be successful. Online games often require teamwork from ad hoc groups of users who work together online collaboratively in a virtual environment to achieve success. High-level skill development through electronic game playing has become so significant that many companies and the military now use computer games and simulations to teach their people. It has already been established that these software experiences can give those who use them an advantage in real-world endeavors. In *Don't Bother Me Mom—I'm Learning,* Marc Prensky states, "in all kinds of jobs and professions, from doctors to lawyers to executives to military officers, we find people being more successful than their peers because of their videogame playing" (Prensky,

2006, p. 79). Not only have current games proven to be effective tools for learning today, they point toward the kinds of firsthand learning experiences we can expect from technology in the future. There is a tendency in some quarters to dismiss such games as wasteful and frivolous. But be aware that something very powerful is taking place beneath our radar.

Related to this, the second development that points toward the technology-based experiences of the future is the emergence of three-dimensional virtual worlds. Games and simulations are no longer limited to a flat, two-dimensional screen display. Today's users can already experience an extensive virtual 3D world in which they can move freely as they engage in the particular task of the game or simulation. Even online experiences are allowing people to move through three-dimensional space. Using a keyboard, mouse, or joystick, a person can control the movements of software characters or vehicles as they go into rooms, around trees, up stairs, or over rocks, fly through the air, or drive down roads. Games like Halo and World of Warcraft provide users with amazingly realistic 3D virtual environments to explore. As impressive as these programs are today, the current capabilities only hint at the kinds of digital experiences that are to come.

The third development that is worth noting is the emergence of virtual role-playing experiences. Many digital games and adventures allow players to assume a virtual identity that they can take on and control while playing. What is of particular note here is that the player can customize the character before assuming that role. A player can choose to be tall or blonde or strong or fast. Just like real life, there may be both advantages and disadvantages to choosing specific physical attributes. For example, if you choose to be tall and strong, then you might not be as fast or as maneuverable. Once a character has been created, the player then becomes that person when playing the game. The movements of the character's body are controlled using a wide range of input devices. The abilities of the character in the game or adventure and the manner in which it interacts with other digital characters are determined by the attributes that were selected when the character was created and combined with the input from the player.

One of the best examples of how the three developments we have just discussed combine to create a powerful virtual experience is found in Second Life (http://www.secondlife.com). Second Life is a simulated world. Just like the games we discussed, users create their own digital version of themselves (called an avatar) and then assume that character in the Second Life world. They meet and interact with the avatars of other people in real time. Second Life avatars are real people talking about whatever is of interest to them, just as you would if you met someone on the street or in an office. Second Life characters can go to restaurants, bars, stores, or nightclubs, visit people's homes, and walk through parks. They buy land (with real money) and then design and build their fantasy home. They can even buy an island. People start virtual businesses in the Second Life world and make real money. For example, IBM has recently purchased more than 60 islands in Second Life from which they plan to conduct future online business. You could also go to school. Several universities have already set up campuses in Second Life and hold real classes in this virtual environment. Students can hear lectures and participate in discussions. This virtual world is astounding in its realism and its extent. It has become quite popular in a very short period of time. There are already several million people inhabiting this world.

But the growing power of new technologies, no matter how impressive they may currently be, only hints at a new generation of online, technology-based experiences that are coming at us very quickly. The exponential growth in technological power over the next few years will result in astounding advances in how and where technology is used in our lives. Although there will be developments in a wide range of applications of technology, let's focus on a few major developments that will have profound implications for instruction and learning.

In *The Singularity Is Near,* Ray Kurzweil says that we will soon have full-immersion virtual reality experiences over the Internet, likely within the next five years (Kurzweil, 2005, p. 105). Users will be able to see, hear, touch, and smell as they travel through three-dimensional virtual worlds. A headset with wrap-around glasses and headphones will provide realistic sights and sounds. Gyroscopes and sensors will allow the technology to know when the user is turning her head and adjust the visual display accordingly. A body suit with similar sensors will allow the technology to know what the person is doing with his arms, hands, and legs. This will enable the user to move an online digital character by simply moving her actual body. A person will be able to literally walk out onto a Web site that will provide a three-dimensional environment that the user will experience. The information from the headset and body suit will be used to determine where the person is in the Web site's virtual world and what he will see and hear there. In addition, the Web site will be able to simultaneously track the position of other users visiting the site. This will allow a person to see and interact with other online characters. What a person sees will be the customized avatars created or selected by the other users.

This will have an amazing impact on the way we use the Internet. For example, when a person wants to go to the Web site for the Louvre in Paris, she will quite literally walk into the three-dimensional online virtual Louvre and saunter down the halls past the *Mona Lisa* and *Venus de Milo* as if she were in the actual museum. People visiting the Web site will be able to view paintings from various angles and walk completely around sculptures and display cases. Further, they will be able to interact with the other people visiting those exhibits at the same time they are. They could ask someone for their opinion of a particular sculpture or eavesdrop on a guided tour that is focused on the paintings of the great masters. Or they could visit the site with a knowledgeable friend and have that person explain the significance of various paintings, sculptures, and other items on display. What will experiences like that do to the nature of teaching, learning, and assessment?

Visitors to the site will interact with virtual guides. These guides will not be human. They will be an artificially intelligent piece of software that produces a realistic, life-sized, three-dimensional character that guides people through the museum. The virtual guide will see where the people are going and what they are viewing and provide appropriate commentary. The guide will also respond to verbal questions. The precursors to these virtual guides already exist. Ananova is a digital character developed by the BBC to read the news. It is a piece of software that takes written text and reads it via a virtual female character that is displayed on the screen. The character reads with appropriate voice inflection and facial expression. The University of Florida has gone one step further and produced an artificially intelligent tutor called Vic who helps medical students with their learning ("Voluptuous artificial patient tests med students," *Vancouver Sun*, March 23, 2005, Page A7). The tutor listens to verbal questions posed by students and provides them with verbal responses. Those responses come from a database of medical information that it accesses intelligently to assist the students with medical problems. But development in this area over the next few years will greatly improve the ability of these virtual guides and tutors to interact naturally with people. Soon these virtual characters will be three-dimensional and you will interact with them in a virtual world by speaking, pointing, and gesturing. It will not be long before it will be impossible to tell them apart from the online characters controlled by people.

Unlike today, where there is an obvious difference between real experiences and technology-based experiences, there will be a blurring of the lines between reality and simulation in the future. We can already see this in high-level simulators today. Flight simulators used to train pilots, for example, are so realistic that many pilots experience real stress when their virtual aircraft has mechanical problems and starts to plummet out of the virtual sky. In the near future, as technology continues to grow in power exponentially, this kind of virtual realism will become much more commonplace. Although the prospect of slipping back and forth between reality and virtual reality may frighten, even shock many older people, kids will embrace this new development and the experiences it offers. Young people will populate these new three-dimensional online virtual worlds immediately and use them for entertainment, business, relationships, and learning. They will not struggle with understanding how it works or marvel at its power or fret about the change this technology is bringing. Instead, they will simply incorporate it into their daily lives and let the technology empower them to do things no one ever dreamed possible.

These developments will have a profound effect for anyone who embraces their use. No longer will devices like keyboards or mice be obstacles to the productive use of digital tools. Interaction will be as natural as seeing, talking, and moving. As the technology becomes more transparent, we will be free to focus more on the tasks we wish to accomplish and be far more productive than we are today. But these developments will be about much more than just increasing productivity. These technologies will also change the nature of interpersonal relationships. Just as the automobile empowered people to have relationships in a far larger community than in horse-and-buggy days, and the telephone redefined communications from face-to-face to global, so, too, will the powerful new communications technology empower people to have relationships with individuals in a much larger global community. However, these relationships will be much more "real" than anything we can imagine today. Instead of exchanging e-mail or text-based chatting, people in the future will interact in three-dimensional virtual worlds complete with all the subtleties of verbal and nonverbal communication. New technologies will allow them to have significant relationships with others from around the globe, complete with all of the natural communication that would occur if they were in the same room.

A Huge Shift in How Kids Will Learn

These technologies will also have profound implications for learning and school organization. Online learning will become an integral part of all students' education, regardless of the type of school they attend, and will provide opportunities to augment the instruction that the school provides. In fact, this is already happening today. Learning has been a natural consequence as digital kids have adopted online computers, cell phones, and other hand-held devices as sources of information, entertainment, and communication. But educators have not widely recognized this development because they don't really participate in this digital world and because this type of learning is not found in traditional subjects taught in school. Unlike traditional schooling, online technology-based learning is far more interest- and needs-driven while at the same time presented to people in a dynamic format. Digital online information is graphical, colorful, accompanied by music, and often in full-motion video. Because it is interactive, this allows kids to quickly move from watching something that is not engaging them to following their own cognitive links to things that do interest and engage them. The online world is one where the learner increasingly controls the media, not the other way round. Online learning is allowing the student to control when the learning will take place, the pace of the presentation, the path through the information, and in many cases, the manner in which the information is presented. Kids often use these online experiences as an antidote to the increasingly tedious, narrowly focused, test-driven instruction found in many schools today. They sit in their bedrooms in the evening and go online to learn how to play the guitar, repair their bikes, learn a new language, play a game, follow the lives of their favorite music group or TV celebrity, start a small business, what to do if they are feeling ill, give first aid to a friend, and on and on. And it's important to note that this is happening today with largely two-dimensional Web sites that still have a great deal of text-based information. Can you imagine the kind of learning that will be available as the online world moves into the three-dimensional virtual world experience with natural interaction and more audio-visual information?

Personal, portable, wearable technology will soon become the prime method for accessing this 3D online world, just as the cell phone and other hand-held devices are poised to supersede the desktop and laptop. Portable headsets and body suits will allow students to access full-immersion, three-dimensional virtual worlds from wherever they are as these new powerful personal devices connect wirelessly to the online world. As this occurs, there will also be dramatic growth in high-speed wireless service areas making anytime, anywhere connections to the online world. Students will have access to an amazing array of new learning experiences from almost anywhere.

A key attribute of technology-based learning will be firsthand experience. This is a new and exciting development in the effectiveness of the learning experience. Most adults reading this book grew up in a world where almost all of their education was secondhand, at best. We read about world events in the newspaper and magazines, often long after they happened. We read textbooks to learn about the workings of legislative assemblies, subatomic particles, and the solar system. We were lucky if these paper-based sources had a diagram or photo to complement the text and help with the explanation. If we were good at constructing mental pictures from text-based explanations, then we were able to learn. But if we had trouble "seeing" what the words were trying to say, our learning suffered. We couldn't learn from the source of the information, so we had to make do with someone writing about it.

But technology is fundamentally changing the way kids learn about the world. Kids are constantly connected to the online world with their cell phones and hand-held devices. They are alerted to major events almost the instant they occur. They can watch events unfold from around the world on webcams. Increasingly, kids are going well beyond the text-based world we experienced when we grew up and are learning from live video and sound. Technology is now letting them learn about the world by watching world events as they happen, learn about the solar system as they ride along in the nose cone of a spacecraft, learn about subatomic particles by watching the electrons circle around the nucleus of an atom, and learn about the democratic process by watching legislators debate new laws. In the very near future, if students want to learn about the work of Michelangelo, they will "go" to Rome and "visit" the Sistine Chapel or "go" to Florence and "walk" around the sculpture of David. They won't just have to read about his work or look at a picture, they can have the firsthand experience of seeing his work in person in a virtual world.

In the future, students will have more access to the actual source of new developments. Technology is already allowing students to make contact with the people who are making news in the world today. Kids are using e-mail and online chatting to talk to experts in a wide range of fields of study. But this communication is still quite slow and difficult because the current technology gets in the way. However, when the technology allows people to interact naturally using their voices and their bodies, communication will be much easier and more effective. And it will greatly increase the immediacy of communication about what is happening in the world.

This leads to another key attribute of technology-based learning. It will occur just when it is needed. Since the online world is never closed, students can access its learning resources whenever and wherever they want or need to. If they are up at 3:30 a.m. and that is their best time for learning, then they will be able to access information and tutorial services when it is right for them. If they are on a field trip touring a factory and want to know how steel is made, or out walking with their family by a stream and want to know about the salmon that are swimming upstream, or if they are going to cut down a tree in their backyard and want to know how to figure out the height of the tree, or if someone they are with becomes sick or injured and they want to know the appropriate treatment, or if they are at a public meeting about the demolition of a church and they want to know the history of the building—all this and much more will be possible with the personal, portable, wireless technology that can access all the resources of the online world whenever, wherever the user wants. Some have called this "just in time learning" because the learning is driven by a need and it happens just in time for the new learning to be applied to solve a problem or meet a need.

To grasp the true power the digital world will have, it is imperative that you understand what information will soon be available to the average person using digital tools. Earlier in this book, we told you about the article written by Kevin Kelly that outlines the work that is underway to convert human knowledge to digital formats (2006, p. 1). It involves the creation of a universal library—an online digital library of literary works, a library distributed over multiple sites across the Internet. The move to digitize significant volumes of printed material began when Google announced in December 2004 it would digitize all of the books in five major research libraries. In addition, Google is now partnering with several major publishing companies to digitize vast numbers of out-of-print books and excerpts from books currently in print. Also in 2004, Raj Reddy, professor at Carnegie Mellon University, began scanning books from his university's library for the Million Book Project, so called because Professor Reddy's goal is a million books scanned by the end of 2008. Superstar, a company based in Beijing, has scanned every book from 200 libraries in China. That represents half of all the books published in the Chinese language since 1949. There is a rapidly growing digital library of digital books being created.

Just think of what these projects will make available when people do searches on the Internet. But this shift to an online digital library is about much more than just access. The magic is in how the information and ideas in one book will be linked to the information in every other book. Imagine being able to jump to each book in a bibliography to see the context of quotes cited in an article or being able to assemble all of the passages from all digital books on a specific term or concept or accessing all of the works with an opinion on a particular issue. But the power of this digital library goes much further than just the linking of information. Kelly goes on to discuss the creation of personalized compilations of references, quotes, and passages gleaned from the massive library of digitized books. People will create these compilations in an area of research or on an area of interest much the same way people create playlists with iPods today. These literary "idea-lists" will then be shared, expanded, annotated, and cross-referenced in the online world. This will greatly alter and extend the pursuit of knowledge, ideas, and opinions. It will also require people to develop whole new skill sets in order to navigate, inquire, analyze, and evaluate in the new digital "ideascape" of interconnected literature. And thus far, we have only been talking about digitizing printed works. What happens when the information in audio recordings and film footage is digitized and cross-referenced to the information in books in the same way? The power of this kind of interconnected digital multimedia ideascape to inform, stimulate, challenge, and engage students will usher in a wonderful new era of learning. It will also force schools to radically shift the focus of their instruction from the 20th-century standards we currently see in education today to the higher level thinking skills required to process information in the rapidly emerging digital ideascape.

Technology is also beginning to facilitate student learning through an advanced trial-and-error approach. Sophisticated educational simulations and games will provide students with powerful tools for learning experientially as they control the variables in the virtual environment the technology provides. As we mentioned previously, games have already proven to be effective teaching tools. Marc Prensky states, "Complex games, already educating our kids after school, also have the potential to be a huge boon to formal education" (2006, p. 63). Some games already offer the potential to learn through a new form of direct experience. Physics teachers use the game "Supercharged," which was developed as part of the MIT Games to Teach initiative, to help students to better understand core principles of electromagnetism (Squire, Barnett, Grant, & Higginbotham, 2003). As a means for learning the laws of electromagnetism through firsthand experience, students navigate electromagnetic mazes by planting electrical charges that attract or repel their vehicles.

Teachers can then build on this intuitive and experiential learning in real and virtual learning environments with their students, introducing equations, diagrams, or visualizations that help them to better understand the underlying principles that they are deploying and then sending them back to play through the levels again and improve their performance.

The games of the future will provide much more powerful learning experiences by making astoundingly real virtual worlds that will teach students as they interact, strategize, create, and collaborate in simulated environments. These firsthand learning experiences will have a far greater impact on student learning than lectures or reading. By varying the inputs to the virtual environment, students can see immediately the impact different combinations have on the outcome. Students will be able to learn about complex, interrelated systems by trial and error. In the future, students will not only control the variables of these simulations, they will also be able to watch the results in three dimensions from whatever vantage point they choose. Technology will allow students to zoom around the points of conflict in the Battle of Waterloo or watch the Invasion of Normandy from the perspective of the Allied forces or the Germans or view the landing of the *Apollo 11* Lunar Landing Module from the lunar surface or from the Lunar Landing Module or watch the behavior of electrons as atoms join to form molecules. Educators have been slow to see the potential of simulations for instruction, and consequently development of this kind of software has been limited. But we are beginning to see an increased demand for these kinds of learning tools. We will soon see the development of much more sophisticated games focused on education designed to teach students a wide range of topics and skills.

The Magic of Artificial Intelligence

And there is still more to consider. New digital tools will increasingly be equipped with powerful, intelligent software that will learn how we ask questions, what we mean when we say certain things, and what information and resources we need on a regular basis. These tools will use this knowledge to "think ahead of us" and retrieve what we will need before we ask. We will communicate with these tools by speaking to them. They will respond by speaking to us. We will carry these tools with us in our cell phones, hand-held devices, headsets, and body suits. They will be the ultimate personal digital assistant, a digital helper that anticipates what we need and want and gets it for us to make our lives easier, more productive, and more enjoyable.

These powerful personal digital assistants will have a profound effect on learning. They will revolutionize information retrieval. They will also put increasing pressure on schools to shift the skills they teach students for information processing. Currently, despite all the rhetoric to the contrary, schools predominantly teach students how to retrieve information.

Students create reports consisting primarily of the ideas of others. Students today are not generally equipped with the higher level thinking skills needed to process the material they find. However, the new digital tools will do more and more of the work of information retrieval for the students. The emphasis of instruction will have to shift to the higher level cognitive skills required to assess the value of the retrieved information to determine its significance. These skills will empower students to form their own ideas about the information they access.

New Educational Resources

There will be a significant change in the kinds of educational resources available to students. Three-dimensional Web sites or portals will allow students to "visit" places around the globe including museums, businesses, libraries, theatres, nonprofit organizations, government departments, and universities. The information students will get at these sites will be audio-visual at the very least, and more than likely a virtual three-dimensional immersion experience. But the emergence of the virtual guides and tutors will have the greatest impact. Nonhuman interaction will become a significant part of every student's education. These Web sites will include virtual characters that will interact with students as naturally as teachers do in classrooms today. Students will increasingly be able to ask questions verbally and listen to answers provided by artificially intelligent software that responds appropriately to student queries.

As natural interaction in 3D virtual environments becomes the norm, there will be a major shift in the way students interact with teachers. Students and teachers will not have to be in the same physical location to have meaningful personal interaction. Students will access teachers from home, the mall, vacation spots, and any other remote location when they have questions. A teacher's class may consist of students from around the city, state, or country, as well as those students physically present in the classroom. Daily lessons, group discussions, and personal interaction could be accomplished completely using new communication technology with a mixture of interaction between physically present and online students.

This new technology will also radically change the traditional notion of the teacher in the classroom. No longer will students be confined to a single teacher. If an elementary school teacher does not have a background in science, students will be able to get expert assistance from a wide variety of science instructors. High school literature students will be able to participate in discussions with many different teachers of literature as well as the authors themselves. The role of the teacher employed by the school district will shift from that of an expert in a particular field to that of a guide or facilitator to learning and who also helps students determine where to best access the instruction needed.

New digital tools will make it incredibly easy for students to produce complex and sophisticated project work that communicates the learning they have done. The projects will be truly multimedia, making the multimedia of today pale in comparison. Online digital tools will empower all students to create videos of original fictional stories and nonfiction documentaries complete with narration and soundtrack. Students will be able to use simulation software to solve problems posed by teachers. Teachers will watch the student's version of the simulation and assess how effective the various inputs have been at reaching a successful solution to the task that was given.

Schools Will Have to Respond to New Online Learning

All schools will be forced to respond to the power of the new online digital learning. The sheer attractiveness of this kind of information presentation combined with the unprecedented level of choice and the increasingly interactive nature of the online world will make the instruction that takes place in traditional classrooms extremely unattractive and undesirable in comparison. Regardless of legislative mandates, schools will have to find ways to shift their instructional approaches to more innovative and interesting ways of engaging students. If they do not, students will vote with their feet and drop out of traditional schools in increasing numbers.

It is important to understand that this technology will have profound effects across all aspects of 21st-century life. As a result, schools will have to shift the focus of instruction so that students are equipped with the skills they will need for success in the technologically infused world they will face after graduation. It will be critical that schools move away from the current focus on low-level content recall skills. Technology will increasingly take over the task of getting information. As this happens, the importance of content-recall skills will decrease while there will be a dramatic increase in the need for higher level metacognitive skills for processing the information the technology retrieves. Schools will also have to teach students the visual design skills necessary for success with the new multimedia technology. As the nature of information presentation changes, students will need new skills for constructing effective presentations of audio-visual material. Students will need to be able to integrate knowledge from multiple sources including music, video, online databases, and other media. This includes the ability to understand the power of images and sounds, to recognize and use that power to manipulate and transform digital media, to distribute them pervasively, and to easily adapt them to new forms of presentation. This will require schools to teach all students graphic and visual design as an essential part of the basic literacy skills everyone will need. This will not only enable the students to use the technology more successfully in school, it will equip them with essential skills for life in the 21st century.

The traditional idea of a classroom, with all its loaded meanings, will change dramatically as this new technology emerges. The kind of online technology we have been discussing will allow students to walk down a virtual hallway to access instructional and informational resources from online sources. Online, interactive, firsthand learning experiences will allow students to learn whenever and wherever they can access the Internet. Wireless access will empower students to learn at exactly the teachable moment regardless of their location. They will access the school, learning resources, and their teacher from their homes, from their cars, on public transportation, walking down the street, from their places of work, and anywhere else the need arises from their own personal digital devices. Not only will access to the school increase, but as we have mentioned, access from the school will increase as well. The learning environment will expand from a 700-square-foot room with desks and a whiteboard to encompass the entire world. It will offer instruction from a wide array of teachers. Students will interact with content experts. They will collaborate with others from around their community and around the world. The power of the new technology combined with the growth in the experiences available in the online world will make digital learning a compelling option for students. All students will benefit from the new instructional opportunities. All teachers will have to adjust to allow for this kind of learning.

As the ability to reach out from the school to access people and educational resources increases at the same time the ability of students to reach into a school from the outside increases, the idea of what a school looks like will also change radically. Technology will force educators to question much of what we currently take for granted in schools. Do students have to be physically present to attend school? If they come to school physically, what kinds of activities will they attend? Do teaching and learning have to occur in classrooms with 25 students, one teacher, and one subject in one-hour periods? Does schooling have to stop for two to three months over the summer? Does access to teachers and learning resources have to end at 3:00 p.m. or on weekends? Do individual students have to learn in a lock-step manner together with all the other students in a school of similar age? Does a student have to stop learning about a particular topic that has sparked her interest and move on to another area of study just because a bell rings? Does a student just have to "tough it out" if he is having difficulty understanding an explanation from a particular teacher? In fact, does a school have to have a physical facility at all?

As technology becomes even more powerful and capable over the next few years (and remember that this will continue to happen exponentially), the answers to these questions will change significantly. The physical configuration and operational organization of schools will need to change as a result. Although technology will affect the learning in every classroom, many school districts will create schools that focus exclusively on learning using technology. These cyber schools will be unlike anything we have ever seen in education. All activities related to learning would be done using online technology.

CHARACTERISTICS OF CYBER SCHOOLS

Cyber schools will be characterized by the following:

- Students may not be physically present in a school building.
- The only physical building might be for staff and the technology required to run the school.
- Students could be drawn from across the town or city that the school serves—possibly from across the region/state/province, even across the country or from around the world.
- Learning will come from multiple sources, including the following:
    - a wide variety of online teachers, both human and nonhuman.
    - a wide range of stand-alone and online digital learning resources.
    - educational games and adventures.
    - simulations of the real world, both current and historical.
- Learning will take place around the clock, seven days a week, 365 days a year.
- Much of the student project work will involve the production of multimedia presentations.
- Instruction will shift to focus on 21st-century literacy skills, including the following:
    - information-processing skills.
    - problem solving.
    - graphic design for multimedia presentations.
- Students will meet with their teacher-advisor using online technology.
- Students will follow their own individual plans for doing the learning required by the school.
- Student progress will be monitored by intelligent digital online tracking systems.
- Staff for these schools will work in shifts to provide access to teacher-advisors over an extended day.

Some cyber schools will be a hybrid of traditional, adapted, and technology-based learning. School districts may decide that there is still a need for students to attend a physical facility for certain activities such as working in groups, playing sports, acting in a play, playing in a musical band, fixing automobiles, or doing certain types of artwork. But these schools will be smaller and organized differently because much of the learning that used to be done at the school will now be done using technology from remote locations. Schools could be housed in small facilities located in the community, close to where students live. Such small schools would allow staff to have more personal relationships with students. The school would provide digital learning resources. Students could choose to learn at school, at home, or in some other remote location. The school would also provide access to technology for students who could not afford to have it at home or those who prefer to work at school. For school districts with large-scale athletic or fine arts programs, students could attend a hub facility for those activities while doing the rest of their school work from smaller community-based facilities or from home.

CYBER SCHOOL SCENARIOS OF THE FUTURE

It is difficult to grasp how these schools could operate because we have never had anything like them before to use as a guide for our thinking. Consequently, it's hard to imagine the huge impact online technology will have on learning. To help you get an idea of what students and teachers will do with technology in the future, we have looked into our crystal ball and created some scenarios for technology use for students and teachers operating in cyber schools.

Andrew and Gus

A student named Andrew wakes up at 11:45 a.m. and has his "breakfast." While he is eating and watching a daytime soap opera on the family's 104-inch-wide screen TV, Gus calls him from his cell phone computer. Gus is his digital personal assistant. Gus is an artificially intelligent piece of software that creates a digital 3D human figure that talks with Andrew. Gus appears on the display created by the glasses Andrew is wearing. Actually, Andrew doesn't need the glasses to correct his vision—it's 20/20—but he wears them because the glasses combined with the built-in earpieces create a three-dimensional audio-visual display that can be turned on and off as needed. This headset communicates wirelessly with the cell phone computer Andrew keeps in his pocket. Gus has realized that Andrew is awake and has waited 30 minutes before speaking (Gus has learned that speaking too soon after Andrew wakes up is not very productive). Gus has remembered that Andrew has an online debate for his social studies class with a student from across town tomorrow on the topic of whether or not the old theatre on Main Street should be torn down for a condo development. Gus has retrieved some information from a number of Internet sources for Andrew to review.

"I have the information you need for your debate tomorrow," says Gus. "Do you want to look at it now?"

"Just give me an overview," says Andrew.

"OK, I have the date of construction for the theatre, a series of historical photos, the name and supporting information for every production ever put on at the theatre, and the plans for the restoration."

"That may be useful, but what I really wanted was how people felt about the theatre. I was hoping to find evidence that people had a fondness for it."

Gus responds, "Let me look for that." He pauses for less than a second. "I have found 73 articles written in local newspapers that express opinions about the theatre. Of those, 65 express positive thoughts and feelings toward the theatre."

"That's great. Rank them in order from most positive to least positive and I'll have a look at them in a minute."

Andrew finishes eating then goes to the bathroom and takes a shower. Then he walks to the couch, picks up his wireless multimedia headset, and puts it on. Gus greets him and shows him a 3D room filled with desks.

"I've ranked the articles, but I thought you might like it if I grouped them by topic. Each desk contains the ranked articles for each group. I thought this desk would be the most appropriate for the debate—it contains all the articles with positive opinions about the building itself."

Andrew looks at the articles on that desk and says, "Yeah, I like these. Can you read me the important parts of the first 10 articles while I choose my pictures?"

Andrew looks for maps and photos for his presentation at the debate while Gus reads him the relevant parts of articles from the newspapers. Through a continuing conversation, Andrew and Gus pull quotes from the articles and create points for the debate. As he works on making his case, Andrew realizes it would be helpful to have a live interview for his presentation. He asks Gus to contact the people who wrote the top 10 articles who are still alive to see if anyone would agree to an interview. The mayor agrees to talk with Andrew for five minutes between meetings. Gus records the conversation.

When Andrew is done preparing for the debate, Gus tells him that a friend called and wants to know if he wants to come over for a game of pool. Andrew tells Gus to let his friend know he'll come and has Gus call a few of his friends to see if they want to join them. Andrew gets changed and heads over to his friend's house. While he is playing pool with his friends, Andrew gets a call from his teacher-advisor. He puts on his multimedia headset and has a video call with his advisor while he stands in the corner of the room. She wants to discuss his progress in his math and science class and go over Andrew's plans for the next two days. She reminds Andrew that his space simulation is due today. Andrew then returns to his game of pool. During the game, he faces a difficult shot. He turns on his headset and asks Gus for some assistance in figuring out the angles necessary to make the shot successfully. After spending a couple of hours playing pool and hanging out, Andrew heads back home.

Andrew plays an online adventure action game when he gets home. In this game, Andrew works with ad hoc groups of players from around the world that form from the people playing the game at that time to accomplish the next task in the game. While he is playing, Andrew also chats with his friends. Each friend's picture appears in the periphery of the display created by his headset. This display is superimposed over the game display. At 4:00 p.m., Gus tells him that it's time for his aerobics class. Andrew puts on his high-tech body suit and goes to the aerobics Web site. There he meets a number of his friends who are also taking this class as part of their physical education course. They gather in a 3D virtual gym and listen to the instructor explain the goals for today's session. Then they begin to do their exercises. Andrew controls the digital image of himself by moving his body. The instructor moves around the virtual gym and gives pointers on each student's exercise technique.

After the aerobics class, Andrew asks Gus to set up the space simulation he has been working on for his math and science course. Andrew has been given the task of taking a lunar landing craft from the International Space Station orbiting the earth to one of the new mining colonies on the moon. His task is a difficult one. He must use physics to calculate the trajectory from the space station to the moon that will use the least amount of fuel because he will be carrying a heavy load of equipment on the landing craft. He must also identify the major lunar features he will use to verify his descent to the moon's surface. Andrew has tried the flight several times, but has yet to successfully land at the colony because he keeps running out of fuel. Andrew still has his headset and body suit on from the aerobics class, so he is ready for the virtual experience of being in a space ship. He sets up for latest attempt and pilots his craft away from the space station. He sets his heading and fires up his main engines. When he nears the moon, he begins his pre-landing checklist. Just then Gus tells him his mother is calling. Andrew continues with his checklist while he talks with his mother in a corner of his display. She tells him she will be late coming home from work, but there is leftover meatloaf in the fridge. Andrew tells his mom he has to go because he is just about to land on the moon and he needs to pay attention. She thinks he is kidding, but says goodbye anyway. Andrew makes his descent to the lunar surface and successfully lands his craft at the mining colony. Excited that he finally got it right, Andrew tells Gus to send the successful simulation results to his math and science teacher right away.

Mrs. Taylor and Jane

Mrs. Taylor, Andrew's math and science teacher, is notified by her own personal digital assistant software that Andrew has just handed in a successful lunar landing simulation. Jane, Mrs. Taylor's digital assistant, calls Mrs. Taylor, who is outside in her garden. Her teaching shift doesn't actually begin until 6:00 p.m., but she has asked Jane to let her know when a student hands in a major assignment. She comes in from outside and has a look at Andrew's work. Mrs. Taylor prefers to use her large 2D screen for her work because she finds the 3D world created by the headset a little disorienting. Unlike her students, she didn't grow up using this device, and its use isn't as natural for her as it is for her pupils. She only uses it to mark 3D simulations like Andrew's lunar landing. The rest of the time she prefers to interact using her flat screen. She asks students to send live video from their cameras instead of interacting with their virtual online selves because she finds it more natural communication. Her students call her old-fashioned, but they comply with her wishes.

Mrs. Taylor is pleased to see Andrew's successful simulation. She asks the simulation program to show the math and physics work behind his lunar landing. She discovers that although Andrew was successful, his fuel tanks were empty at touch down. This is cutting it too close. When she looks at the time of his departure, she realizes that if Andrew had waited for 11 hours, the orbits of the space station and the moon would have been much more in sync for his trip. Then she checks the lunar features Andrew used to verify his descent. She notices that Andrew has missed a major lunar feature, so she asks Jane to call him. Once Andrew appears on her screen, they have a two-way video conversation. Mrs. Taylor begins by congratulating Andrew on successfully landing his craft on the moon. She points out the omission of the lunar feature and asks Andrew to update his flight plan. Then she asks Andrew to check his fuel tank levels after he has landed. Andrew re-enters the simulation and gives Mrs. Taylor the readings. The tanks are empty. Mrs. Taylor asks if she can come along for another attempt at the landing. She puts on her headset and joins Andrew as he goes through the landing phase of his trip once more. This time he runs out of fuel before landing. They discuss the problem, and Andrew sees that no matter how well he pilots the spacecraft, he will be lucky to land successfully. After a short discussion, Andrew realizes there is a problem with the physics of his trip. Mrs. Taylor suggests that Andrew look at the timing of his departure from the space station and see if he can find a better time for the trip that will allow him to land with the required reserve fuel in his tanks. Andrew agrees, and she decides to extend his deadline until tomorrow.

When the conversation with Andrew ends, Jane reminds Mrs. Taylor that the chemistry lecture from the school district will begin in 15 minutes. She asks Jane to call the members of her chemistry discussion group to remind them to listen in to the lecture. The lecture is actually an online multimedia presentation by one of the school district's master chemistry teachers on the impact laundry detergent, shampoo, and other household cleansers are having on the pollution of a local river. As the lecture is ending, Mrs. Taylor asks Jane to tell her students to join an online discussion about the content of the lecture. The students begin appearing on Mrs. Taylor's screen as they sign in. Several simultaneous conversations begin as they wait for everyone to join the group. Then Mrs. Taylor calls the group to order and begins throwing out questions for the students to discuss. They have a spirited discussion for the next 35 minutes. When there is disagreement over what was said in the lecture, Mrs. Taylor asks Jane to replay the appropriate part of the presentation to set the record straight. At the end of the discussion, Mrs. Taylor asks all the students to do some further research into the chemical reactions taking place in the river due to the dumping of untreated sewage.

Over the course of her shift, Mrs. Taylor gets numerous calls from students asking for help with their science research and projects. One student calls to ask about a virtual physics experiment that is not going as planned. The student is recreating a motor vehicle accident that occurred recently, but cannot match the actual final locations of the cars in the real accident. Again Mrs. Taylor dons her multimedia headset and joins the student inside the 3D simulation to see what is going wrong. After looking at the setup for the collision, Mrs. Taylor cannot see anything that has been set improperly. She asks Jane to retrieve all the information collected by the police at the scene of the accident. Mrs. Taylor realizes that the student has not factored in the nearly empty gas tank into the weight of one of the cars. She guides the student through the data that Jane has accessed so the student can discover the error for himself.

During a break in her interactions with students, Mrs. Taylor asks Jane to see if there are any local companies that manufacture batteries. Mrs. Taylor wants her students to see a practical application of chemistry in the workplace and is wondering if anyone is producing batteries in the area. Jane locates three battery companies within a 20-mile radius. Since it is now late in the evening, Jane talks with the digital assistant software for the communications people for the three companies and sets up online interviews for the next afternoon.

Susan and Theo

Another student named Susan wakes up at 8:00 a.m. the next morning. After breakfast and spending some time in the bathroom getting ready, Susan heads out the door to go to school. It's just three short blocks to the small shopping center that houses her school, and Susan enjoys her walk in the cool crisp morning air. She reaches the shopping center, passes the 7-Eleven store on the corner, opens the glass door in the next storefront, and goes into her school. Susan walks down a short hallway past some offices and out into a large open area. There are several students sitting on couches and large overstuffed chairs. Some are talking to each other. Others are immersed in some kind of digital experience using their multimedia headsets. One student gets up and goes to one of the offices for a face-to-face meeting with his teacher-advisor. Susan goes over to a counter at the back of the room and signs in with the attendance clerk. She signs out one of the school's headsets and then heads for her favorite chair and makes herself comfortable.

The first thing Susan does is put on her headset and connect with the school district's online service center to get access to her personal digital assistant. Susan calls him Theo.

"Good morning, Susan," says Theo.

"Hey Theo, how are you doing?"

"I'm fine thanks, Susan, and I'm ready to get going on the work we have to do today," replies Theo. "Would you like to go over your schedule?"

"No thanks, not right now. What I really need is for you to get hold of Mr. Walters. I have a question for him."

Mr. Walters is Susan's English literature teacher. In a few moments, Theo informs Susan that he has Mr. Walters on the line.

"Hey Mr. Walters, how are things?" says Susan.

"I'm great, Susan, how are you?" he replies.

"I'm OK, but I'm having trouble understanding something in *Lord of the Flies*. It's when Piggy gets killed. Can you help me understand the symbolism when the conch gets smashed?"

"Let's see if we can find you some people with an opinion on that. Come with me to the LitNet Web site."

"I'll follow him for you," says Theo.

Susan meets Mr. Walters at the LitNet site. They enter the room called "Prose" and are greeted by a digital character.

"Hello, my name is Christine," says the digital character. "How can I help you?"

"We are looking for some opinions on the symbolism in *Lord of the Flies*," replies Mr. Walters.

"Can you tell me more specifically what you are looking for?" asks Christine.

"We would like to understand the symbolism in the scene when the conch is smashed," replies Mr. Walters.

"Of course," says Christine. "Please go in the door to your right and I'll meet you there with some people with knowledge of *Lord of the Flies*."

Susan and Mr. Walters enter the room and are met by Christine. Behind Christine are three other characters. Unlike Christine, these are images of real people.

"These people are experts on *Lord of the Flies*," says Christine. "The first is Dr. Musgrave. She is a professor of English at Oxford University. The second is George Wilcox. He the editor of *The Canadian Journal of Literature*. The third is Cecil Thompson. He is the literature critic for the *New York Times*. Each of these people have recorded opinions on the symbolism in *Lord of the Flies* that includes a reference to the significance of the conch being smashed."

"It looks like you're in good hands, Susan," says Mr. Walters. "I'll leave now and let you listen to what they have to say"

"Thanks Mr. Walters," says Susan. "I have another question for you, but I'll contact you when I'm finished here."

Mr. Walters leaves the site, and Susan then listens to the opinions recorded by the three literature experts. Susan likes what Dr. Musgrave has to say and wants to include it in her video project. She checks with Christine to see if it is possible to record part of Dr. Musgrave's video presentation. When Christine indicates that this is acceptable, Susan gets Theo to record the desired clip.

When she is finished at the LitNet site, Susan asks Theo to contact Mr. Walters once again. While she is waiting, Susan opens up the documentary movie on *Lord of the Flies* she is working on for her English literature class. She adds the clip of Dr. Musgrave and some commentary on the symbolism of the conch being smashed. Susan references the opinions she heard at the LitNet site in her commentary. When Theo tells her he has Mr. Walters on the line, Susan asks him how to create a multi-image overlay effect that is synchronized to the music track. Mr. Walters walks Susan through the steps required to create the effect for her movie. Susan says goodbye to Mr. Walters and works on her movie for about an hour. While she works, she listens to music and carries on several simultaneous online conversations with her friends.

Before she has completed her work on the movie, Theo interrupts Susan.

"Don't forget you have the appointment with Dr. Henderson this afternoon," says Theo. "You asked me to remind you to do the online eye dissection before meeting him."

"Thanks, Theo. I'll just save my work and do that," replies Susan.

"Would you like me to get the eye dissection up and ready to go?" asks Theo.

"That would be great. I'll be ready in about two minutes."

Susan finishes her work on the movie and tells Theo she is ready for the dissection. Theo brings up a biology Web site on Susan's screen. She sees a virtual laboratory. On the table is a dish with a human eye from a patient with glaucoma. There are also all of the tools necessary to do a dissection. Susan's work on the eye is directed by David, an artificially intelligent virtual tutor. David outlines the procedure to Susan and then monitors her progress. He also responds to Susan's questions. David waits patiently while Susan stops her work on the dissection to take notes. When Susan makes mistakes on the dissection, David takes her back a step or two and lets her redo her work. Susan wants to learn as much as she can from this dissection because she is interested in ophthalmology and the school district has set up a mentorship for her with a local ophthalmologist. Susan meets with him online once a week. When the dissection is completed, Susan goes to the 7-Eleven and has a hot dog for lunch.

After lunch, Susan asks Theo to set up her meeting with Dr. Henderson and let her know when he is ready. Susan reviews her notes from the dissection because today she is watching as Dr. Henderson treats a patient with glaucoma. Dr. Henderson wears a special headset that allows Susan to see and hear everything that the doctor does. Susan joins Dr. Henderson in the exam room. She is introduced to the patient, and then the doctor begins his examination. As the session progresses, Dr. Henderson speaks both to the patient and to Susan. After the patient leaves, Dr. Henderson spends five minutes talking with Susan and answering her questions.

Now it's almost 2:00 p.m. and Theo reminds Susan that she had better catch her bus or she will be late for her basketball practice. Susan returns her headset and heads out the front door to catch a city transit bus. She is heading for the physical education and career center for the school district located in a suburb of the city. Her basketball team meets at the center every day at 3:00 p.m. While she is on the bus, Susan listens to music on her cell phone and talks with her friends. Just before arriving at the gymnasium, Susan uses her cell phone to look up her team's schedule for the next week on the school district's Web site. At the practice, Susan's coach notices that Susan is having some trouble with her jump shot. Near the end of the practice, the coach hands Susan a headset and a high-tech body suit. She asks Susan to go to the Shooter Tutor Web site for some help with her shooting. Susan puts on the gear and goes to the site. She meets with a virtual shooting coach who asks her to take some jump shots. Susan shoots on an actual basketball hoop in the gym that has been fitted with special sensors. The virtual tutor monitors Susan's movements from the data generated by the body suit and the sensors on the hoop. With that information, the tutor can analyze Susan's body mechanics and shooting technique. Susan adjusts her shooting according to the feedback from the tutor, and her shooting has improved markedly after 20 minutes.

Summarizing the Scenarios

These scenarios illustrate the increased role technology will have in daily life in the future. They also illustrate the power technology will have to help students learn. As far out or improbable as they may seem, it is critical to remember that the power of technology is increasing exponentially. This means that while there will be more and more power in technology in the future, it will take less and less time for it to appear. The technology we outline in the scenarios will enter our lives sooner than you think.

Let's summarize the changes we outlined in the scenarios.

- Online communication will become much more natural and interactive than today.
- Communication will be a combination of face-to-face and online conversations. People will slip seamlessly from real to virtual communications and back.
- Kids will do a significant amount (but not all) of their socializing with online technology.
- Instruction will come from a multitude of sources, both virtual and real.

- Learning will happen almost anywhere.
- Instruction and learning will take place at any time.
- Learning will be customized for each individual student.
- Technology will be essential for schools. Learning cannot take place without it.
- Technology will be just a tool, albeit a very powerful one. Its use will become increasingly transparent, leaving the mind of the student free to focus on the task to be accomplished.
- Students will learn from highly interactive three-dimensional Web sites with artificially intelligent virtual tutors.
- Students will have access to master teachers through online technology.
- Teachers will do less direct teaching. Instead, they will assume the role of a guide and an advisor.
- The focus of instruction will shift to 21st-century literacy skills like problem solving, information processing, and graphic design.
- All teachers will possess information access skills for a digital online world.
- All teachers will posses information-processing skills.
- All teachers will posses multimedia design skills.
- There will truly be no more cookie-cutter schools. School and schooling will be tailored to the specific needs of students and parents in a particular community.

This last point is an important one. Technology will bring unprecedented levels of flexibility to education resulting in a far greater range of learning possibilities for each individual student. It will be necessary for those responsible for planning and designing schools to let go of the idea that there is a single configuration for a high school that can adequately handle all of the instructional needs and preferences of all the students who attend. Instead, school designs for the 21st century must be configured to allow for maximum flexibility in meeting the learning needs of individual students. To achieve this customization of instructional approach, school designs may borrow ideas from a number of the models we have outlined.

Many of you reading this chapter may be thinking that the kind of education we have just discussed sounds like science fiction—a great exercise in whimsical fantasy with no real bearing on what will actually happen in the schools we build. Although we agree that the content of this chapter seems impossible, it would be a grave mistake to dismiss it as pure fantasy. Much of the foundational work for the technology necessary for the cyber school learning we predict in this chapter has already been done. And in an environment of exponential change, development of the astounding technological power required to make the learning we have just outlined will occur much faster than anyone has ever experienced before. This exponential advancement in the capability of technology will soon make the instructional applications of intelligent devices we project a reality very quickly. This is of great importance for anyone involved in designing new schools. If planning is limited to what exists today or only looking at what will be coming just a few years into the future, then the design of the school will be quite out of date by the time it is actually built. It is critical that all those involved in education immediately begin to embrace the kind of instruction we outline in this chapter and start making plans for how to implement and manage the cyber learning we discuss because its emergence will explode onto the educational landscape much faster than we can imagine.

PRECEDENTS

Precedents include the following:

- Virtual High School Global Consortium (http://www.govhs.org/website.nsf).
- Florida Virtual School (http://www.flvs.net).
- Illinois Virtual High School (http://www.ivhs.org/index.learn?action=inquiry).
- Kentucky Virtual Schools (http://www.kvhs.org).
- Michigan Virtual School (http://www.mivhs.org).
- Arkansas Virtual High School (http://arkansashigh.k12.ar.us).
- Maryland Virtual High School of Science and Mathematics (http://mvhs.shodor.org).
- Georgia Virtual School (http://www.gavirtualschool.org).

FOCUS ON TEACHING OR LEARNING?

Teacher Centered **Student Centered**

						●

Learning is customized for each student.

GROUP OR INDIVIDUAL TEACHING AND LEARNING?

Group Teaching and Learning **Individual Teaching and Learning**

						●

Learning is customized for each student.

TRADITIONAL TEACHING VS. DIGITAL LEARNING

Teacher, Text **Digital**

This is a cyber school. There is no direct teacher-to-student instruction.

21ST-CENTURY THINKING SKILLS

Knowledge Skills **Content + Problem-Solving Skills**

Both content and problem solving will be integrated into all instruction.

ASSESSMENT

Content Skills **Content + Problem-Solving Skills**

Assessment will be an integral part of instruction and continuous as students progress.

LEARNING FOCUS

Traditional Content **21st-Century Literacies**

Twenty-first-century literacy may be an issue for teachers, but not for students. It is the vehicle by which the school functions.

INSTRUCTIONAL ORGANIZATION

Departments and Disciplines **Interdisciplinary**

Set within real-world contexts, cyber instruction is inherently interdisciplinary.

APPLICATION OF LEARNING

Classroom Theory **Real-World Relevance**

There are no classrooms in the cyber school. Instruction is relevant to students because of the medium, its content, and the real-world context within which students work.

RESPONSIBILITY FOR LEARNING

Teacher **Student**

Students have the primary responsibility for their learning. Teachers guide and support only.

TIME—SCHOOL YEAR

Fixed **Flexible**

Teaching and learning occur 24/7/365.

TIME—SCHOOL DAY

Fixed **Flexible**

Teaching and learning occur 24/7/365.

STUDENT SUPPORT

Counselor **Teacher-Advisor**

Students, teachers, advisors, and counselors work together in many different ways with cyber instruction. Communications may be more distant, but more frequent.

STUDENT LEARNING SPACES

Teachers' Rooms **Individual Workstations**

Students may work anywhere. School may not be a place. A student's workstation may be in her bedroom.

SPATIAL FLEXIBILITY

Durable, Permanent **Responsive, Flexible**

Spatial flexibility is irrelevant. Cyber schooling is a process, not a place.

SCALABILITY—SCHOOL SIZE

Large Enrollment **Small Enrollment**

School size has no impact on offerings or learning environment.

COURSE OFFERINGS

Core + Broad Elective Subjects **Core Subjects**

Offerings are not limited by the size or nature of the school. So long as the digital courses are accredited, students may go "anywhere" for instruction.

EXTRACURRICULAR ACTIVITIES

Extensive **Minimal**

There are no conventional extracurricular activities such as athletics, but there may be digital extracurricular activities. Students may participate in local community programs.

COSTS—STAFF

High Cost per Student **Low Cost per Student**

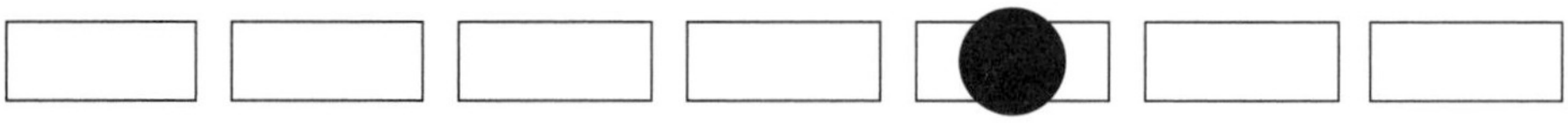

The ratio of students to teachers is comparable to that in a conventional school. The ratio of students to administrative staff is high. There is no extracurricular staff. The costs of creating digital instructional materials are high, but may be distributed over very large numbers of students.

COSTS—FACILITIES

High Cost per Student **Low Cost per Student**

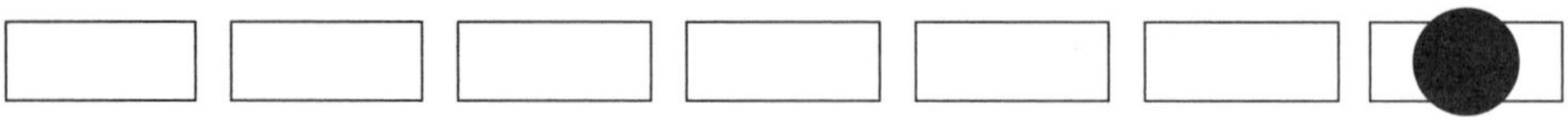

Except for administrative offices and servers, there are no facility costs. Instructional staff work in their homes or anywhere. The school does incur costs for digital equipment and networks to connect teachers and students.

Reflect on the Cyber School and Consider Your Own High School(s)

- Do you think the kind of cyber learning we outline here is impossible?
- If this kind of real cyber learning emerges, what changes do you see in the role of the teacher in the learning process?
- How does the breadth of course offerings in your school compare to those in cyber schools?
- Is coursework available anytime? Is work self-paced?
- Are your teachers able to respond to all students' queries about their studies? How do your students communicate with each other verbally and digitally?
- Can your schools and campuses accommodate the varied instructional needs of the students in your community?
- How do your students do research?
- Do your students maintain digital portfolios of their work?

14

Diverse Learning Communities

The diverse learning community school provides students with multiple choices of instructional programs, teaching methods, and learning methods, all on a single campus.

- Each community provides a different mode of teaching and learning, has different spaces, and may have a different schedule (school day and year).
- Each is a multidisciplinary group with all of the core subjects for grades 9–12.
- Students work within their learning community with the same group of teachers for their four years on the campus.
- Some students may work on the campus, whereas others are part of a cyber community.
- The campus affords students opportunities for extracurricular activities.

Instructional/Spatial Organization
The school is organized into learning communities, each with different teaching/learning methods, different calendars and school days, different elective strands, and different priorities. The entire school may be located on a single campus, or some of the learning communities may be off site.

Diverse Learning Communities on a Campus

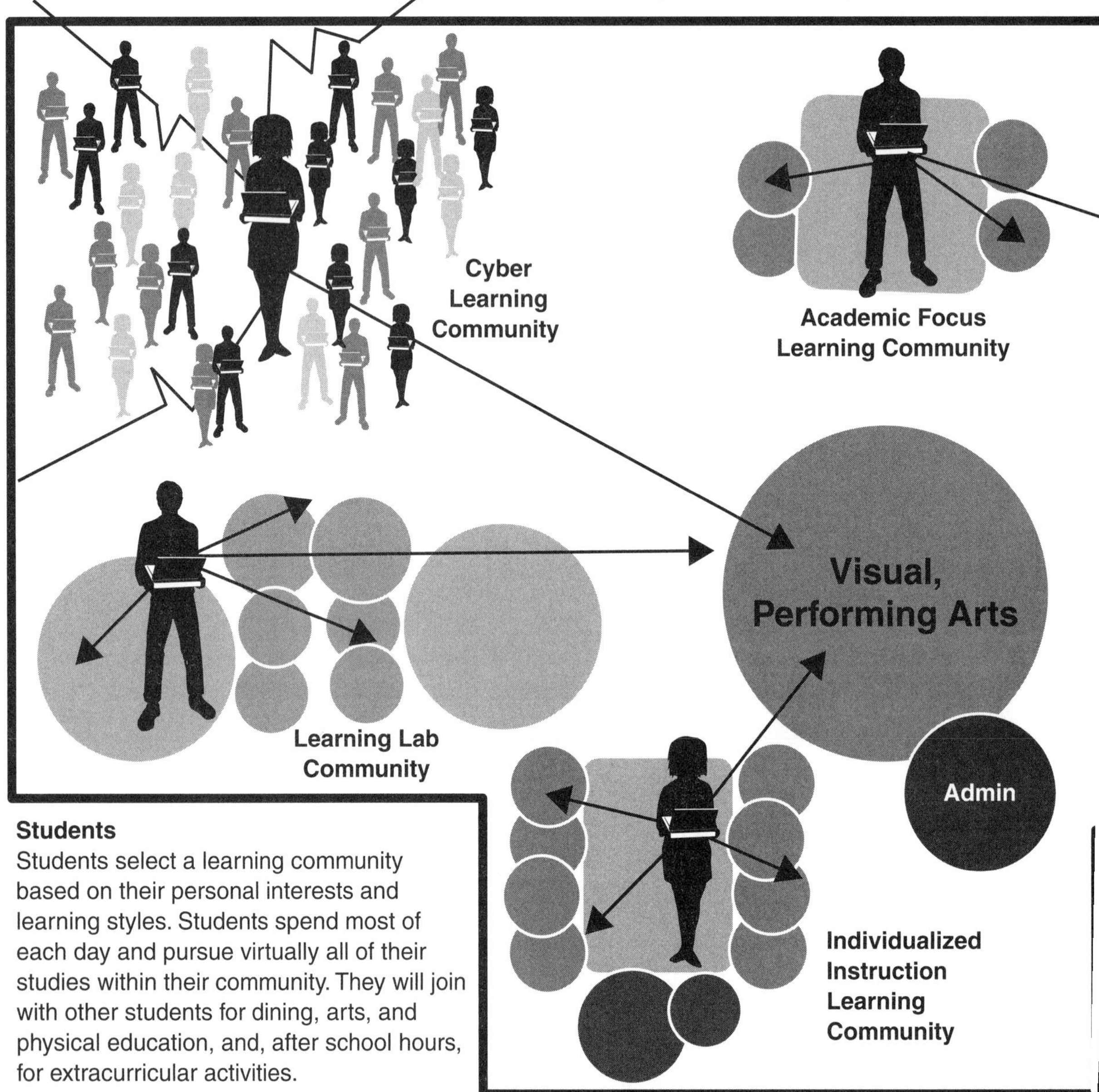

Students
Students select a learning community based on their personal interests and learning styles. Students spend most of each day and pursue virtually all of their studies within their community. They will join with other students for dining, arts, and physical education, and, after school hours, for extracurricular activities.

School Year

The length and structure of the academic year in each community reflects its teaching and learning process. Some are organized around defined periods, whereas others run continuously all year 24/7.

J	F	M	A	M	J	J	A	S	O	N	D
Continuous 12-month instruction services											
1st Quarter			2nd Quarter			3rd Quarter			4th Quarter		

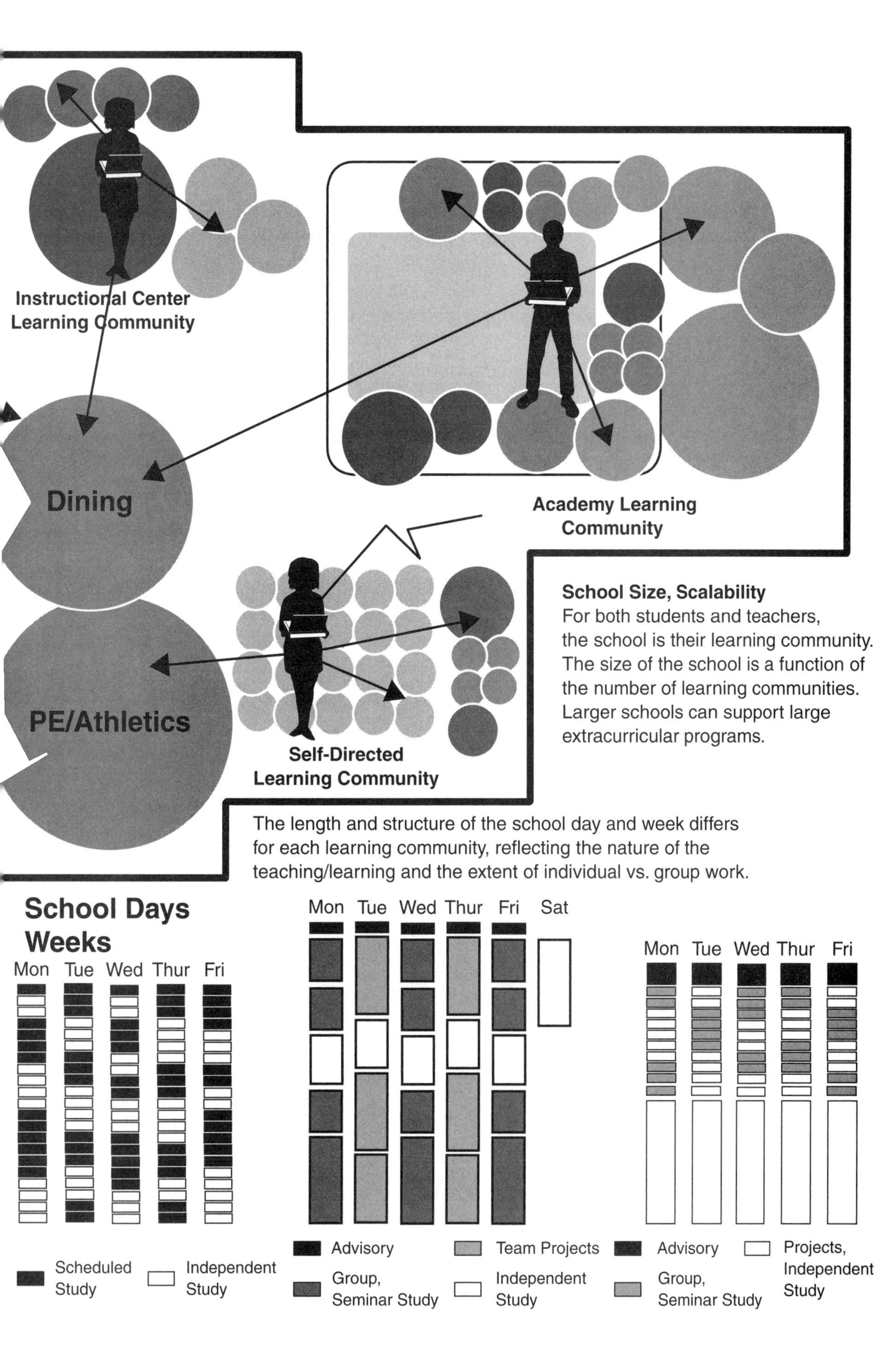

Instructional Center
Learning Community
Dining
PE/Athletics
Academy Learning
Community
Self-Directed
Learning Community
School Size, Scalability
For both students and teachers,
the school is their learning community.
The size of the school is a function of
the number of learning communities.
Larger schools can support large
extracurricular programs.
The length and structure of the school day and week differs
for each learning community, reflecting the nature of the
teaching/learning and the extent of individual vs. group work.
School Days
Weeks
Mon Tue Wed Thur Fri
Scheduled Study
Independent Study
Mon Tue Wed Thur Fri Sat
Advisory
Team Projects
Group, Seminar Study
Independent Study
Mon Tue Wed Thur Fri
Advisory
Projects, Independent Study
Group, Seminar Study

In the early drafts of this book, the Industrial Age model was followed by one based on small learning communities that reflected the recommendations of the NASSP's *Breaking Ranks: Changing an American Institution* (1996). Although that model addressed some shortcomings of the Industrial Age school, in other regards, it remained firmly rooted in early 20th-century instructional thinking. So, we modified "small" into "diverse" learning communities and relocated this model from its spot near the beginning of our list to the end because it draws on thinking from all the other models.

The diverse learning community model recognizes that small learning communities on a campus do not have to be identical and that one school may offer students widely varied teaching and learning opportunities. It further recognizes that many districts have only one high school and thus have limited possibilities for creating different types of schools.

This model seeks to be diverse in both the breadth of offerings and the teaching and learning methods to serve the needs of many different students on a single campus. However, it is ***not our intent*** to create a new type of comprehensive high school to be replicated across districts with fixed attendance zones. Although this school may have its place, it will be a challenge to create and operate.

Diverse learning community schools are characterized by the following:

- The school is divided into **small learning communities**, each serving students in grades 9–12. Students work with the same group of teachers throughout their years at the school. Teachers and students come to know each other well.
- Learning communities vary in size **from 150 to 600** students depending on teaching and learning methods.
- All of the communities adhere to the same **core curriculum** required for graduation, but offer different electives or draw on different resources appropriate to their teaching and learning methods and the interests of the students.
- **Each community is different** in its teaching and learning approach to serve the varying needs and interests of individual students. It is expected that over time, some communities will evolve, some will grow, and others will be replaced in response to changing needs. Thus, it is anticipated that the composition of the school will change over time.
- On entering the school, students **select a learning community** based on their personal interests and learning styles. The school works with students in grades 6–8, who will come to the high school in grade 9, to inform them of the important choices they will be offered. As students progress through their studies, they may elect to move from one community to another as teachers and space become available.
- Every student and teacher has a **personal portable digital device**. Access to technology and the Internet is critical to instruction in each of the learning communities.

- The school provides learning services **12 months per year, 7 days a week.** The organization of the school year and day varies from learning community to learning community. School days are similarly varied. Some students set their own pace, whereas others have more structured days. There are no bells.
- Some teachers and students work entirely on campus, whereas others divide time between **campus and community-based** activities.
- One of the learning communities may be **cyber based,** with most of its students working off campus. These students may come to the campus to access specialized equipment (for example, science labs or some career programs) and to participate in group activities such as performing arts or athletics.
- The learning communities are very different spatially, and each has its own **unique identity**. Each is shaped to serve its teaching and learning concepts. There is a huge need for spatial flexibility to accommodate changes in instruction and in the sizes of communities as demand varies. Anticipating that change will occur regularly, spatial flexibility is more important than permanence and durability.
- The school is a **single large building** instead of a campus of separate structures for each of the learning communities. Small separate structures would discourage the reallocation and reconfiguration of spaces as instructional programs change over time. The school has a durable exterior shell and structural system. Mechanical, plumbing, electrical, and data systems are planned to accommodate future changes. But, everything inside the building shell is designed to be quickly and economically reconfigured to accommodate changing instructional programs. Such structures are typical in office and retail buildings where spaces are regularly changed to meet the needs of different tenants.
- Some of the learning communities may be located off campus in **leased commercial space**. Leasing permits the school to expand, contract, or relocate learning communities as needs evolve.
- **Learning communities** in the school are supported by and share some spaces and services such as administrative offices, food services, library, performing arts, and physical education and athletics.
- **Teachers and students** spend the majority of each day within their communities, but some may go to other communities on occasion to access teachers or specialized courses, spaces, and equipment.
- **Extracurricular activities** may be generated within individual learning communities, whereas major programs that require specialized costly facilities such as performing arts and athletics draw participants from across the campus. Given that each of the learning

communities operates on a different school year and day, extracurricular activities occur outside typical school hours. Students who participate in seasonal extracurricular activities are responsible for coordinating these with their studies.

- School **faculty** are organized around both their disciplines and their small learning communities. All of the faculty in the school in each discipline work together to share expertise and resources in their field. Similarly, within each small learning community, faculty from multiple disciplines join together to integrate their teaching and address the needs of their students.
- Given the diverse methods of instruction and evolving learning communities, **teachers must be highly flexible**, and staff development is critical. Over time, most teachers will work in several learning communities and use very different teaching and learning methods. The school is a learning community for both students and teachers.
- The school provides **places for students and teachers to work** in each learning community. The work of both students and teachers is equally critical to the success of the school.
- The school may have a **library** or share a library (on or off the campus) with the community. If the school does not have a library on the campus, it will have librarians to help students effectively use the Internet for research.
- Each learning community has it own **administration suite** appropriate to the nature and scale of the group. Wherever possible, teachers also serve as advisors, counselors, and assistant principals. Virtually every adult on the campus has some teaching role and works directly with students.
- With widely varied and highly flexible schedules, students and faculty eat when they wish. **Food services** are continuous throughout the school day in an open space that also serves as a social center for the campus.
- The school is very **open visually**. As students move about the campus, they are exposed to the activities, spaces, and equipment of each learning community. Student work is prominently exhibited. The intent is to expose students to different fields of study and different teaching and learning possibilities. Like a retail center, the school puts its "wares" on display to attract students and teachers. The school is a fascinating place to attend and to visit.

For **teachers**, the school offers the same choice it does for students—to teach and learn in ways suited to their own interests and capabilities. Within a single school, there are multiple opportunities to teach in very different ways. The challenge is for teachers to embrace new possibilities—and then to have the flexibility to change over time. With the close student-teacher relationships encouraged in each community, teachers have a broader role as advisors and counselors to provide individual support and direction to students. Although teachers have contact with colleagues in their own field, they work most closely with teachers from other disciplines within their small learning community. The overall school might be large, but day to day, the much smaller learning community is the teacher's working environment.

For **students**, the challenge is to know their own interests and how they learn best, and to make good choices about learning communities. Teachers and advisors support and guide the students in making these important choices. Flexible scheduling allows all students the opportunity to succeed, but they must assume real responsibility for the management of their time. The presence of several different learning communities gives each student the opportunity to see other ways to learn and other areas of study and to confirm the choice they made. Although students will use the school's shared facilities, most of their day is spent in their learning community.

For **administrators**, the challenge is to operate concurrently multiple schools, each with different teaching methods, different sorts of teachers and kids, different schedules, different spaces, and different costs—but all striving to graduate students ready for success in the 21st century. Compounding the challenge is that, with student choice, learning communities compete within the school for enrollment. Administrators must forecast and recognize what works in terms of outcomes and what attracts students and teachers—nothing is fixed or guaranteed for long in the diversified learning community school.

For **architects**, the challenge is to make the school exceptionally flexible to accommodate change. Historically, school districts have given priority to durability and permanence over flexibility and adaptability, when in fact even industrial model schools evolve in terms of enrollment, programs, educational, and life safety codes. Through additions and renovations, high schools are often substantially modified long before their life expectancy has expired, and in the process can become poorly organized, inefficient, and disorienting.

Aside from the design challenge, district administrators and architects will have to convince the public and facility personnel that parts of schools are short term, in effect, disposable instead of permanent. This requires new mindsets about the use of funds, selection of building materials, and different ways to handle mechanical, electrical, plumbing, and data systems.

With regard to both **construction and operating costs**, the diverse learning community and industrial model schools are comparable, but the funds are spent and utilized differently. In the diverse learning community school, more money is spent on the building shell and furnishings, but less on interior partitions and finishes that will be changed multiple times over the life of the building. In the future, changes to keep the facility current with instructional needs will cost less. Because the school operates 12 instead of 9 months per year, the facility serves a larger enrollment each year. Similarly, teachers working 12 months per year teach and earn more, but fewer teachers are required.

PRECEDENTS

As noted in the previous chapters, there are substantial precedents for each of the learning communities suggested above, but at this date, the authors are unaware of any one school that has provided the diversity of instruction outlined here.

FOCUS ON TEACHING OR LEARNING?

Teacher Centered **Student Centered**

						●

The school is student centered by virtue of the broad choices it offers students and parents.

GROUP OR INDIVIDIUAL TEACHING AND LEARING?

Group Teaching and Learning **Individual Teaching and Learning**

						●

The diverse learning communities offer varying degrees of individualized instruction.

TRADITIONAL TEACHING VS. DIGITAL LEARNING

Teacher, Text **Digital**

					●	

Every student and teacher has a digital device, and digital instruction is used in all of the learning communities.

21ST-CENTURY THINKING SKILLS

Knowledge Skills **Content + Problem-Solving Skills**

The development of both content and problem-solving skills varies between the learning communities.

ASSESSMENT

Content Skills **Content + Problem-Solving Skills**

Methods of assessment vary among the diverse learning communities.

LEARNING FOCUS

Traditional Content **21st-Century Literacies**

Twenty-first-century literacy is the key to effective use of technology for learning.

INSTRUCTIONAL ORGANIZATION

Departments and Disciplines **Interdisciplinary**

The extent of interdisciplinary instruction varies among the learning communities.

APPLICATION OF LEARNING

Classroom Theory **Real-World Relevance**

The learning communities relate instruction to the real world outside the campus in varied ways.

RESPONSIBILITY FOR LEARNING

Teacher **Student**

All of the learning communities require that students assume significantly more responsibility for their own learning than does the traditional industrial model school.

TIME—SCHOOL YEAR

Fixed **Flexible**

Taken together, the diverse learning communities offer students great flexibility in selecting a school year best suited to their individual interest and needs.

TIME—SCHOOL DAY

Fixed **Flexible**

All of the communities provide significant flexibility for the use of time in the typical school day.

STUDENT SUPPORT

Counselor **Teacher-Advisor**

Most of the communities provide a teacher-advisor for every student. Some may use counselors that serve larger numbers of students.

STUDENT LEARNING SPACES

Teachers' Rooms **Individual Workspaces**

The communities provide very different teaching and learning spaces.

SPATIAL FLEXIBILITY

Durable, Permanent **Responsive, Flexible**

The entire school provides spatial flexibility to accommodate changes in instructional methods and the programs offered.

SCALABILITY—SCHOOL SIZE

Large Enrollment **Small Enrollment**

The size of the school is a function of the number and type of learning communities. The larger the enrollment, the more diverse the types of learning communities that can be offered.

COURSE OFFERINGS

Core + Broad Elective Subjects **Core Subjects**

The elective offerings vary with each learning community. Overall, the school offers broad elective choices for students. Students may be able to take some elective courses outside their own community.

EXTRACURRICULAR ACTIVITIES

Extensive **Minimal**

The school offers a full range of extracurricular activities.

COSTS—STAFF

High Cost per Student **Low Cost per Student**

The ratio of students to staff will be similar to that in a traditional industrial model school.

COSTS—FACILITIES

High Cost per Student **Low Cost per Student**

The building area per student will be comparable to that in a traditional industrial model school, but with the school operating 12 months per year, the facility may serve more students per year.

Reflect on the Diverse Learning Communities School and Consider Your Own High School(s)

- How are the students served by your high school alike or different? Are their backgrounds, interests, and learning styles all similar or are they diverse?
- How do your instructional methods reflect the diversity of our students?
- In your school, how is time in the school day and year organized to meet the diverse needs of your students?
- How are you ensuring that all of your students graduate ready for work and/or college?

15

Diverse High Schools

No More Cookie-Cutter High Schools

In a diverse high school district, most or all of the high schools provide different teaching and learning methods to serve students with varied interests and learning styles.

- Each campus may be different in its teaching methods, course offerings, facilities, and schedule.
- Students and parents select a high school on the basis of their interests and needs. There are no attendance zones.
- Parity among the schools is measured in terms of outcomes for students.
- Over time, the schools change their programs in response to changing needs in the community and to attract students.

Diverse High Schools Within a District
No More Cookie Cutter-High Schools

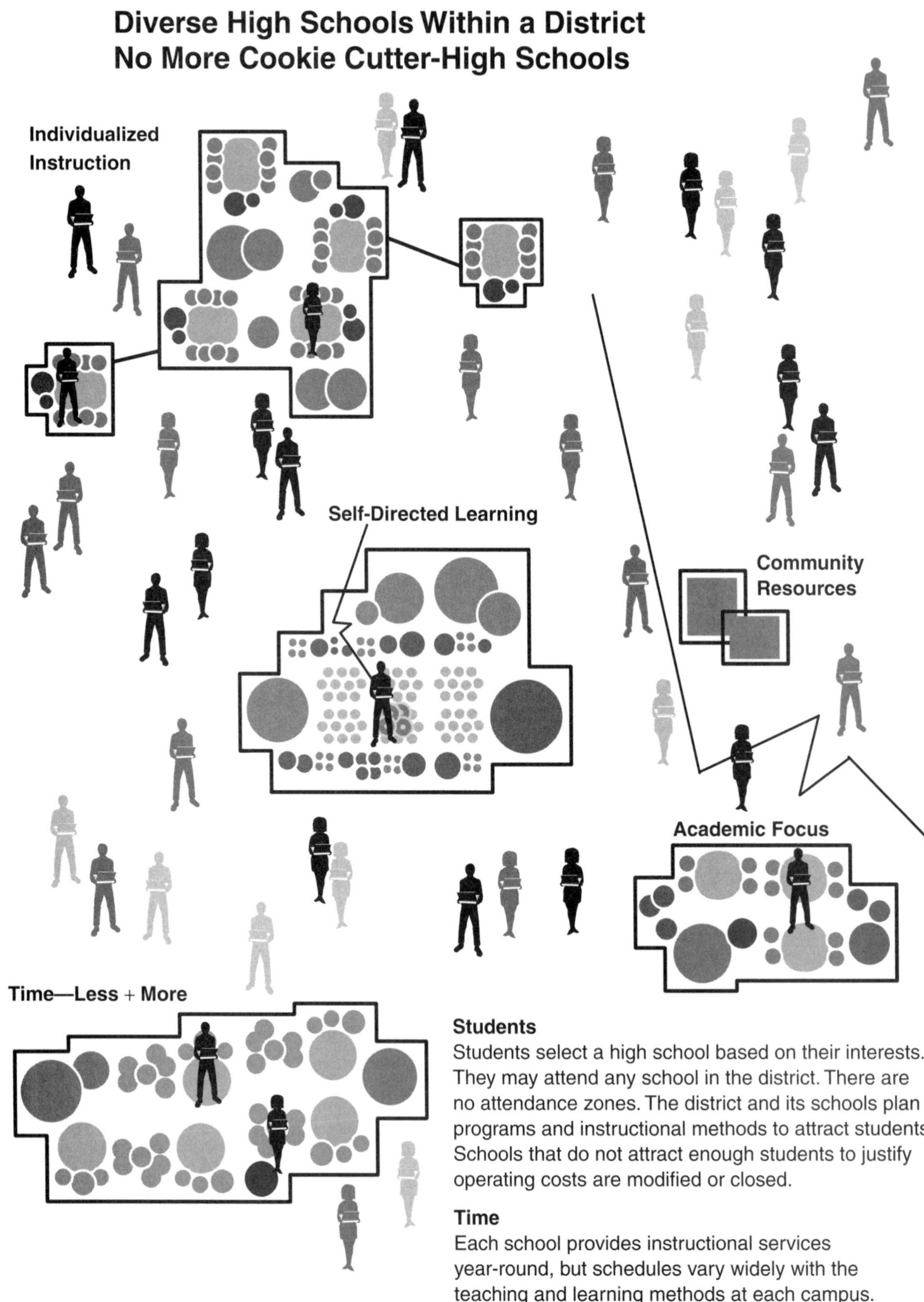

Students

Students select a high school based on their interests. They may attend any school in the district. There are no attendance zones. The district and its schools plan programs and instructional methods to attract students. Schools that do not attract enough students to justify operating costs are modified or closed.

Time

Each school provides instructional services year-round, but schedules vary widely with the teaching and learning methods at each campus.

Types of High Schools

The district provides multiple types of high schools with diverse instructional programs reflecting the needs of the students and communities they serve. Each offers all the courses required for graduation but within very different instructional contexts. Beyond the core subjects, elective, career, performing arts, and extracurricular offerings vary widely from campus to campus. Parity is measured by student outcomes vs. course offerings, facilities, and expenditures.

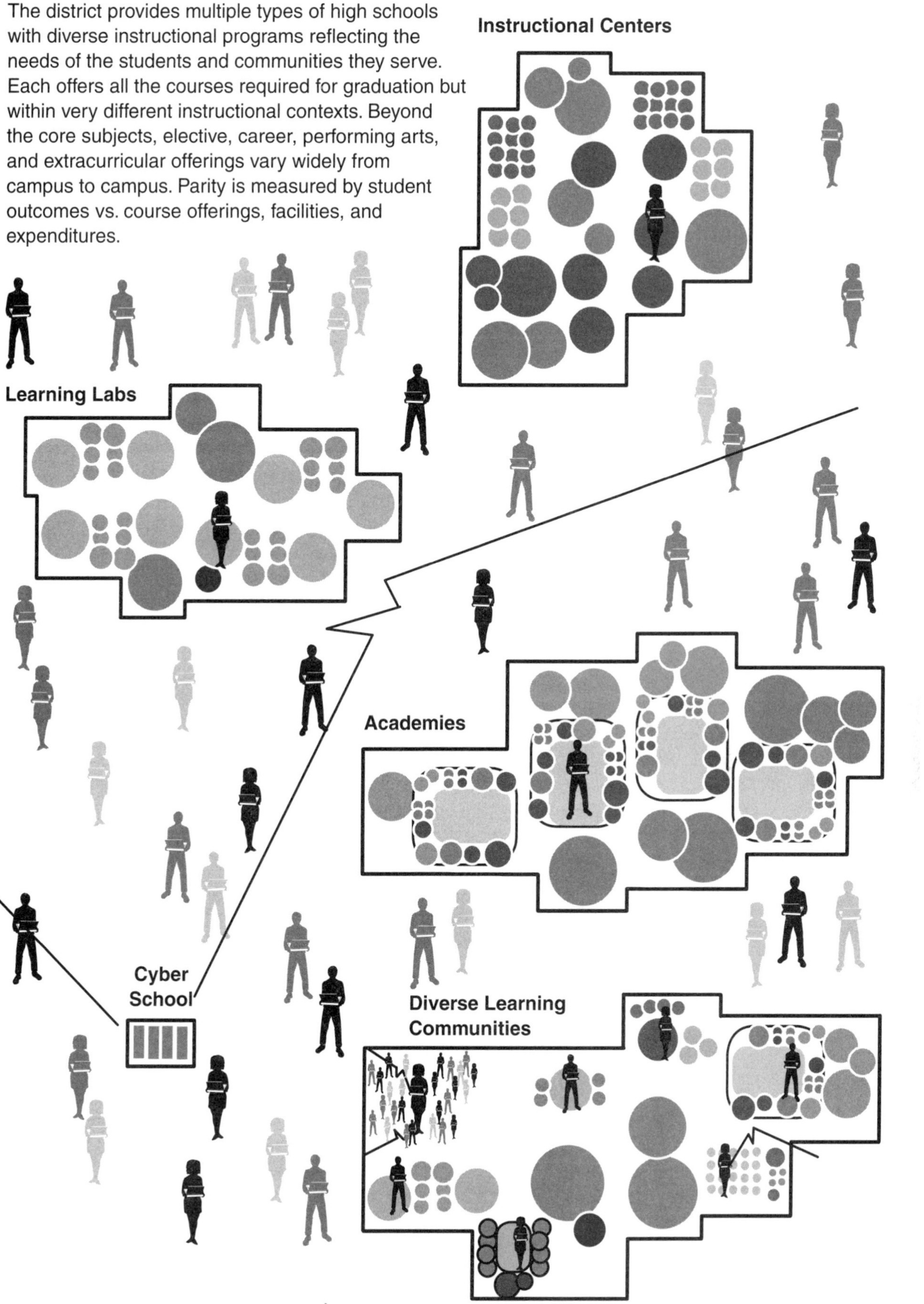

This book is about making high schools fit students in the 21st century rather than fitting students into high schools. It recognizes that students are very different from one another and that no single school or instructional approach has achieved or can achieve comparable or even acceptable outcomes for all students. The industrial model described in Chapter 5 has tried to be comprehensive in its offerings and to serve all students, but nationwide serves many students very poorly.

We propose to realize "comprehensive" instruction in districts with multiple high schools by creating different types of schools that allow students and parents to select the school best suited to the student's interests and learning style. The models previously described are indicative of the range of school types that might be considered to create such a district.

Districts with multiple types of high schools are characterized by the following:

- Districts must have **sufficient enrollment** to support multiple high schools of different types and sizes. Small districts with a single high school may consider the diverse learning communities model we discussed in Chapter 14.
- Students and parents must be able to **select a high school** solely on the basis of their learning needs and interests, not where they live. This precludes the assignment of students to schools based on attendance or catchment zones and precludes feeder patterns.
- The **composition of the student body** at each campus reflects the choices made by students and parents among instructional programs and methods offered across the district. Admissions to each high school are based on students' interests, not their academic capabilities or socioeconomic factors.
- **Parity** among schools means comparable outcomes instead of comparable programs, facilities, and expenditures per student. Different types of high schools have different priorities, different course offerings, and different facilities. Just as different programs in industrial model schools vary widely in cost per student, different types of high schools vary in their total cost per student. The community and district determine priorities for the use of available funds. For students and parents, parity is the opportunity to select, without constraints, where they want to go to school and how they want to learn.
- Diverse high school districts provide and maintain **schools that are responsive to the market** (students and parents) they serve. School districts modify schools, course offerings (including state mandated requirements), instructional methods, and extracurricular activities as demand changes over time. School districts and individual schools have an entrepreneurial perspective and adapt over time to serve and attract students. School districts must not constrain the options of students and parents by retaining schools and programs

that do not attract sufficient students to justify their costs. Consequently, the location, number, and types of schools evolve over time as the needs of the community and its students change.

- Diverse high school districts have campuses with **different enrollments and schedules** (both school days and school years). Extracurricular activities vary widely from school to school. Some have competitive athletic programs, others do not. Some have performing arts programs. Different schools have widely varied career technology programs. Students and parents select schools on the basis of their academic and extracurricular interests.
- Without attendance zones and with widely varied school days and school years, the diverse high school district may not provide **transportation** for all high school students. The use of personal or public transportation is a factor parents and students may have to consider in selecting a high school.

PRECEDENTS

The Dallas Independent School District has announced (Fischer, 2008) that it will create varied types of career academies at its more than 20 high schools and allow students and parents to choose the school that best serves their needs and interests. The district plans to begin the transformation in the 2008–09 school year and have all the academies in operation by 2012.

Reflect on the Diverse High Schools District and Consider Your Own District

- How do the high schools in your district reflect the differences in the communities and students they serve? Do they all have similar programs and facilities?
- How different or similar are your high schools with regard to instructional methods and program offerings?
- How do your students and parents select the high school best suited to their needs and interests? Is the high school a student attends determined by an attendance zone, catchment area, or other factor?
- How do you ensure that high school graduation rates and readiness for work or college are comparable for students from all the communities across your district?

Summary

At the risk of sounding repetitive, we need to restate what we wrote at the very beginning of this book. We want our readers to understand and believe that there are many ways to organize high schools—not just one. We need our readers to understand and believe that the industrial model is not the "standard" school suitable for most students. We want our readers to understand that all the models we have described are not merely "special" for small numbers of "special" students. We need our readers to understand that there should be no "base," "standard," "normal," "conventional," or "traditional" high school. If we are to create new high schools that truly work, we must be willing to reexamine our assumptions about teaching and learning every time we build or renovate a school for each community it will serve.

Further, we need our readers to understand that this book is not a comprehensive catalog of high school models from which to make selections. Rather, it is intended to provide illustrative examples exploring a range of viable possibilities. There are clearly many variations and derivatives for each of the models described, not to mention many other models we've yet to imagine. The challenge is not just to find new ways to make high schools, but also to muster the courage to seek them out.

If we are going to prepare our students for life and work in the world that awaits them beyond school, rather than the world we knew when we grew up, we must rethink traditional schools, we must rethink learning, we must rethink teaching—and we need to do it now! All the models examined here can do more for less—the issue of change is far more about a poverty of attitude than it is a poverty of dollars.

Reflect on your high schools, consider the guiding principles (from Chapter 2), and ask yourself if your high schools are geared for the 21st century.

i. How have your schools shifted the focus from teachers and instruction to students and learning?
ii. What are your schools doing to prepare students for a world of constant change?
iii. How are your schools providing students with opportunities to develop 21st-century thinking and 21st-century fluency skills?
iv. How do teaching, learning, and assessment in your schools reflect the new digital reality?
v. How have assumptions about teaching, learning, and assessment been adapted to support interdisciplinary learning opportunities?
vi. How have your schools adapted to meet the learning needs and learning styles of individuals?
vii. What strategies have your schools developed to better engage 21st-century digital kids?
viii. How do your schools connect teaching and learning in the classroom to the outside world?
ix. What have your schools done to ensure that learning opportunities are available 24 hours a day, 7 days a week, and 365 days a year?
x. What strategies have your schools developed to ensure that learning is the constant and the time it takes to learn is the variable?
xi. How are your schools ensuring that students assume more responsibility for their own learning?
xii. What strategies have your schools developed to ensure that every student has a close working relationship with at least one adult in the school?
xiii. What strategies do your schools use to provide students with their own personal place to work?
xiv. What assessment models have your schools developed to ensure that evaluation encompasses both knowledge skills and higher order thinking skills?
xv. What strategies have your schools developed to ensure that all of your students are properly prepared so they can go on to some form of postsecondary studies?
xvi. What strategies have your schools developed to ensure that the configuration of spaces within the school building is more flexible?
xvii. What steps will you take starting right now to begin moving your school, your faculty, your district staff, and your community from where they are to where they need to be?

"You see things that are and say why. I dream things that never were and say why not?"

George Bernard Shaw (1889)

If you always believe
What you have always believed;
You will always feel
What you have always felt.
If you always feel
The way you have always felt;
You will always think
The way you have always thought.
If you always think
The way you have always thought;
You will always do
What you have always done.
If you always do
What you have always done;
You will always get
What you have always got;
If there is no change,
There is no change.

–Author Unknown

References

Abramson, P. (2005). 10th annual school construction report. Dayton, OH: *School Planning & Management Magazine.* Retrieved May 13, 2008, from http://www.peterli.com/global/pdfs/SPMconstruction2005.PDF

Anderson, C. (2006). *The long tail: Why the future of business is selling less of more.* New York: Hyperion.

Belfield, C. R., & Leven, H. M. (2007). *The price we pay: Economic and social consequences of inadequate education.* Washington, DC: The Brookings Institution.

Botstein, L. (1997). *Jefferson's children: Education and the promise of American culture.* New York: Doubleday.

Boyer, E. L., & Mitgang, L. D. (1996). *Building community: A new future for architecture education and practice.* Stanford, CA: Carnegie Foundation for the Advancement of Teaching.

Bridgeland, J. M., DiIulio, J. J., Jr., & Morison, K. B. (2006). *The silent epidemic: Perspectives of high school students.* Washington, DC: Civic Enterprises, LLC. Retrieved May 14, 2008, from http://www.civicenterprises.net/pdfs/thesilentepidemic3-06.pdf

Darling-Hammond, L. (1997). *The right to learn: A blueprint for creating schools that work.* San Francisco: Jossey-Bass.

Fischer, K. (2008, January 16). DISD is looking to the future with high school career academies, *The Dallas Morning News.* [Electronic version.] Retrieved January 16, 2008, from http://www.dallasnews.com/sharedcontent/dws/news/localnews/stories/DN-highschools_16met.ART.State.Edition1.377a7ca.html

Friedman, T. L. (2005). *The world is flat: A brief history of the twenty-first century.* New York: Farrar, Straus and Giroux.

Gates, B. (2005, February 26). *What's wrong with U.S. high schools—and how we can make them better.* Talk presented at the National Summit on High Schools, Washington, DC.

IDC. (2007). *Expanding digital universe.* Framingham, MA: Author. Retrieved May 13, 2008, from http://www.emc.com/collateral/analyst-reports/expanding-digital-idc-white-paper.pdf

Kelly, K. (2006, May 14). Scan this book, *New York Times* [Electronic Version]. Retrieved May 13, 2008, from http://www.nytimes.com/2006/05/14/magazine/14publishing.html?_r=1&oref=slogin&pagewanted=all

Kurzweil, R. (2005). *The singularity is near: When humans transcend biology.* New York: Penguin.

Levine, E. (2002). *One kid at a time: Big lessons from a small school.* New York: Teachers College Press.

Lindstrom, R. (1994). *The Business Week guide to multimedia presentations.* New York: McGraw-Hill.

Littky, D., & Grabelle, S. (2004). *The big picture: Education is everyone's business.* Alexandria, VA: Association for Supervision and Curriculum Development.

Machiavelli, N. (2005). *The prince.* Lawrence, KS: Neeland Media. (Original work published 1513.)

Master, D. (1999, December 7). Keynote speech given at Southwestern Ohio Instructional Technology Association (SOITA) Conference, Dayton, OH.

McCain, T. (2005). *Teaching for tomorrow: Teaching content and problem-solving skills.* Thousand Oaks, CA: Corwin.

McCain, T., & Jukes, I. (2001). *Windows on the future: Education in the age of technology.* Thousand Oaks, CA: Corwin.

National Association of Manufacturers. (2005). *2005 skills gap report—a survey of the American manufacturing workforce.* Washington, DC: Author.

National Association of Secondary School Principals. (1996). *Breaking ranks: Changing an American institution.* Reston, VA: Author.

National Association of Secondary School Principals. (2004). *Breaking ranks II: Strategies for leading high school reform.* Reston, VA: Author.

National Center for Education Statistics. (2002). *The condition of education 2002,* NCES 2002–025. Washington, DC: Author.

National Education Commission on Time and Learning. (1994, April). *Prisoners of time.* Washington, DC: Author. (2005 reprint.) Retrieved May 13, 2008, from http://www.ed.gov/pubs/PrisonersOfTime/index.html

National Governors Association. (2005). *An action agenda for improving America's high schools.* Washington, DC: Achieve, Inc., and National Governors Association. Retrieved May 14, 2008, from http://www.nga.org/Files/pdf/0502ACTIONAGENDA.pdf

Nearly half of Texas students entering college now must take remedial classes. (July 7, 2006). *Houston Chronicle,* p. B1 [Electronic version]. Retrieved July 7, 2006, from http://www.chron.com/disp/story.mpl/metropolitan/4029961.htm

New Commission on the Skills of the American Workforce. (2006). *Tough choices or tough times.* San Francisco: Jossey-Bass.

Partnership for 21st Century Skills. (2006). *Results that matter: 21st century skills and high school reform.* Tucson, AZ: Author. Retrieved May 13, 2008, from http://www.21stcenturyskills.org/documents/RTM2006.pdf

Peters, T. (2001). *Education and third millennium work: We've got it dangerously wrong.* Boston: Tom Peters Company.

Pink, D. H. (2001). *Free agent nation: The future of working for yourself.* New York: Warner Books.

Pink, D. H. (2005). *A whole new mind: Moving from the information age to the conceptual age.* New York: Riverhead Books.

Popham, W. J. (2005, April). F for assessment: Standardized testing fails. *Edutopia,* p. 41. Retrieved May 13, 2008, from http://www.edutopia.org/f-for-assessment

Prensky, M. (2006). *Don't bother me mom—I'm learning.* St. Paul, MN: Paragon House.

Robinson, M. (2003). *What box? Creating a problem-based learning program. The story of Star Lane Center.* Casper, WY: Natrona County School District Print Shop.

Schlechty, P. C. (1997). *Inventing better schools: An action plan for educational reform.* San Francisco: Jossey-Bass.

Shaw, G. B. (1891). *Fabian essays in socialism,* ed. H. G. Wilshire. New York: The Humboldt Publishing Co. (Original work published 1889.)

Squire, K., Barnett, M., Grant, J. M., & Higginbotham, T. (2003). *Electromagnetism supercharged! Learning physics with digital simulation games.* Retrieved May 13, 2008, from http://www.educationarcade.org/supercharged

Toch, T. (2003). *High schools on a human scale: How small schools can transform American education.* Boston: Beacon.

Toffler, A. (1970). *Future shock.* New York: Bantam.

Trump, J. L. (1959). *Images of the future: A new approach to the secondary school.* Urbana, IL: Commission on the Experimental Study of the Utilization of the Staff in the Secondary School, National Association of Secondary School Principals.

Trump, J. L. (1977). *A school for everyone: Design for a middle, junior, or senior high school that combines the old and the new.* Reston, VA: National Association of Secondary School Principals.

Tuchman, B. W. (1984). *The march of folly: From Troy to Vietnam.* New York: Alfred A. Knopf.
Voluptuous artificial patient tests med students. (2005, March 23). *Vancouver Sun,* Page A7.
Worzel, R. (2006, May/June). *Teach Magazine,* p. 7.

Schools Referenced

Bard High School Early College (http://www.bard.edu/bhsec/)
Canadian Coalition for Self-Directed Learning, http://www.bchs.calgary.ab.ca/ccsdl/
Member schools:
Banff Community High School, Banff, Alberta, http://www.crsd.ab.ca/bchs/
Bishop Carroll High School, Calgary, Alberta, http://www.bchs.calgary.ab.ca/
Bishop O'Bryne High School, Calgary, Alberta, http://www.bishopobyrne.ca/
Frances Kelsey Secondary School, Mill Bay, British Columbia, http://www.fkss.ca/
Mary Ward Catholic Secondary School, Scarborough, Ontario, http://home.eol.ca/~maryward/
St. Joseph High School, Edmonton, Alberta, http://www.stjoseph.ecsd.net/
Thomas Haney Secondary School, Maple Ridge, British Columbia, http://www.stjoseph.ecsd.net/
Carl Wunsche Senior High School Career Academy, Spring, Texas, http://academy.springisd.org/
Department of Curriculum & Instruction, School of Education, University of Wisconsin-Madison
Early College High Schools, www.earlycolleges.org/
Gary & Jerri-Ann Jacobs High Tech High School, San Diego, California, http://www.hightechhigh.org/
KIPP Schools, Houston, Texas, http://www.kipphouston.org/
New Technology Foundation, http://www.newtechfoundation.org/
School of the Woods, a Montessori high school, Houston, Texas, http://schoolofthewoods.org
The MET School/The Big Picture Company, Providence, Rhode Island, http://www.whatkidscando.org/portfoliosmallschools/met/metintro.html
Westside High School, Westside 66 School District, Omaha, Nebraska, http://www.westside66.org/westsidehs/site/default.asp
YES (Youth Engaged in Service) College Preparatory Charter School, Houston, Texas, http://www.yesprep.org

Index

The Corwin Press logo—a raven striding across an open book—represents the union of courage and learning. Corwin Press is committed to improving education for all learners by publishing books and other professional development resources for those serving the field of PreK–12 education. By providing practical, hands-on materials, Corwin Press continues to carry out the promise of its motto: **"Helping Educators Do Their Work Better."**